PHOTOGRAPHER'S AMERICA

Forever Brooklyn

Images from New York's Most Iconic Borough

Liz Cooke and Andy Milford

AMERICA THROUGH TIME

America Through Time®
An imprint of Sutton Publishing Inc.
www.through-time.com

First published 2025

ISBN 978-1-63499-559-7

Typeset in Gotham Book
Printed and bound in England

Contents

Introduction

This is a book of stories. Some are told with words, but most are told with images. Much like Brooklyn itself, this is a book full of life, energy, and hope. At its heart, this is a book about people. About struggle and perseverance. About food and family. And like Brooklyn, it is about permanence and change.

Andy and I come from different parts of the globe and bring different perspectives to our photography. I am a Brooklyn-born, dyed-in-the wool street photographer. When I look for shots, all I see are faces, body language, and moments. Andy is a British-born artist, with a lifelong interest in the craft of photography, street art, and urban exploration. He comes to this project with a much different take, seeing light and shadow, reflections and grit—the very texture of Brooklyn is in all his work. Together, we looked at this as a chance to go beyond the obvious and get to something deeper—the Brooklyn I've always loved and the Brooklyn Andy came to love, one story, one person, and one picture at a time.

When we speak of Brooklyn, it's hard to know exactly what we're speaking of. If nothing else, Brooklyn is a study in contrasts—a place with both spectacular wealth and extreme poverty. A place of modest bungalows and grand brownstones. A place for stockbrokers and bus drivers, aspiring rappers and tech entrepreneurs, Michelin-rated restaurants and street-corner taquerias. On a good day, Brooklyn is a whirlwind, and on a bad day, a tornado.

Since my earliest days here, Brooklyn has only gotten more interesting, more compelling, and more exciting. In fact, Brooklyn has become something of a phenomenon—a global brand attracting thousands of tourists and would-be residents every year. In the Hudson Valley where Andy and I both live, we frequently hear of small towns being referred to as the "new Brooklyn," bespeaking, we suppose, the arrival of hipsters, high-end shops, and a diverse art and music scene. We hope that's a good thing.

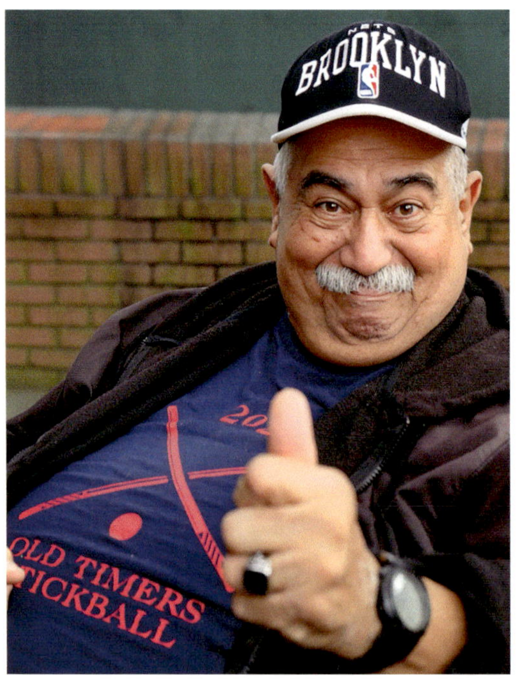

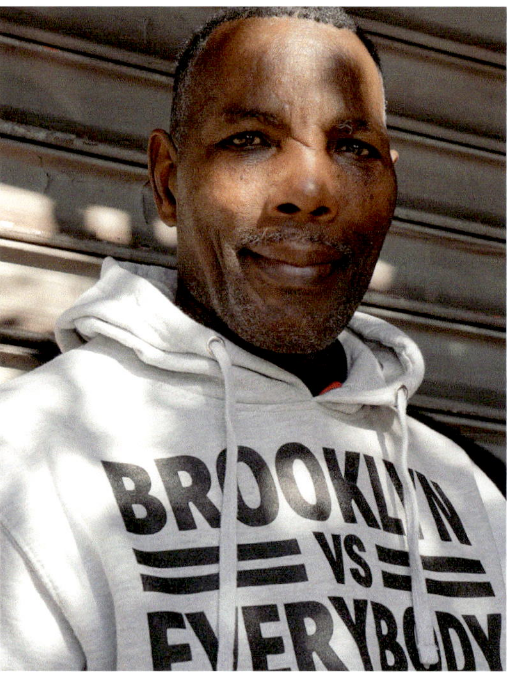

Above left: Brooklynites are friendly! This old-timer gives a big thumb's-up at the American Legion Hall in Gowanus. (*Photo: Liz Cooke*)

Above right: What is more Brooklyn than a "Brooklyn vs. Everybody" hoodie, seen here on a resident of Sunset Park? (*Photo: Liz Cooke*)

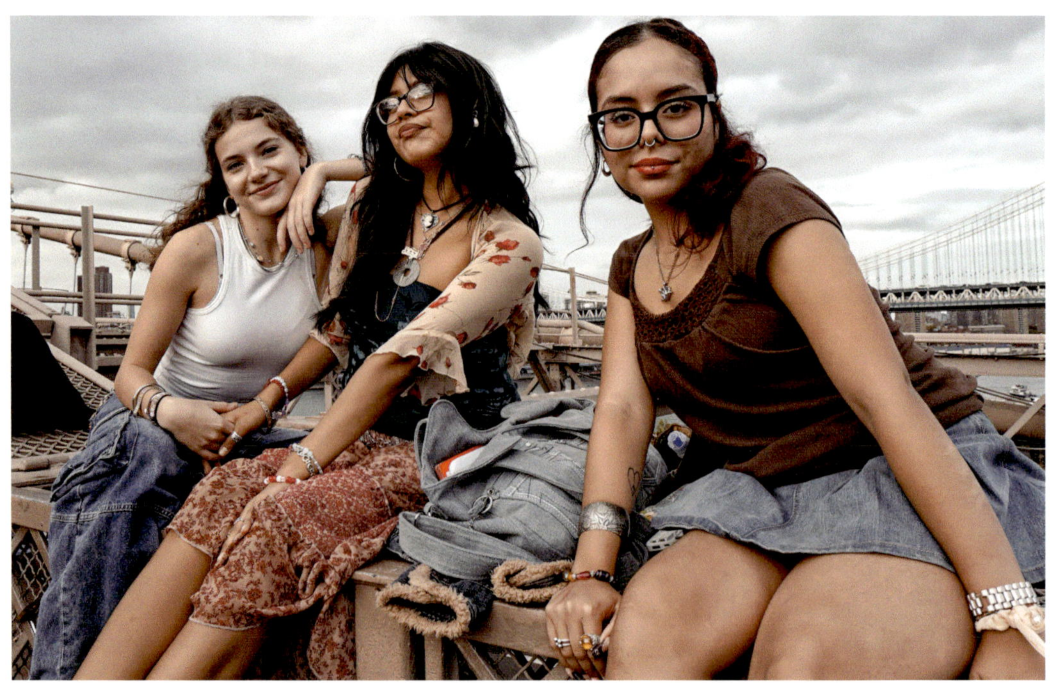

Students from nearby Murry Bergtraum High School strike a pose on the Brooklyn Bridge. (*Photo: Liz Cooke*)

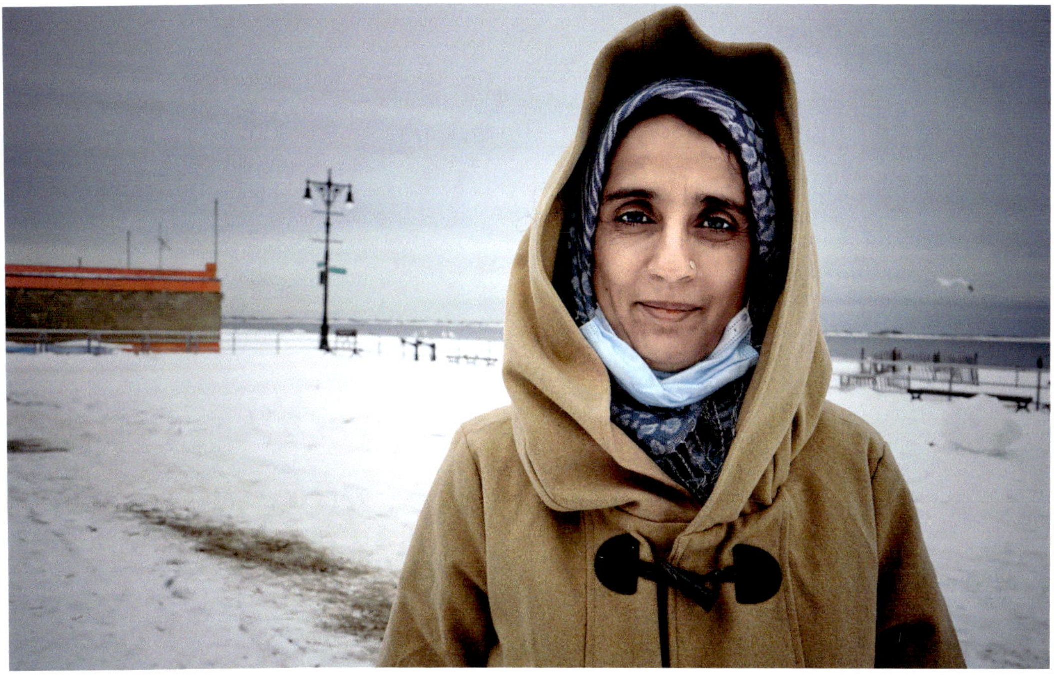

A cold winter's day did not stop this woman from strolling on the boardwalk in Brighton Beach. (*Photo: Liz Cooke*)

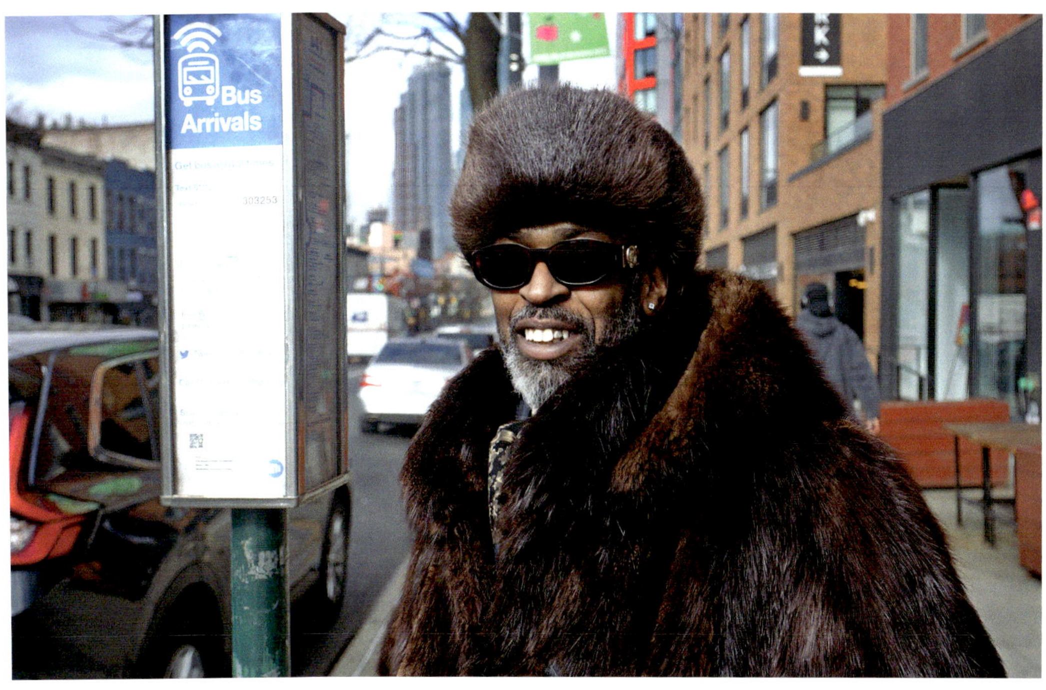

Bold style choices are very Brooklyn, exemplified by this gentleman in Prospect Heights. (*Photo: Andy Milford*)

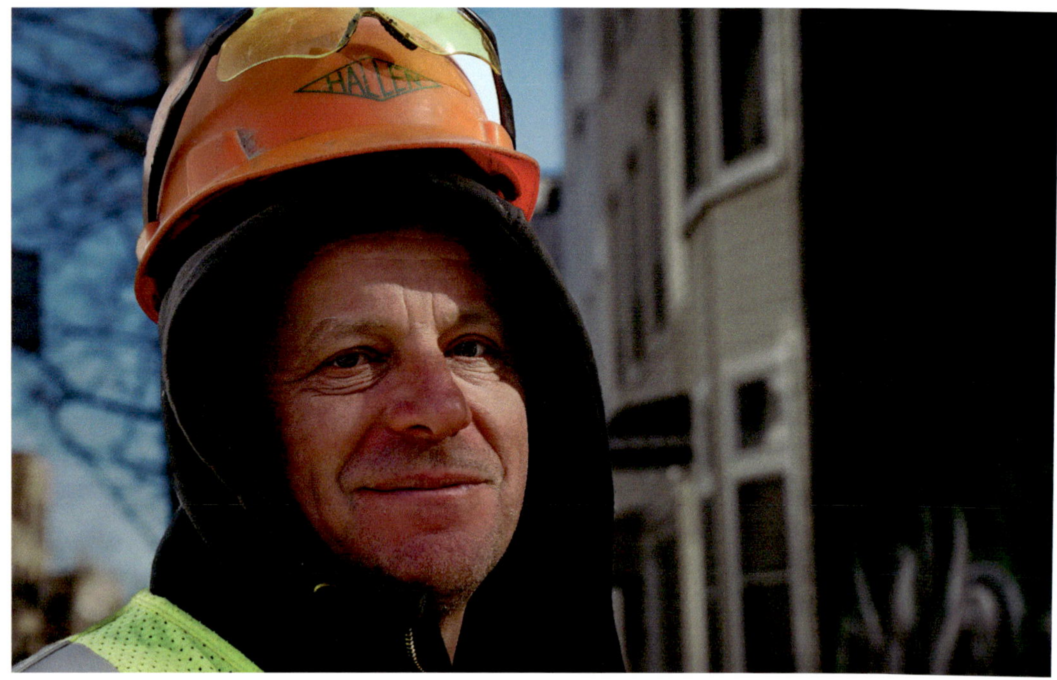

If you are hungry in Greenpoint, look for this man. He will tell you where to get the best paczki (Old Polish Bakery). (*Photo: Liz Cooke*)

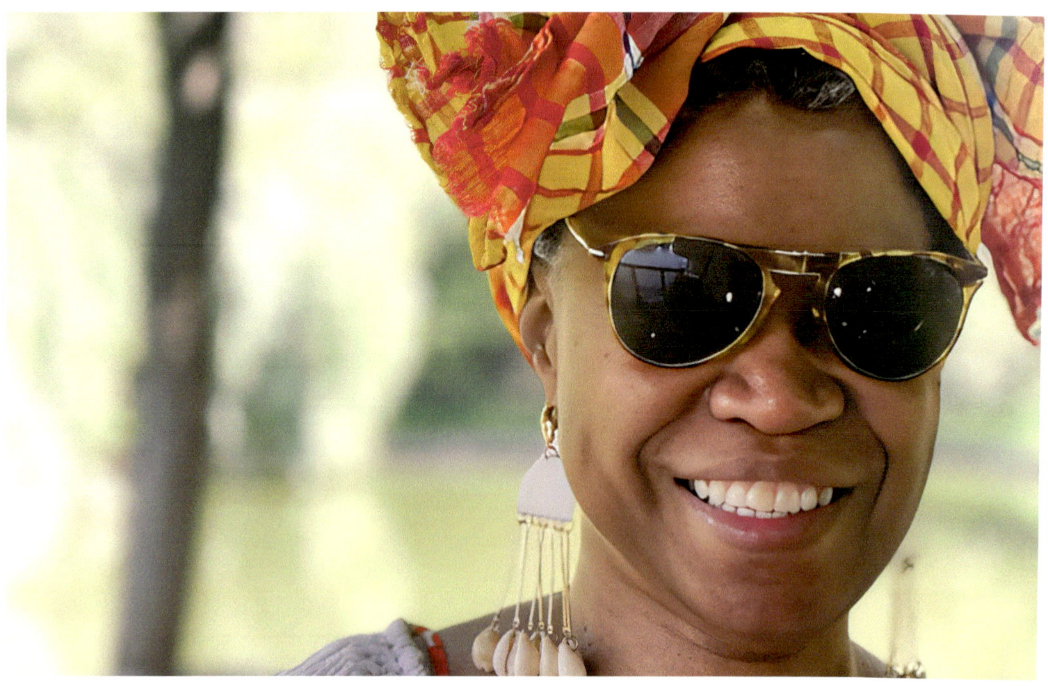

Queenie, enjoying a day at the Brooklyn Botanic Garden. (*Photo: Liz Cooke*)

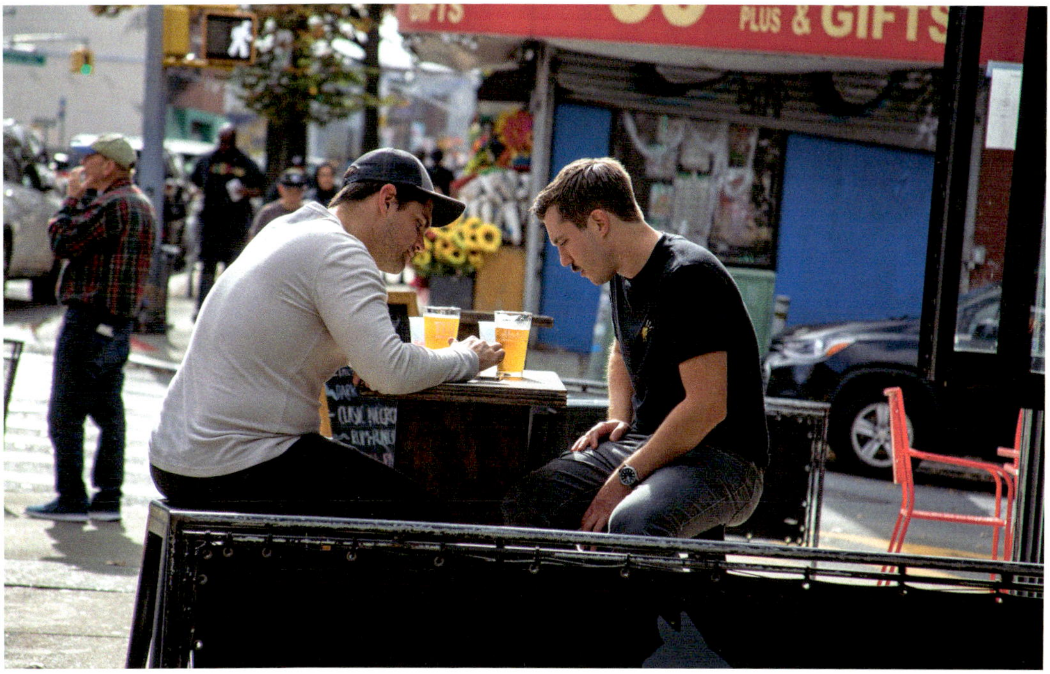

Enjoying the outdoors and a pint on a busy Bushwick street. (*Photo: Andy Milford*)

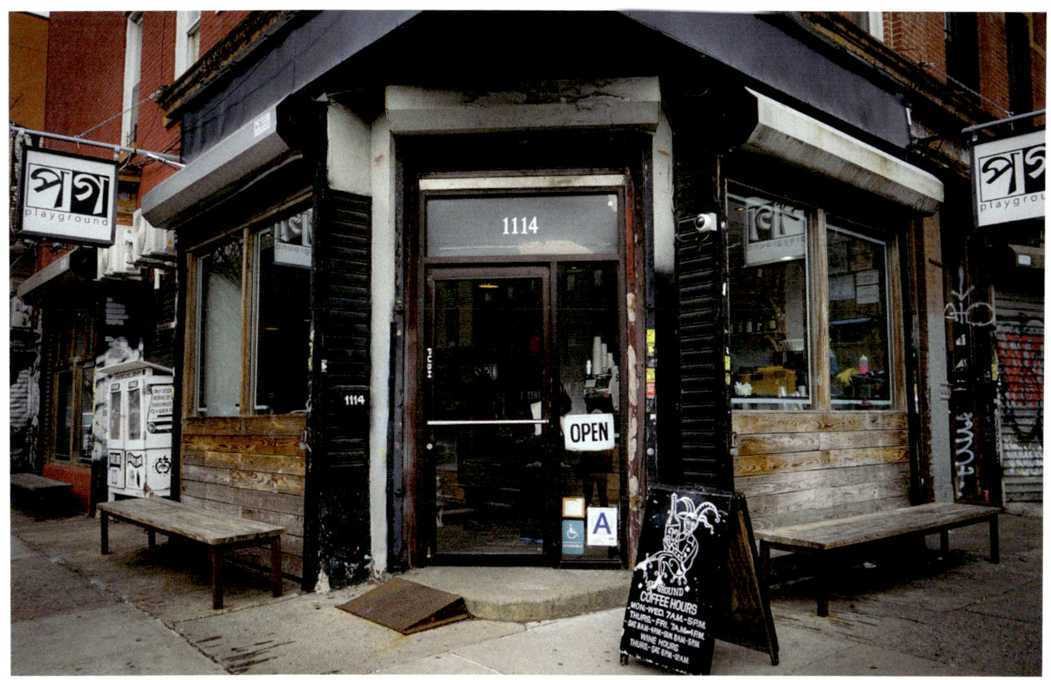

Trendy coffee shops like this one in Bed-Stuy are everywhere in gentrified Brooklyn. (*Photo: Liz Cooke*)

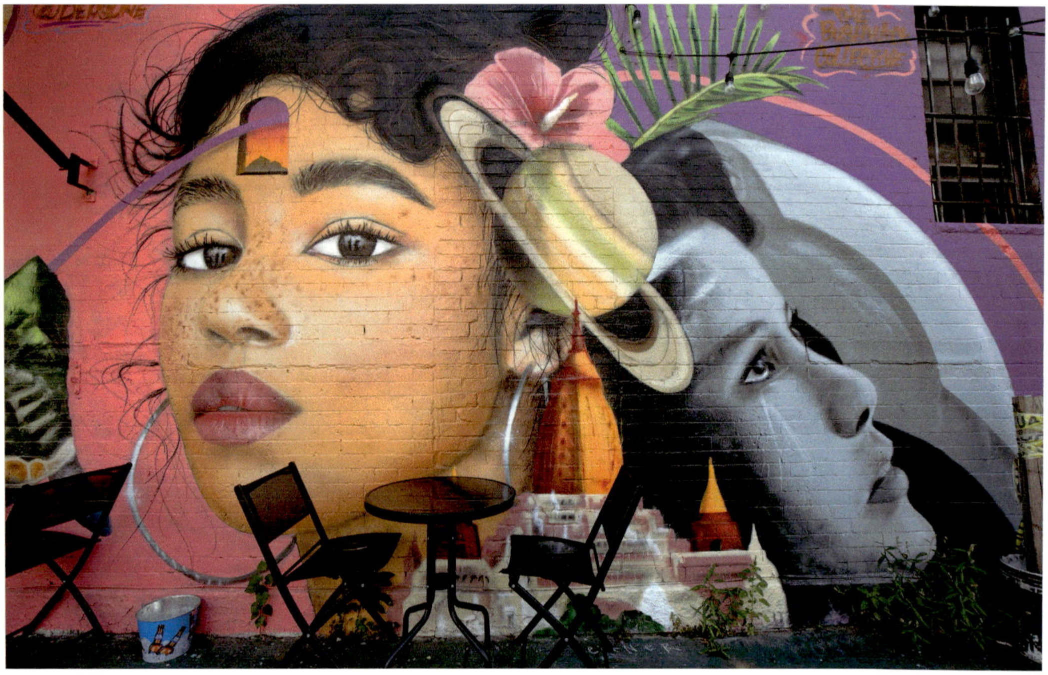

Colorful mural by DepsOne (Carson Deyoung) at the Bushwick Collective. (*Photo: Andy Milford*)

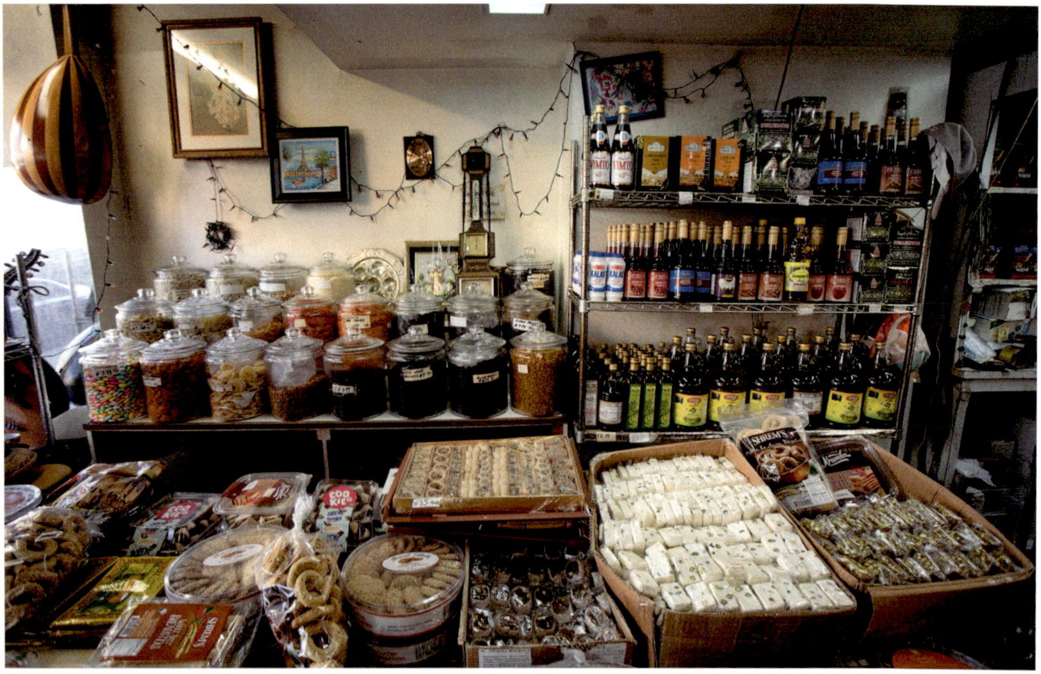

Middle Eastern pastries and groceries at Malko Karkanni Bros. Imports on Atlantic Avenue. (*Photo: Andy Milford*)

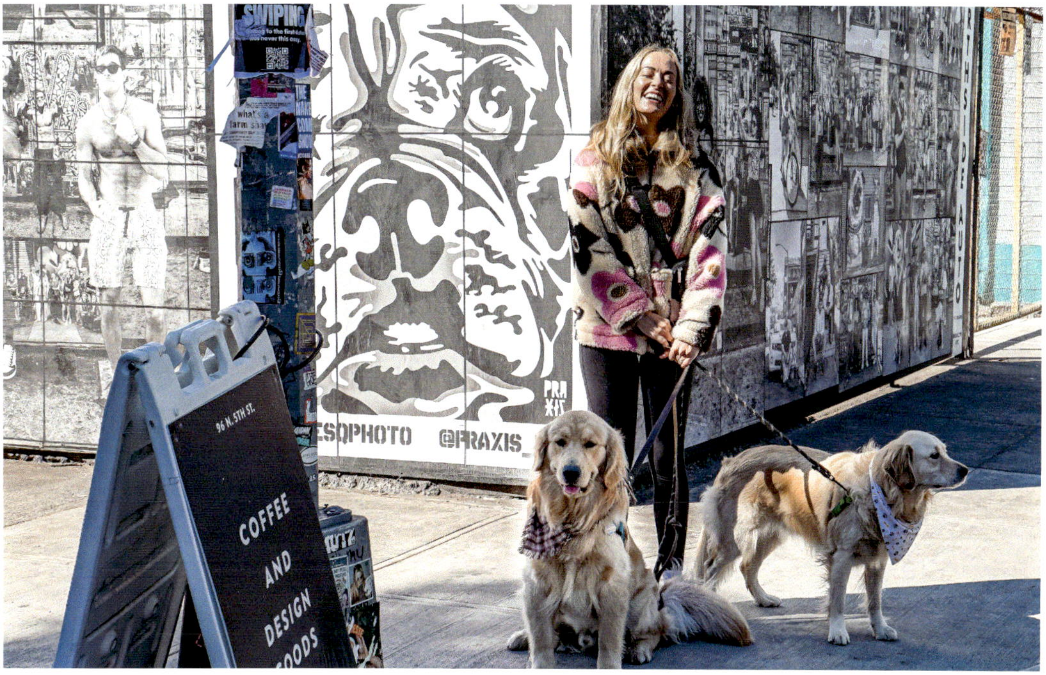

Happy dogs and a happy dogwalker in Williamsburg. (*Photo: Liz Cooke*)

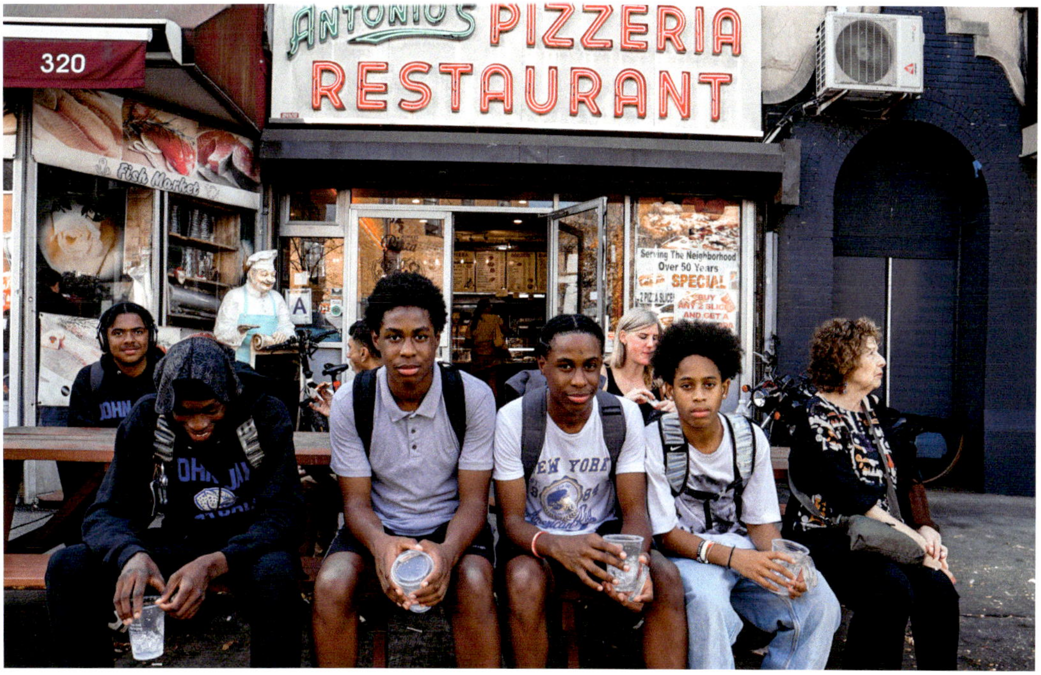

Kids gather after school at Antonio's Pizzeria on Flatbush Avenue in Park Slope. (*Photo: Liz Cooke*)

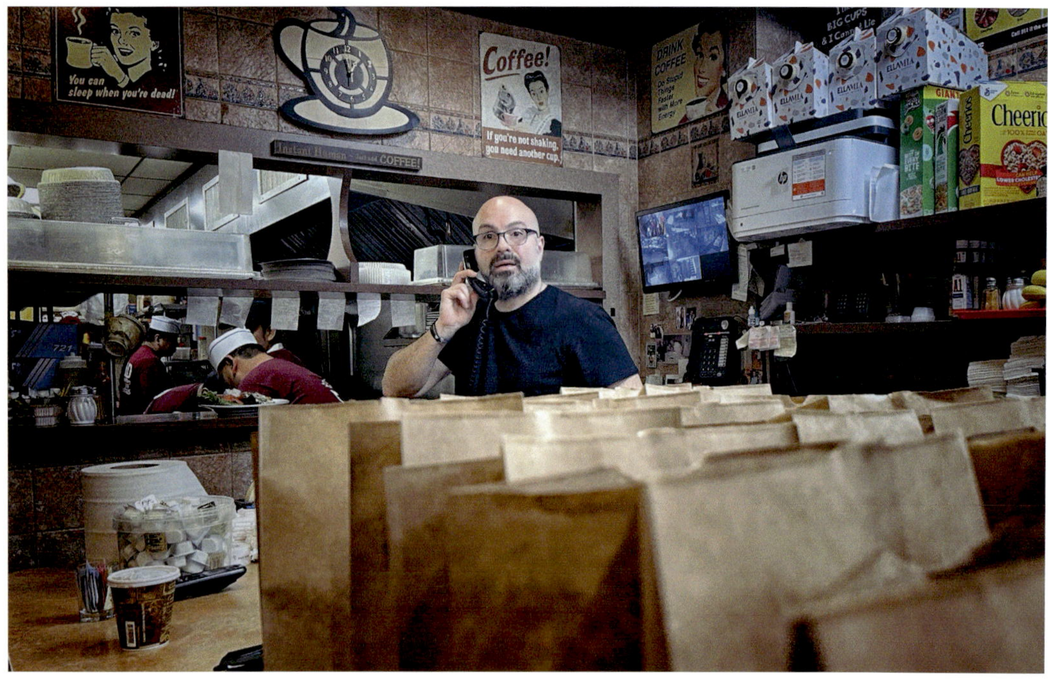

Busy time for takeout at Best Coffee and Luncheonette in Borough Park. (*Photo: Liz Cooke*)

With a land mass of just under 70 square miles, Brooklyn is New York City's second largest borough and arguably, its most iconic. On any street corner, on any day of the week, there will be someone with a story to tell. With more than 2.7 million residents, that is a whole lot of stories. And because Brooklynites are not known for their shy or retiring nature (*fuhgeddaboutit*!), you are bound to hear more than a few colorful tales. You might hear parents bragging about their children's new jobs or complaining about their choice of partners. You might hear about landlords jacking up the rent while withholding heat. You might hear about a new jerk chicken place that opened down the block or a gluten-free bakery with people lined up outside. You'll hear what's worth the money and what's a waste of time. You'll hear old-timers cursing "Dem Bums" for abandoning Brooklyn for Los Angeles almost sixty years ago. You'll hear it all. But it won't all be in English, because in Brooklyn, some 200 languages are spoken, and almost half the population speaks a language other than English at home. And amid all the noise of the trains overhead, the cars jockeying for position, and the sirens blaring, you will hear music, because in Brooklyn—inevitably—someone, somewhere will be blasting music—be it rap, soul, salsa, opera, or klezmer.

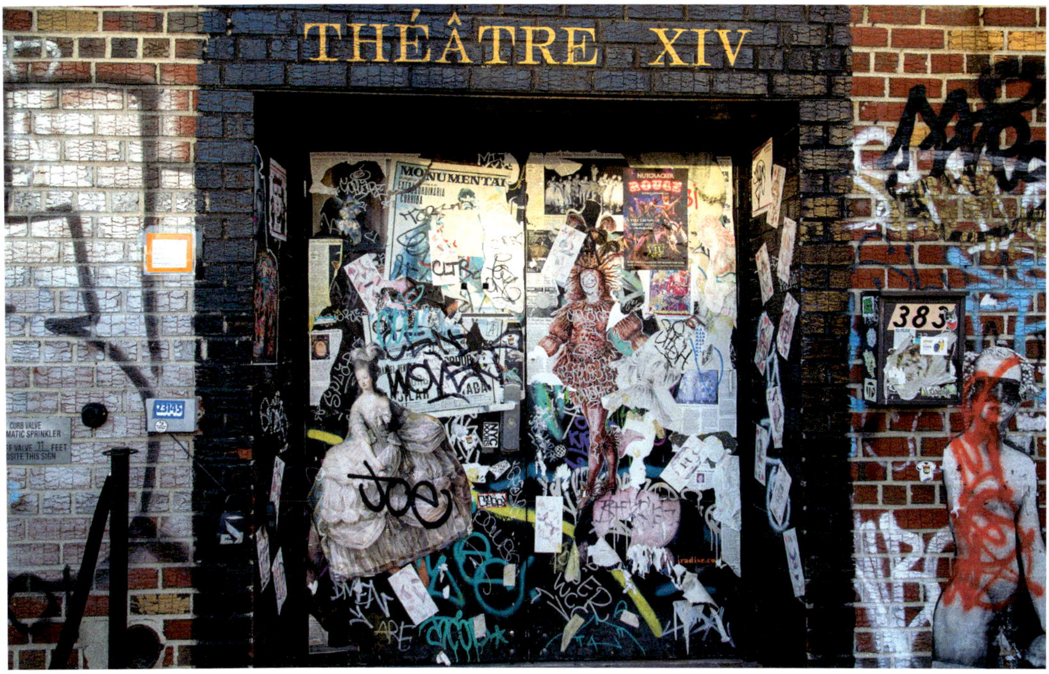

A "phantasmagoria of miracles" awaits at Theatre XIV in Bushwick. (*Photo: Andy Milford*)

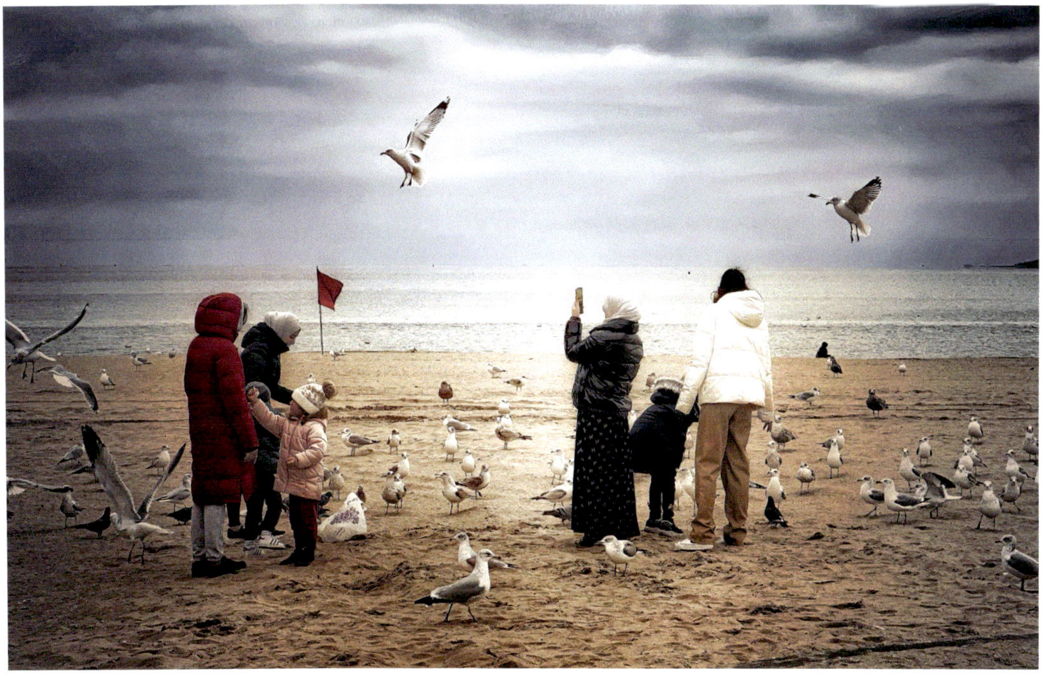

Seagulls gather around a family on a winter's day on Brighton Beach. (*Photo: Liz Cooke*)

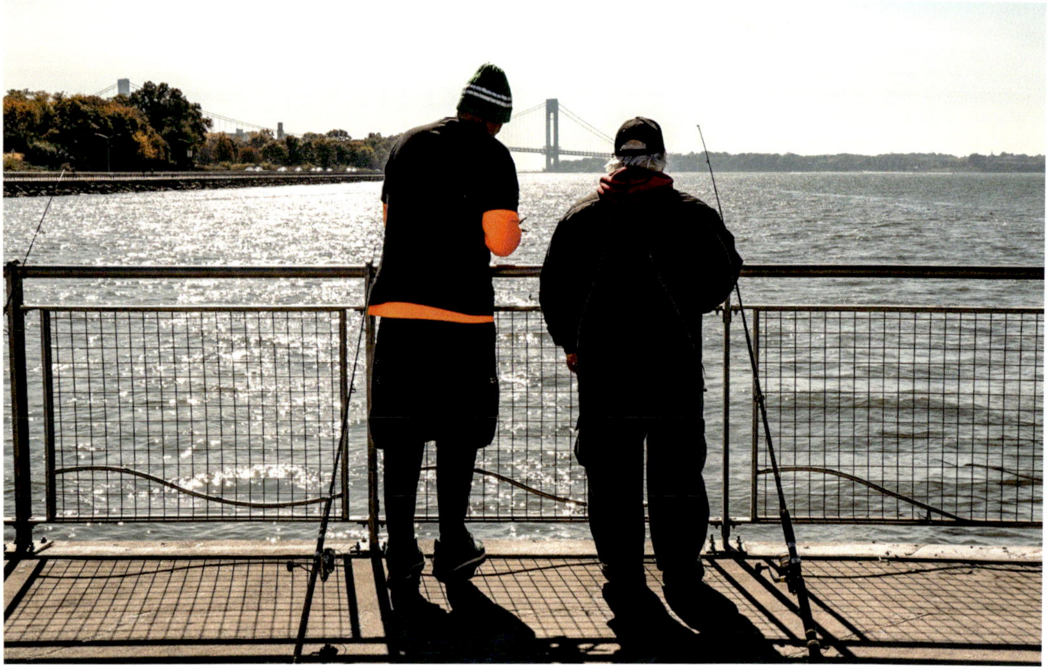

Fishermen enjoying the view of the Verrazzano Bridge from the American Veterans Memorial Pier in Bay Ridge. (*Photo: Liz Cooke*)

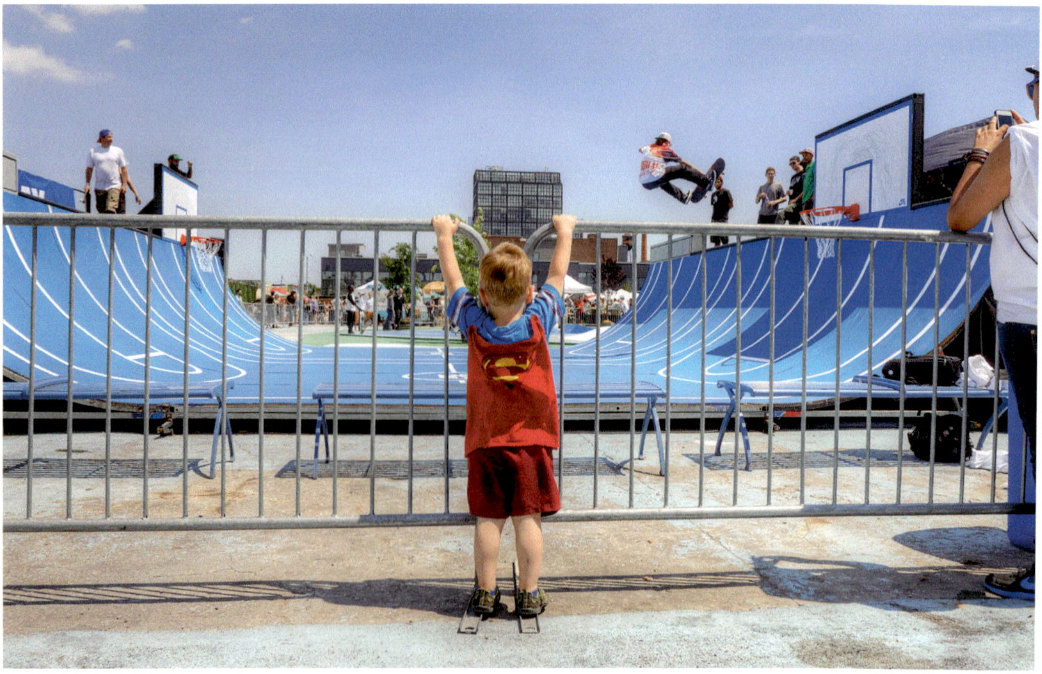

A young boy is fascinated by the skateboarders on "Go Skateboarding Day" in Williamsburg. (*Photo: Andy Milford*)

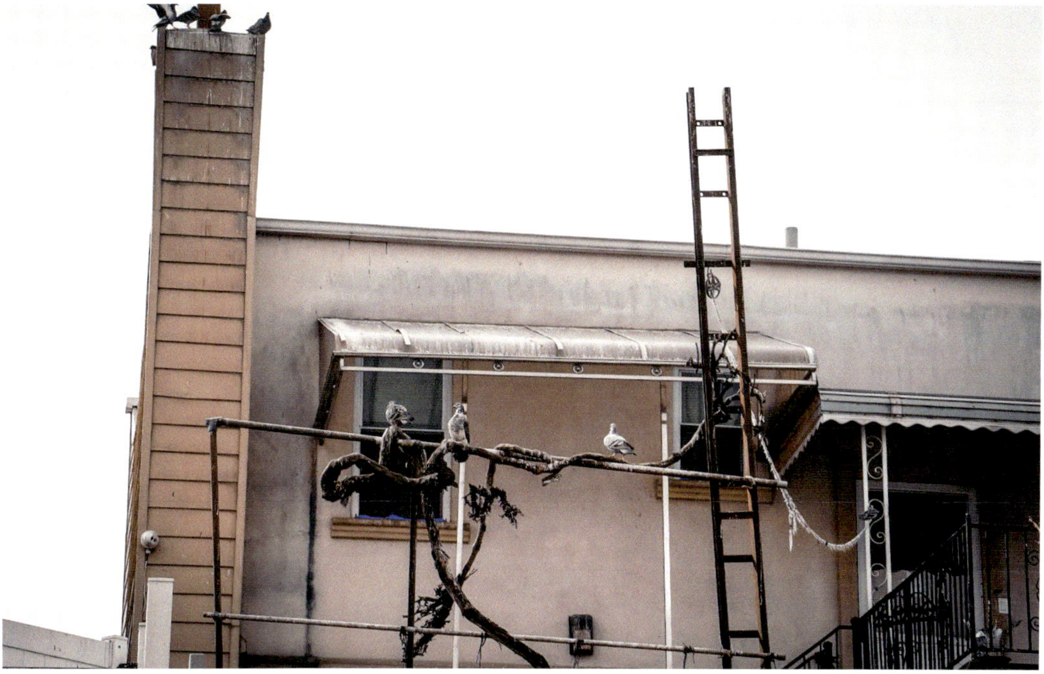

Pigeon racing was once a major sport in Brooklyn. Now, only a handful of "pigeon fanciers" pursue the hobby. This set-up was spotted in Bensonhurst. (*Photo: Liz Cooke*)

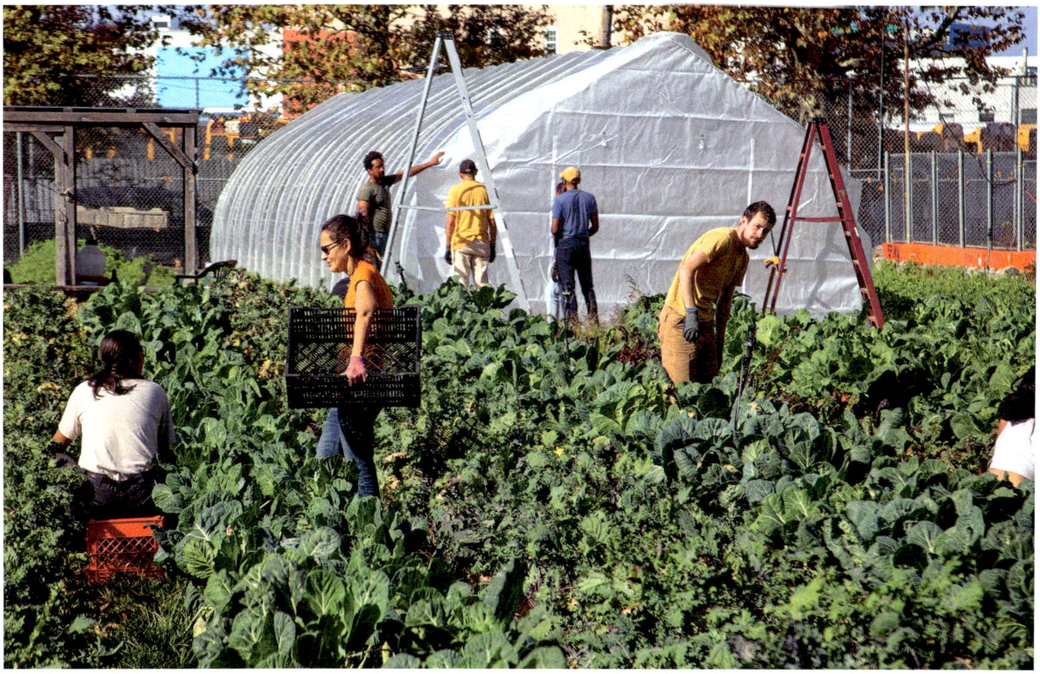

Community members harvesting vegetables at Red Hook Farms, a "youth-centered urban agriculture and food justice program." (*Photo: Andy Milford*)

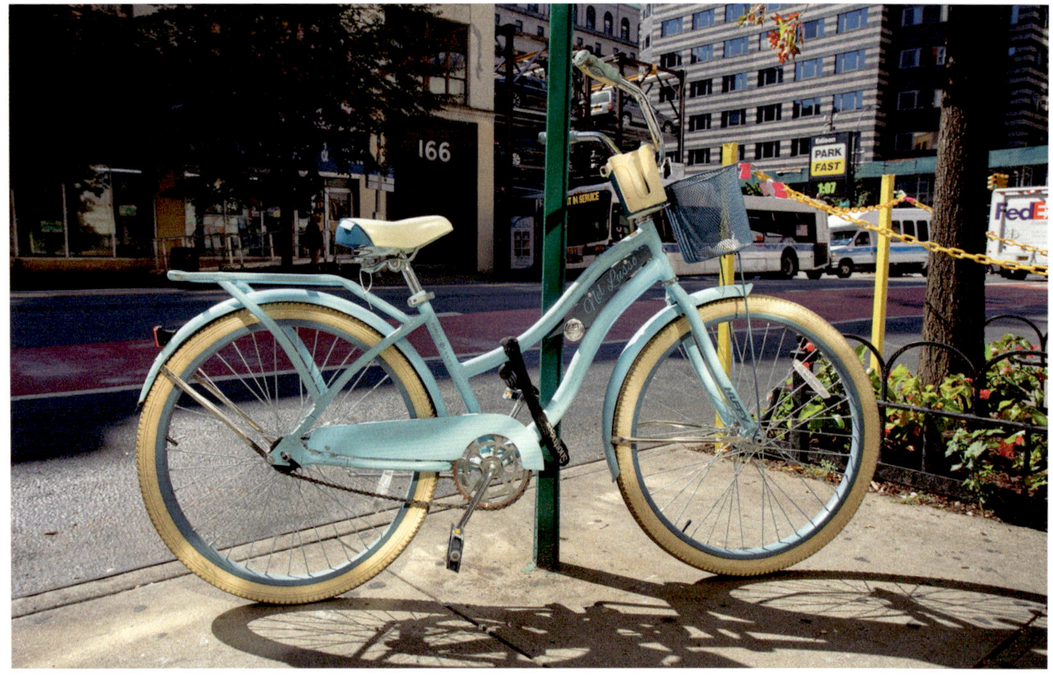

With over 36,000 Citi Bikes and countless other bicycles, scooters and motorcycles, cars may soon be outnumbered on Brooklyn's busy streets. (*Photo: Andy Milford*)

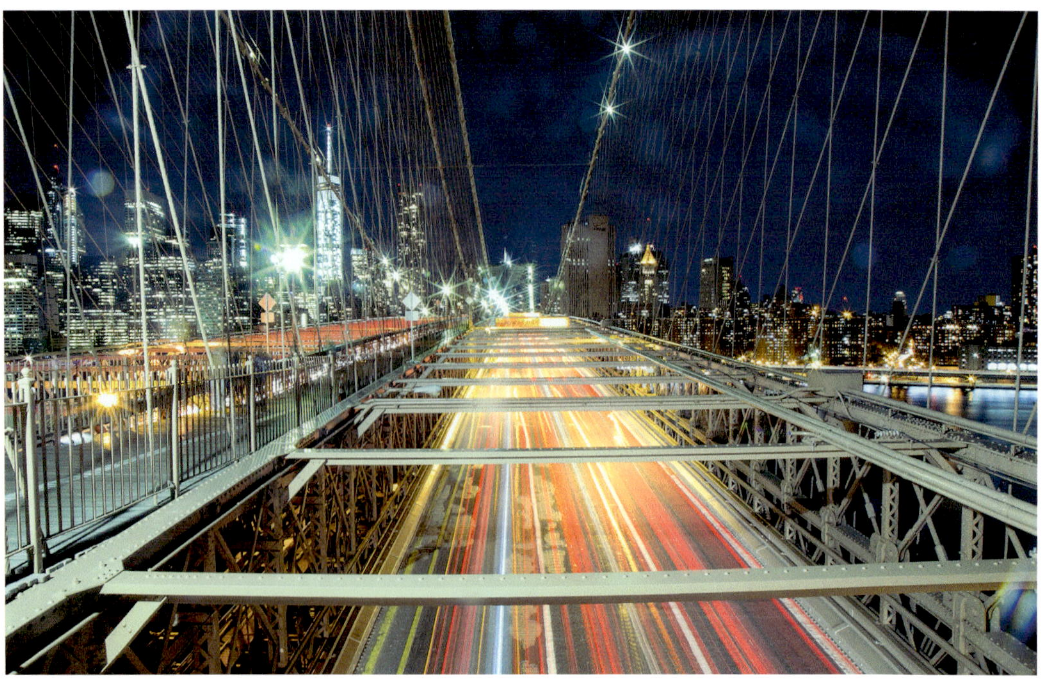

On average, more than 100,000 cars cross the Brooklyn Bridge each day. (*Photo: Andy Milford*)

For some, this cultural kaleidoscope can be overwhelming. But we wouldn't have it any other way. And why wouldn't a photographer want to try to capture it? This book represents that effort. Andy and I have worked together for years, and it did not take much for this Brooklyn girl to persuade a British-born guy to explore Brooklyn together. It has been an utter thrill to see his expression as we move from block to block, visiting pizzerias and places of worship, world-famous landmarks and forgotten back alleys, art galleries, music venues, high rise luxury condos and humble rowhouses, brownstones and bars, all of it beckoning us to come closer and take the shot. We hope you enjoy coming along with us as we share the experience of discovering that there isn't just one Brooklyn, but many.

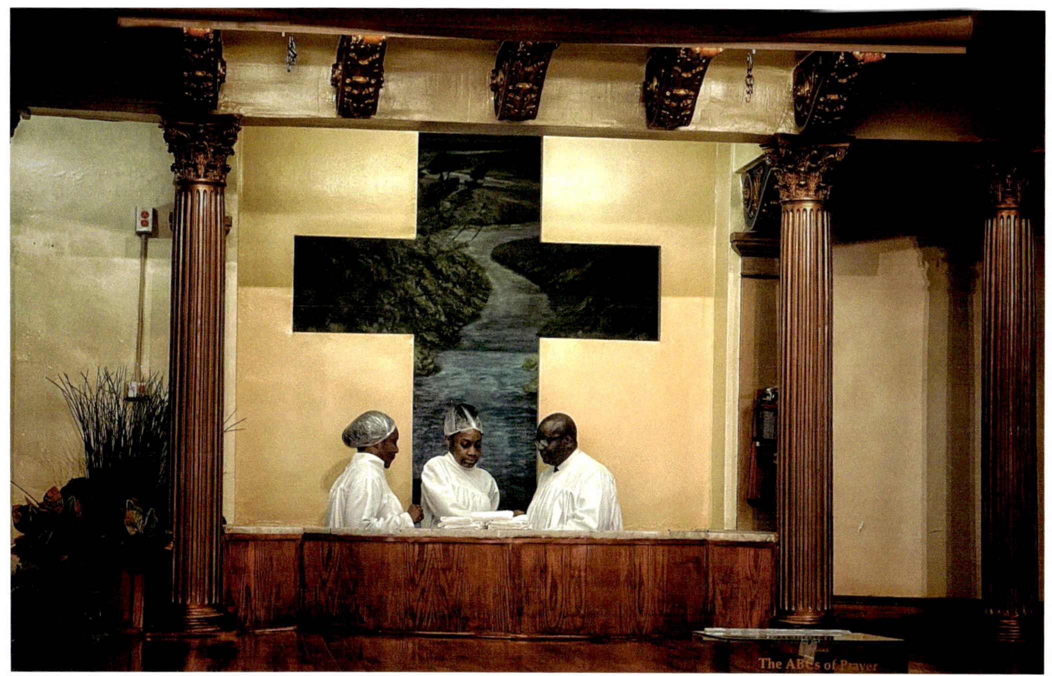

Baptism at the Hanson Place Seventh Day Adventist Church in Fort Greene. (*Photo: Liz Cooke*)

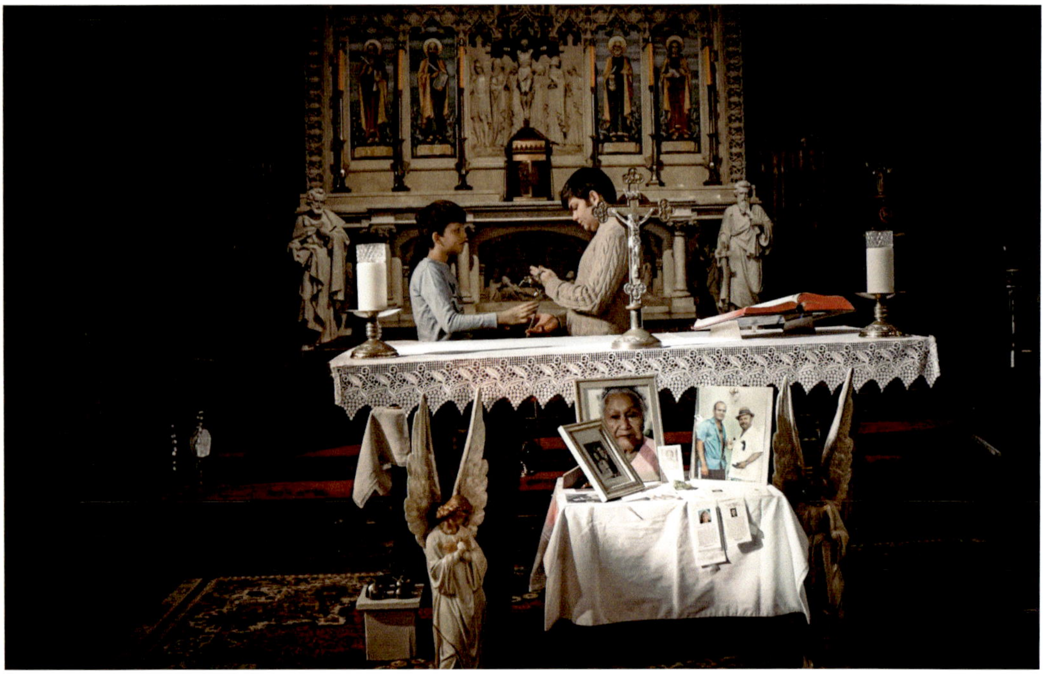

Prepping the altar at St. Paul's Roman Catholic church in Cobble Hill. (*Photo: Liz Cooke*)

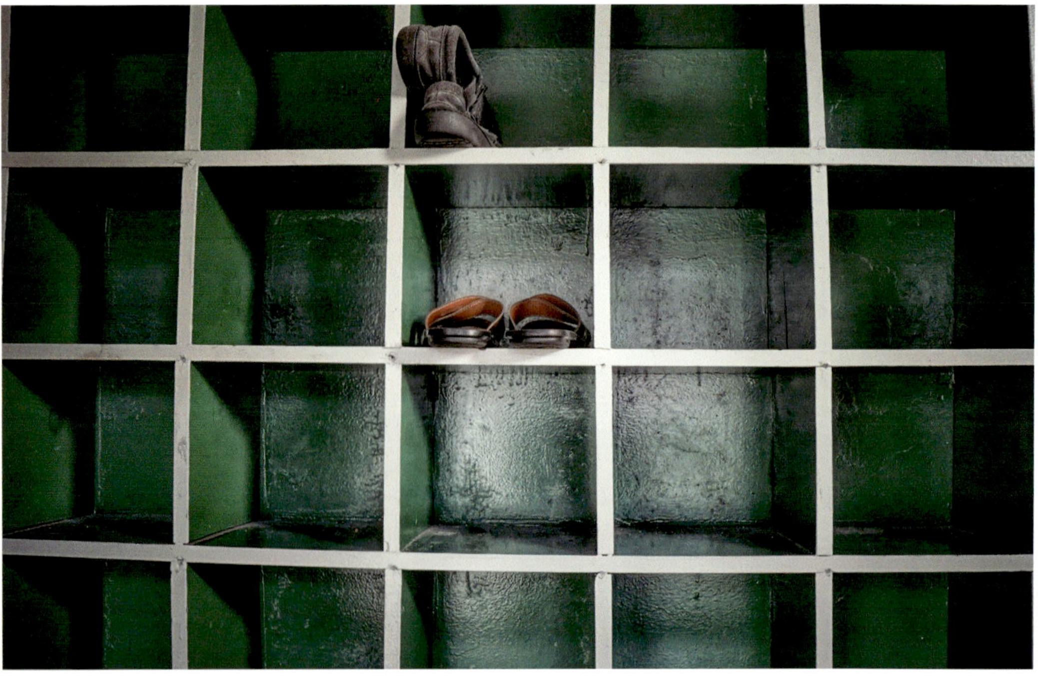

Shoes at the Masjid Al-Ihsaan Mosque in Crown Heights. (*Photo: Liz Cooke*)

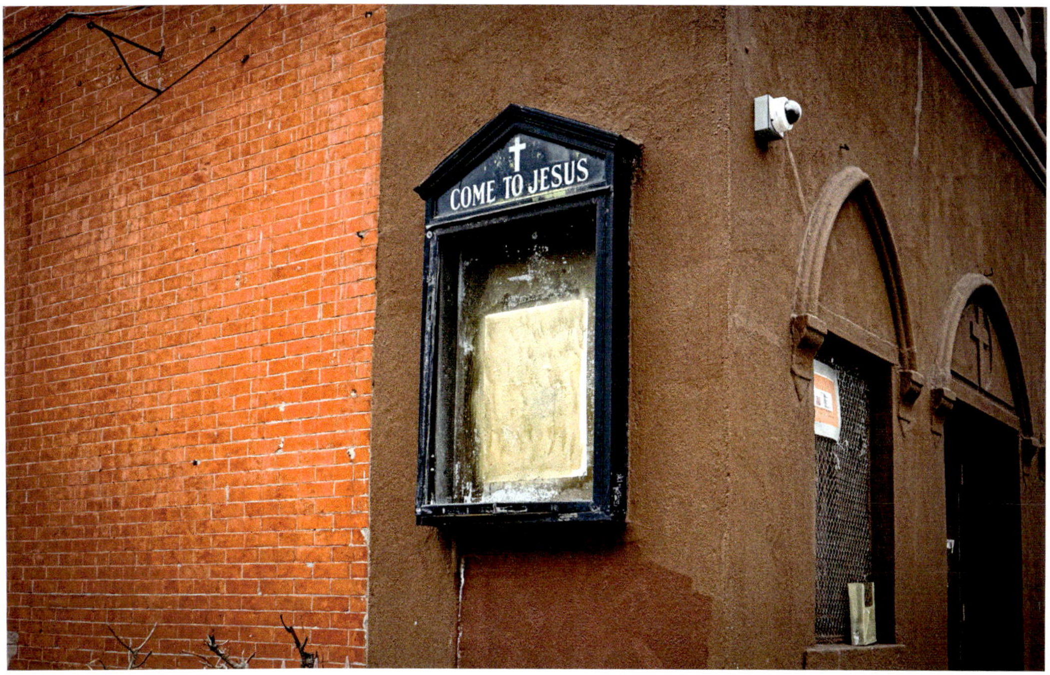

"Come to Jesus" at a Bedford Street church in Bed-Stuy. (*Photo: Liz Cooke*)

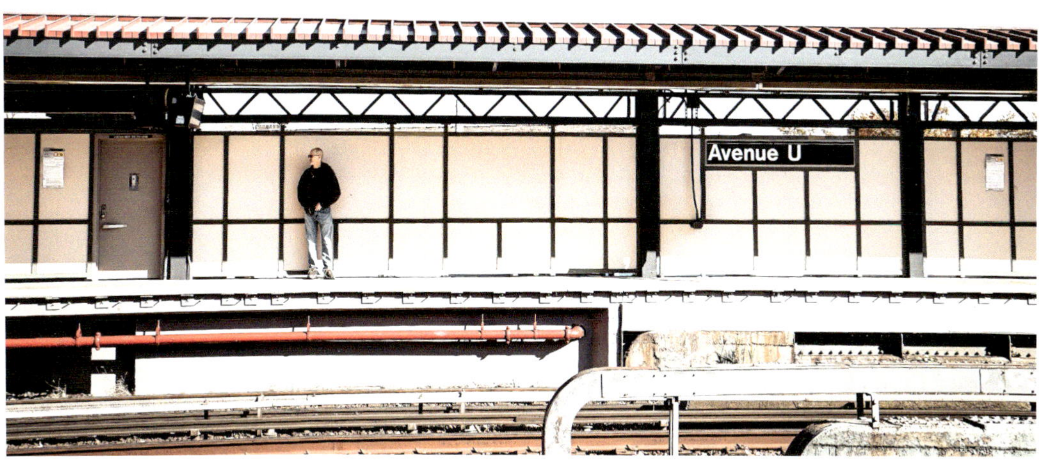

Waiting for the Manhattan-bound train at the Avenue U stop in Homecrest. (*Photo: Liz Cooke*)

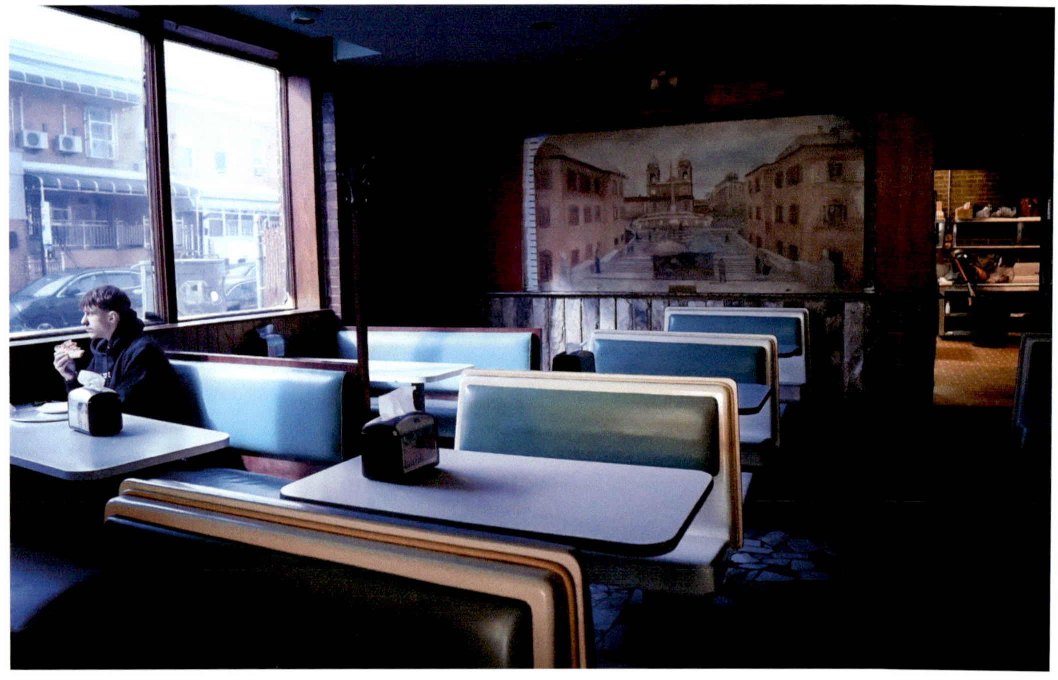

Quiet time after the lunch crowd at J&V Pizzeria on 18th Avenue in Bensonhurst. (*Photo: Liz Cooke*)

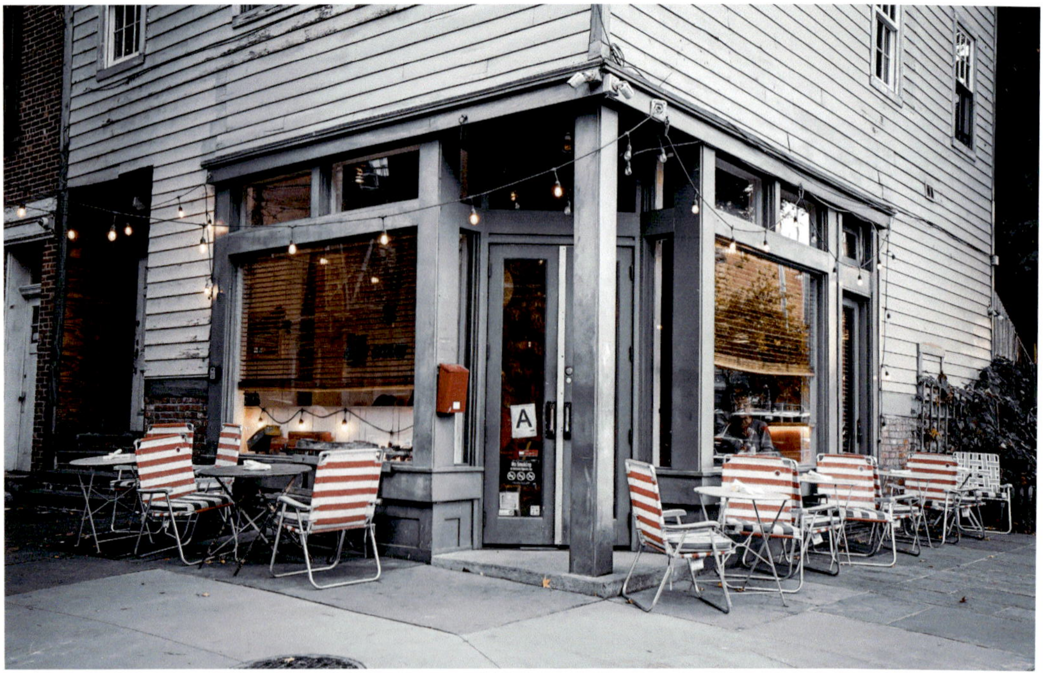

The unhurried pace of Vinegar Hill is the perfect setting for brunch at Cafe Gitane. (*Photo: Liz Cooke*)

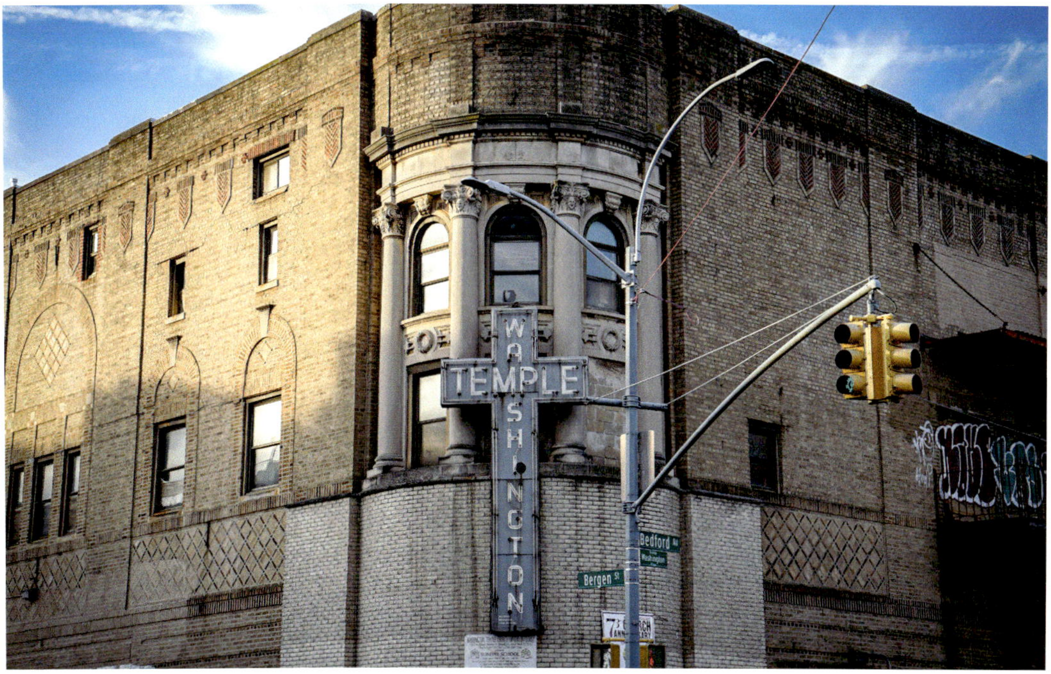

Above: Washington Temple Church of God In Christ in Crown Heights. (*Photo: Liz Cooke*)

Right: Observant Jews walk everywhere on Shabbos. This group is seen on Fort Hamilton Parkway in Borough Park. (*Photo: Liz Cooke*)

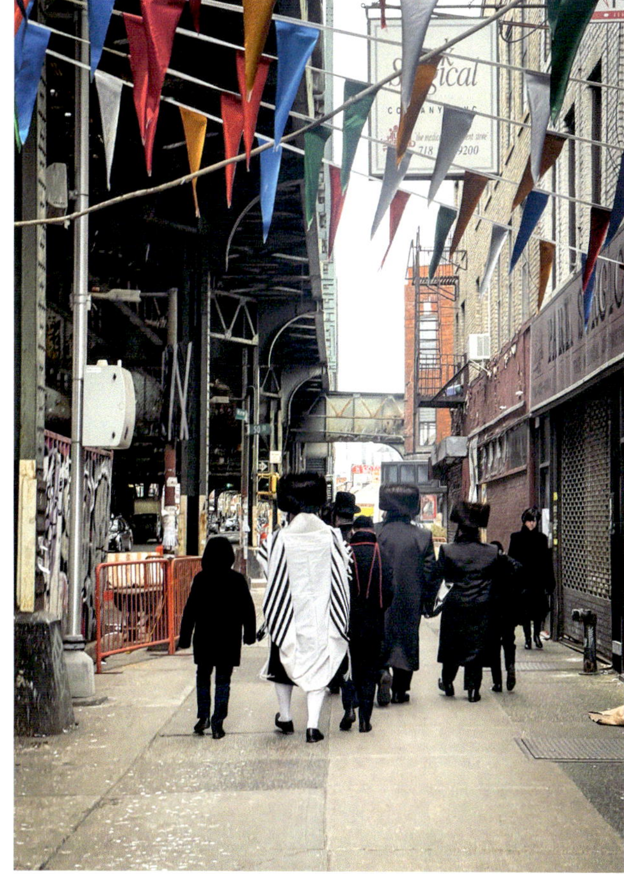

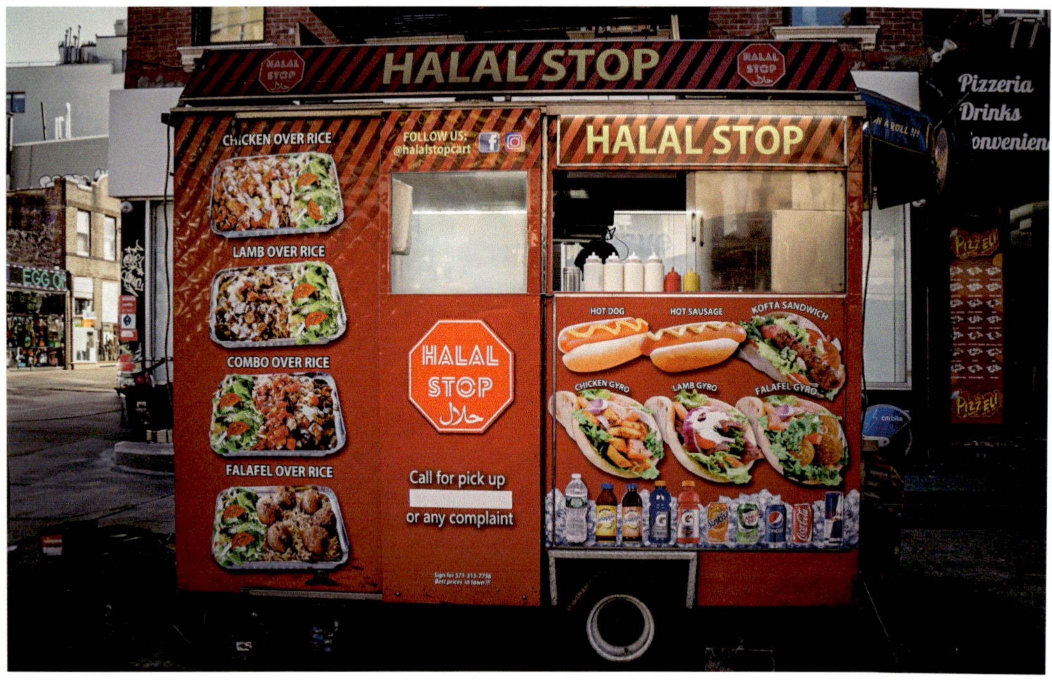

The Halal Stop cart in Williamsburg offers an alternative to the high-priced fare found in neighborhood restaurants. (*Photo: Liz Cooke*)

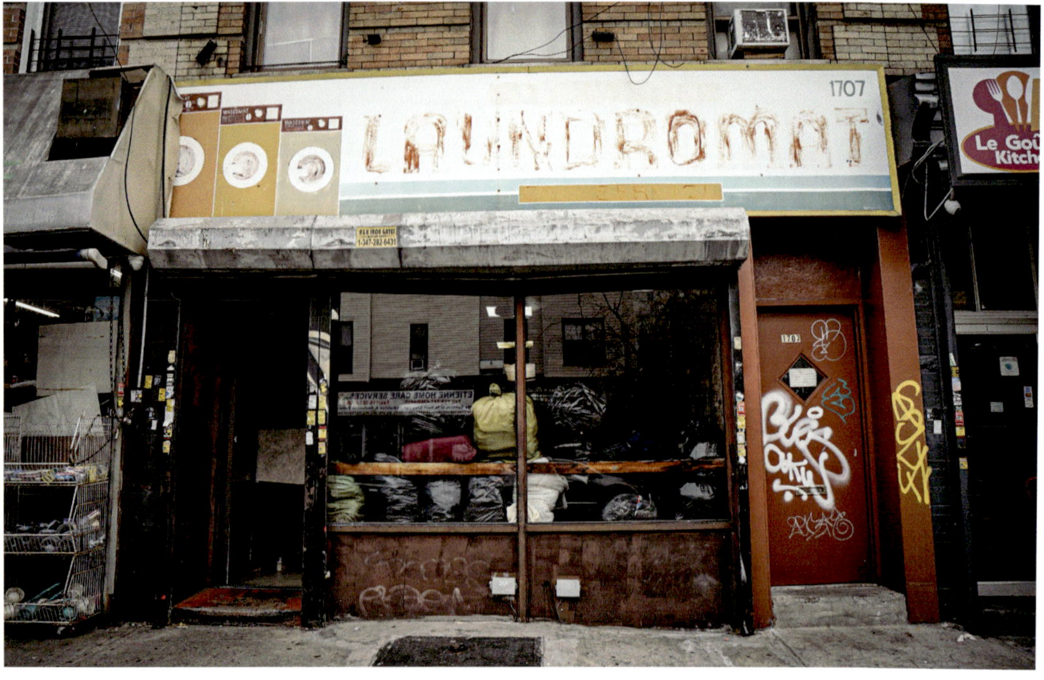

A faded sign above a laundromat in Little Haiti. (*Photo: Liz Cooke*)

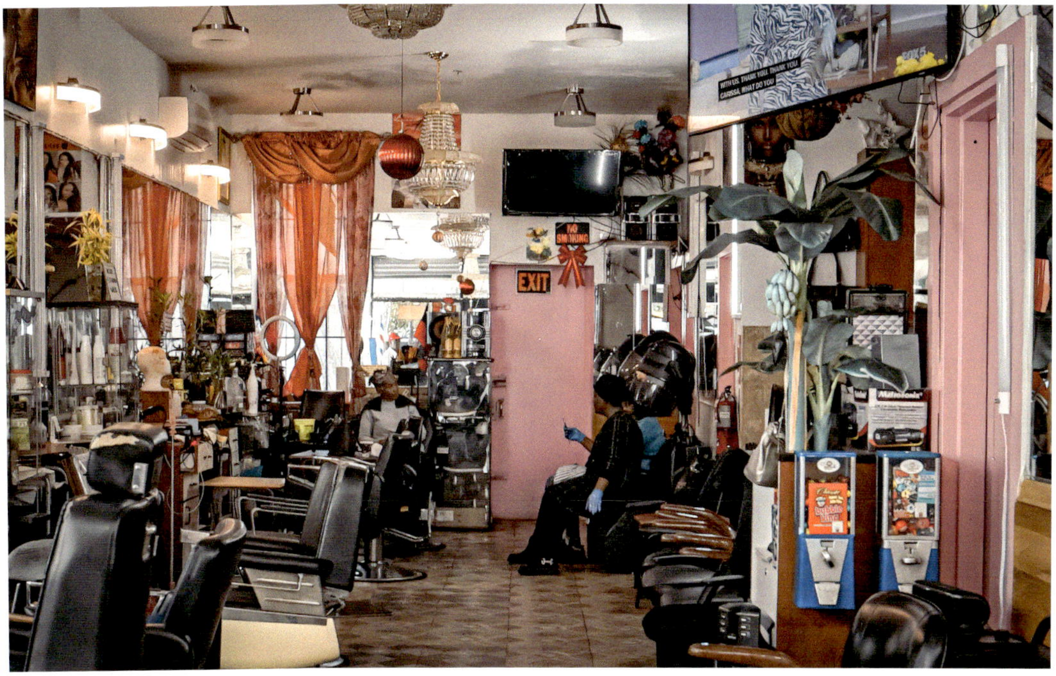

This Little Haiti beauty salon is more than a place for a new hairdo; it is a vibrant community gathering place. *(Photo: Liz Cooke)*

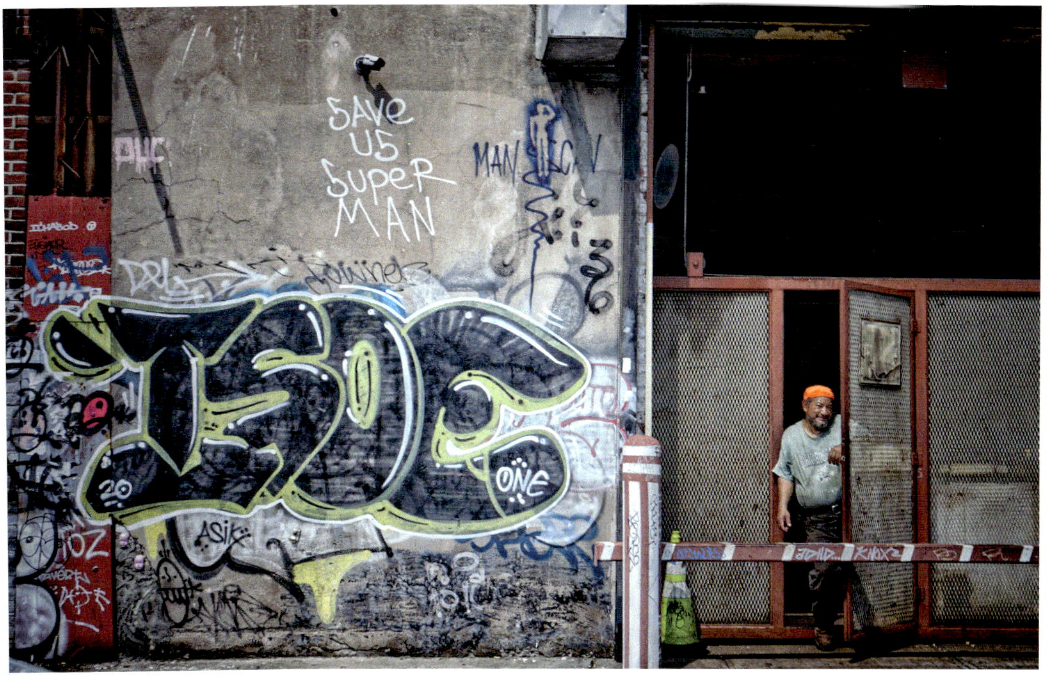

"Save us Super Man" and a friendly worker, seen in Gowanus. *(Photo: Liz Cooke*]

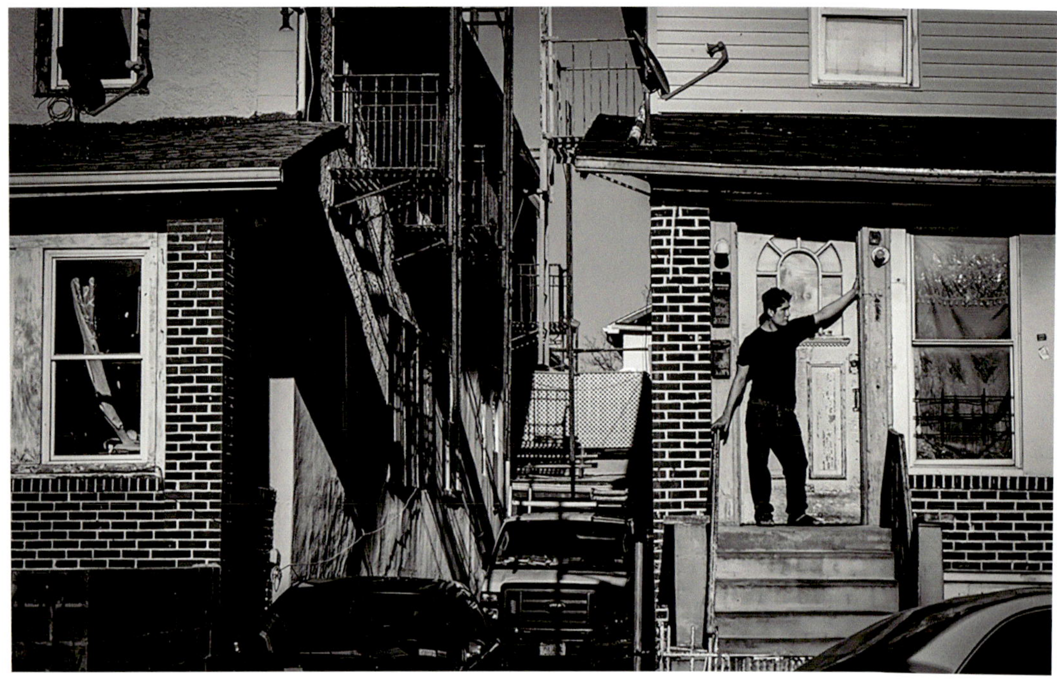

Brighton Beach has an eclectic mix of homes and apartments, including Art Deco pre-war buildings and modest brick houses and bungalows. (*Photo: Liz Cooke*)

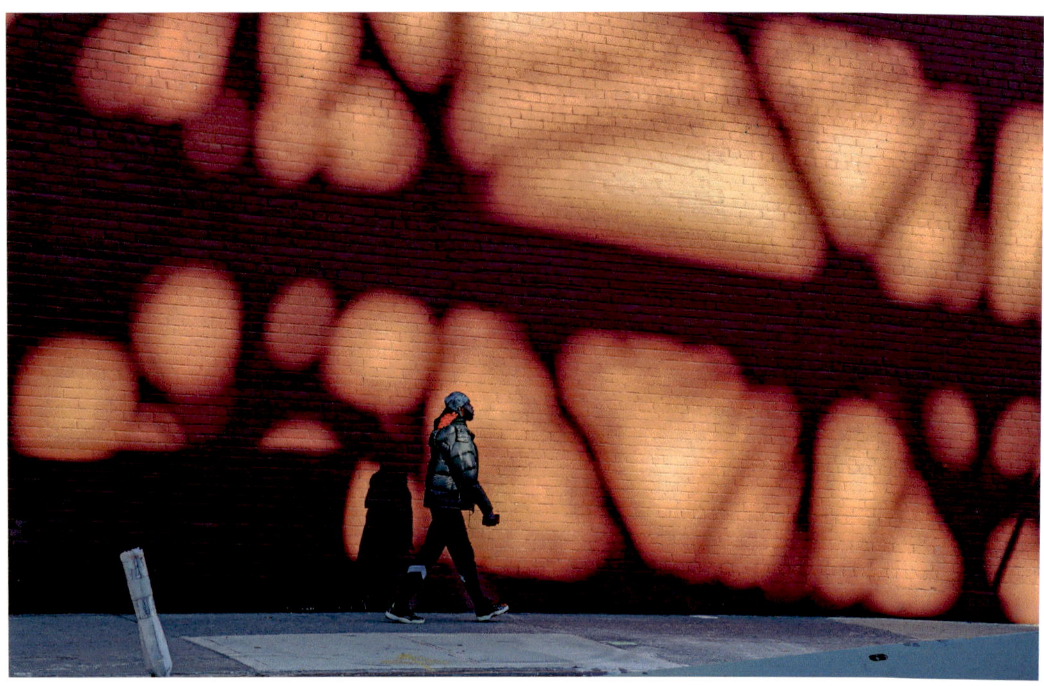

The concrete and steel Culver Viaduct casts colorful shadows in Gowanus. (*Photo: Liz Cooke*)

1

Gentrified Brooklyn

Gentrification in Brooklyn is one of those topics upon which everyone has an opinion. For some, it's a story of revival—formerly neglected neighborhoods becoming safer and more vibrant. For others, it's a tale of loss, with communities pushed out by skyrocketing rents and luxury condos replacing longtime staples. Either way, the changes in Brooklyn over the last few decades are undeniable, reshaping the borough from a working-class stronghold to one of the trendiest and most expensive places to live in the country.

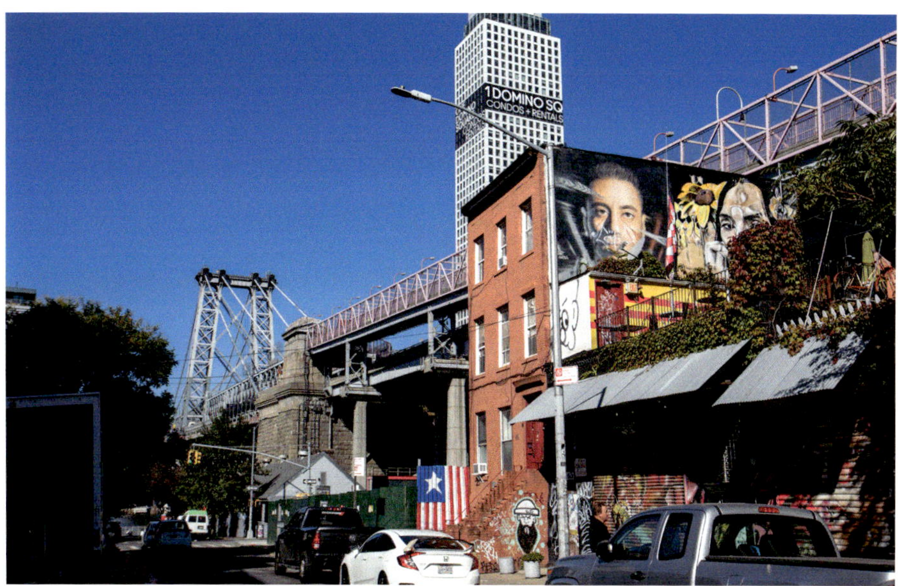

Modern and historic architecture meet at the entrance to the Williamsburg Bridge. (*Photo: Andy Milford*)

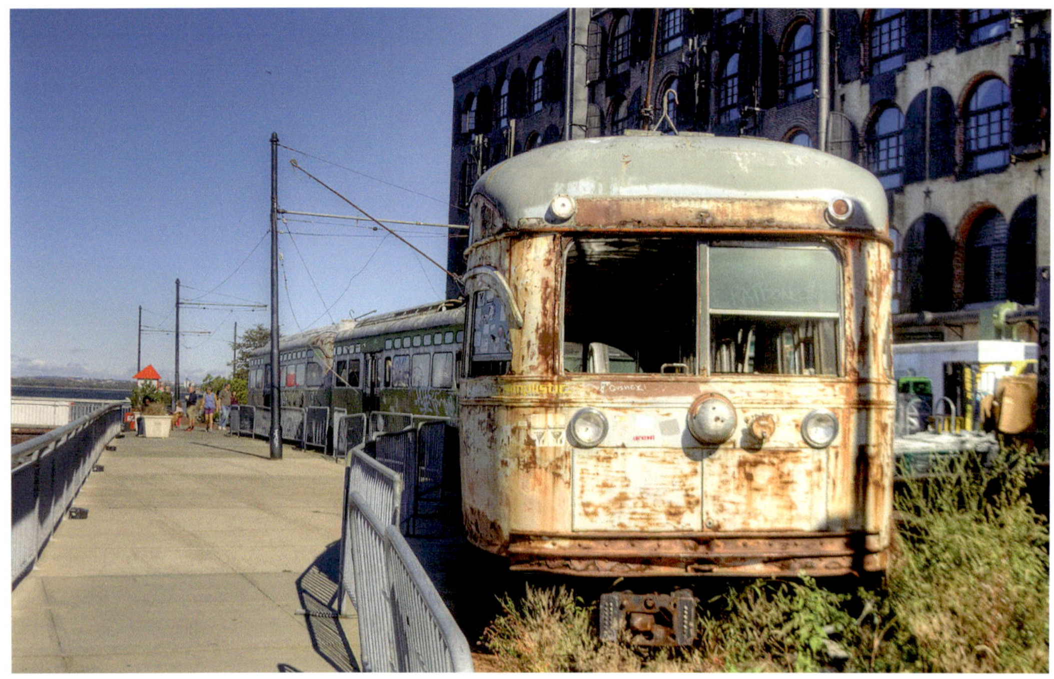

These old streetcars were meant to connect Red Hook with the rest of the borough. The dream never came to pass and they are now deteriorating in plain sight. (*Photo: Andy Milford*)

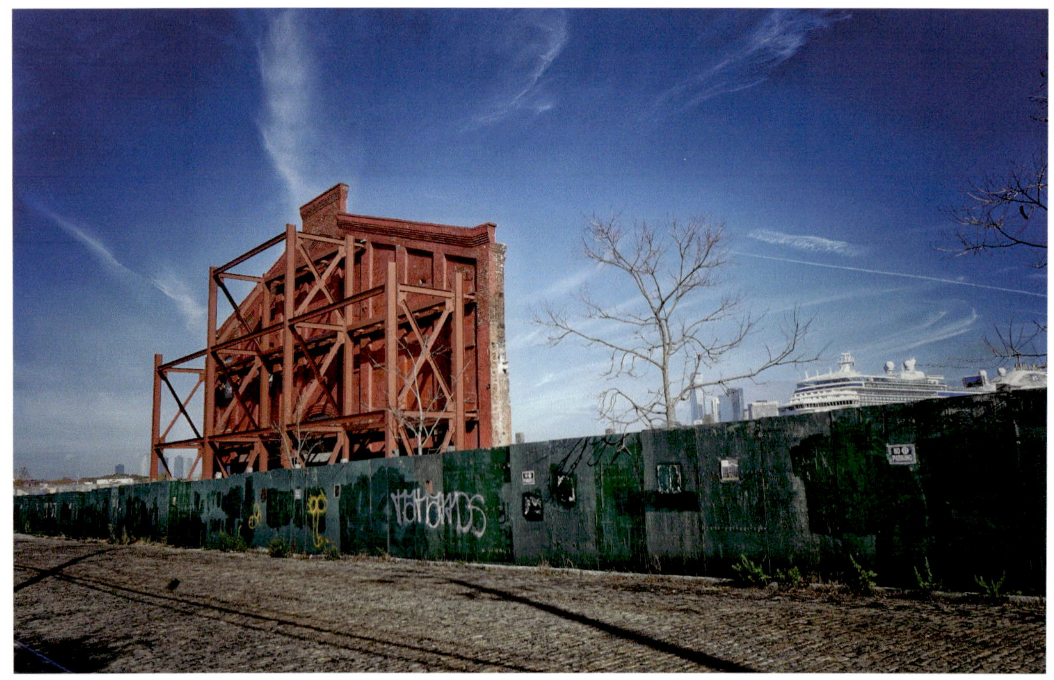

The remains of the Potemkin Building, a nineteenth-century grain terminal, are visible from the Brooklyn Cruise Terminal in Red Hook. (*Photo: Andy Milford*)

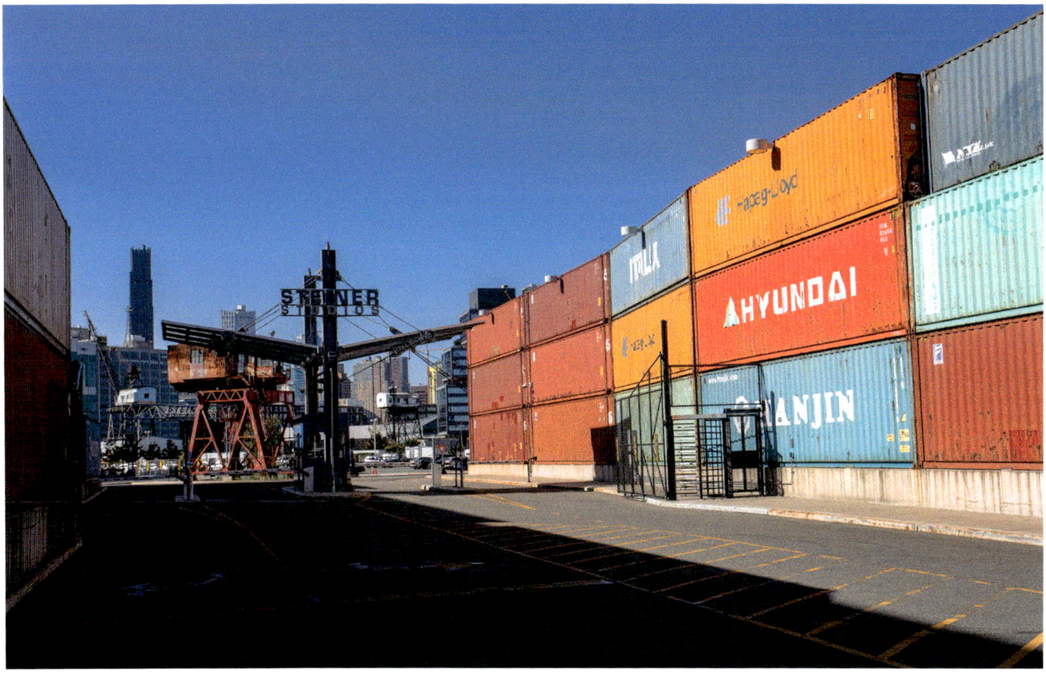

These containers mark the entrance to Steiner Studios in the Brooklyn Navy Yard. Opened in 2004, Steiner Studios is the largest television and film production studio outside Hollywood. (*Photo: Andy Milford*)

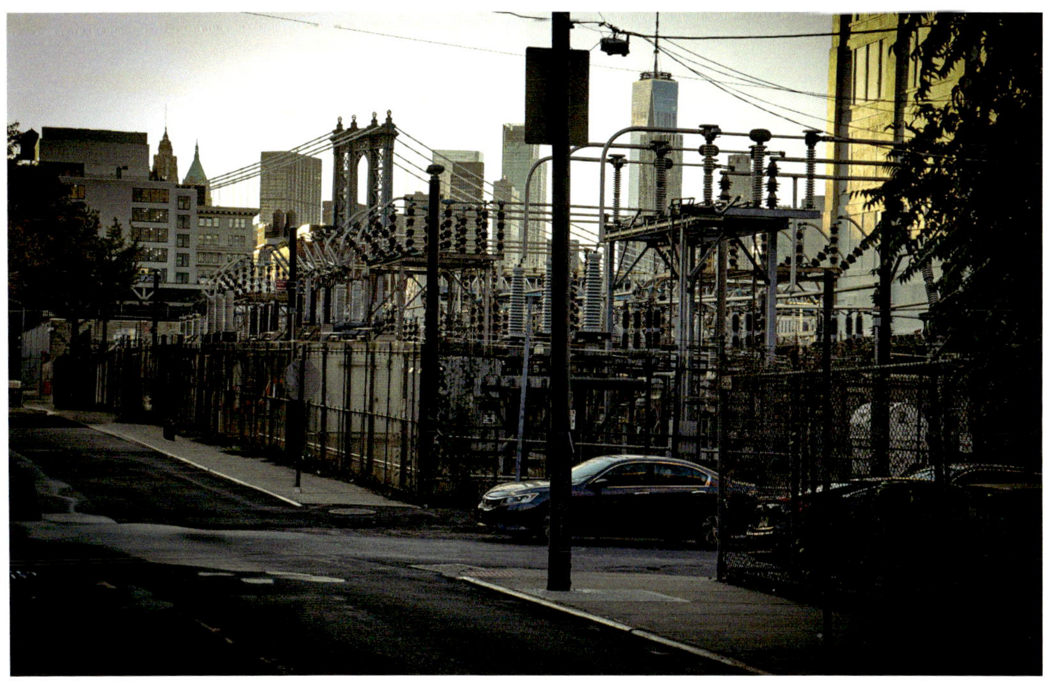

Vinegar Hill was once filled with factories, warehouses, and power plants. The area is seen here with the towers of the Manhattan Bridge in the distance. (*Photo: Liz Cooke*)

In the 1970s and 1980s, Brooklyn was a very different place. Areas like Williamsburg and Greenpoint were largely industrial, with abandoned warehouses and a struggling blue-collar population. Brownstone neighborhoods like Park Slope, Brooklyn Heights, and Cobble Hill were seen as unsafe and undesirable. Services in historically Black neighborhoods like Bushwick, Bedford-Stuyvesant, and Brownsville were severely underfunded. Immigrant neighborhoods like Flatbush, Crown Heights, and Sunset Park were experiencing high levels of crime and disruption. All over Brooklyn, businesses were shutting down and people were moving out.

Things began to change in the 1990s. Artists, priced out of Manhattan neighborhoods like SoHo and the West Village, began crossing the river in search of affordable studio space. Williamsburg became a magnet for creatives and the tree-lined neighborhoods of Brooklyn Heights, Park Slope, and Cobble Hill attracted young professionals. In the 2000s, the rezoning of Williamsburg and Greenpoint allowed residential development along the waterfront. As a consequence, many working-class Puerto Rican and Dominican families struggled to stay in "Los Sures," or South Williamsburg. With a growing demand for luxury developments, the cost of living soared, trendy cafes, upscale restaurants, and designer boutiques followed, leaving shuttered groceries, bakeries, and bodegas in their wake.

During this period, many other parts of Brooklyn were experiencing their own transformations. Dumbo ("Down Under the Manhattan Bridge Overpass") was a virtual no-man's-land in those earlier days. It now boasts multi-million-dollar lofts, galleries, coffee shops, and markets. Nearby Vinegar Hill, also a bit of a no-man's-land, offered little in the way of amenities. It now has a handful of inviting shops and restaurants. Red Hook, once a busy port and later a forgotten piece of real estate, is now home to a sprawling Ikea and a growing art and restaurant scene. Fort Greene, known for its African American cultural and literary roots, saw an influx of wealthier residents drawn by its stunning brownstone-lined streets. Bushwick and Bedford-Stuyvesant, long centers of Black culture and history, became prime spots for gentrification. Even Gowanus, which for years was known primarily for the spectacularly polluted Gowanus Canal—a Superfund site since 2010—is emerging as a desirable residential and arts hub.

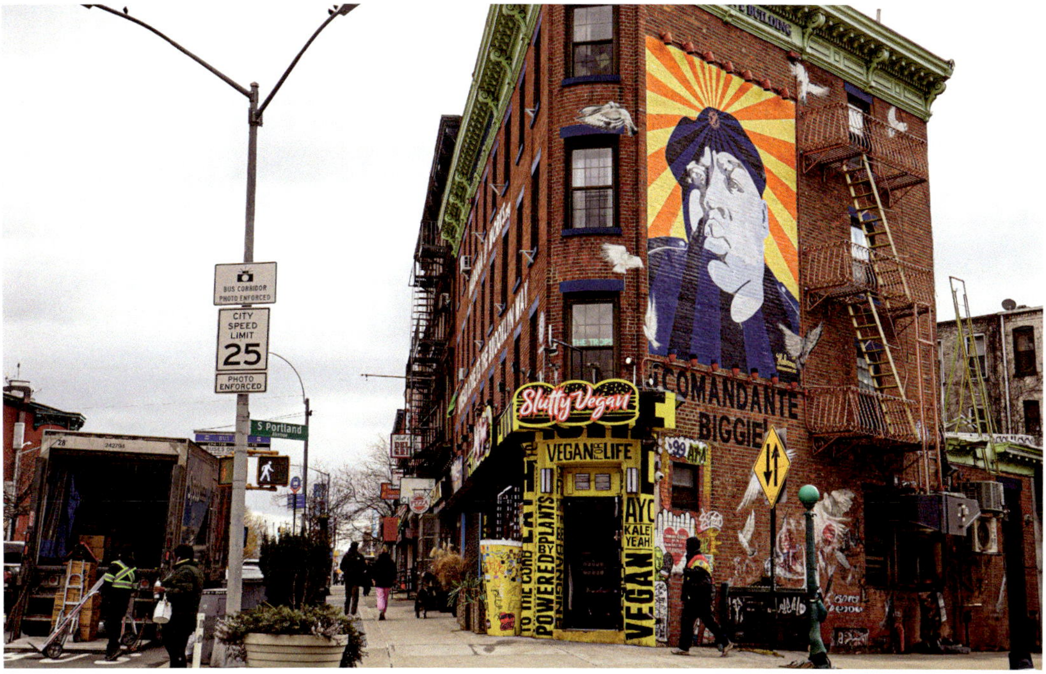

"Comandante Biggie" welcomes guests (lovingly called "sluts") to Slutty Vegan, a vegan burger joint in Fort Greene. (*Photo: Liz Cooke*)

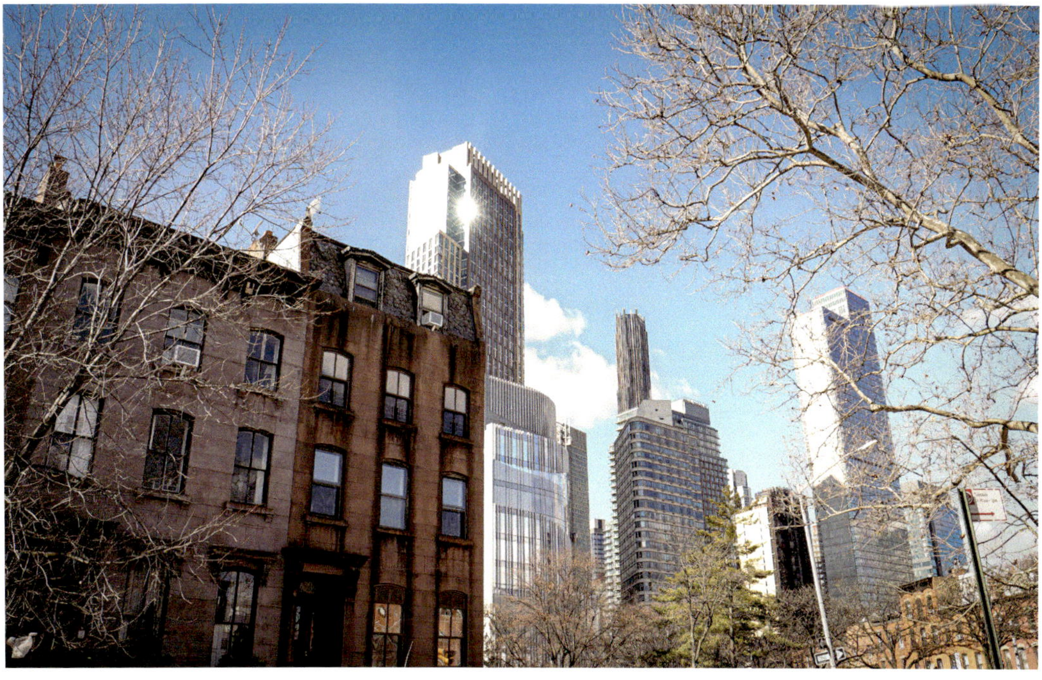

A mix of old and new buildings in the Fort Greene/Downtown Brooklyn area. (*Photo: Liz Cooke*)

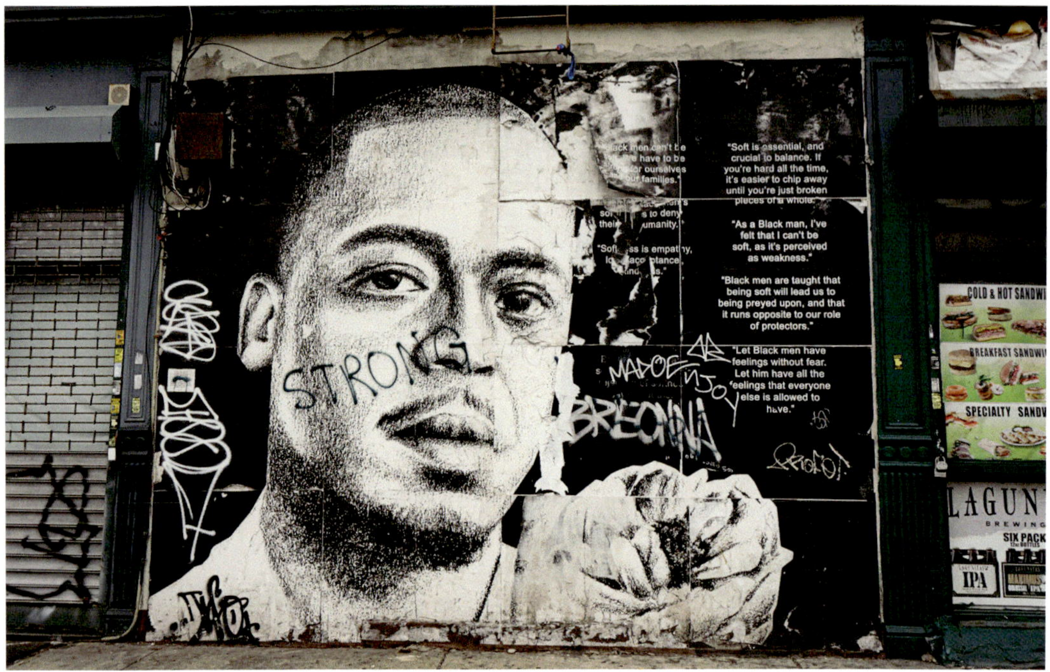

"Let Black Men Be Soft" is the work of artist and cultural worker Tatyana Fazlalizadeh, seen here in Bed-Stuy. (*Photo: Liz Cooke*)

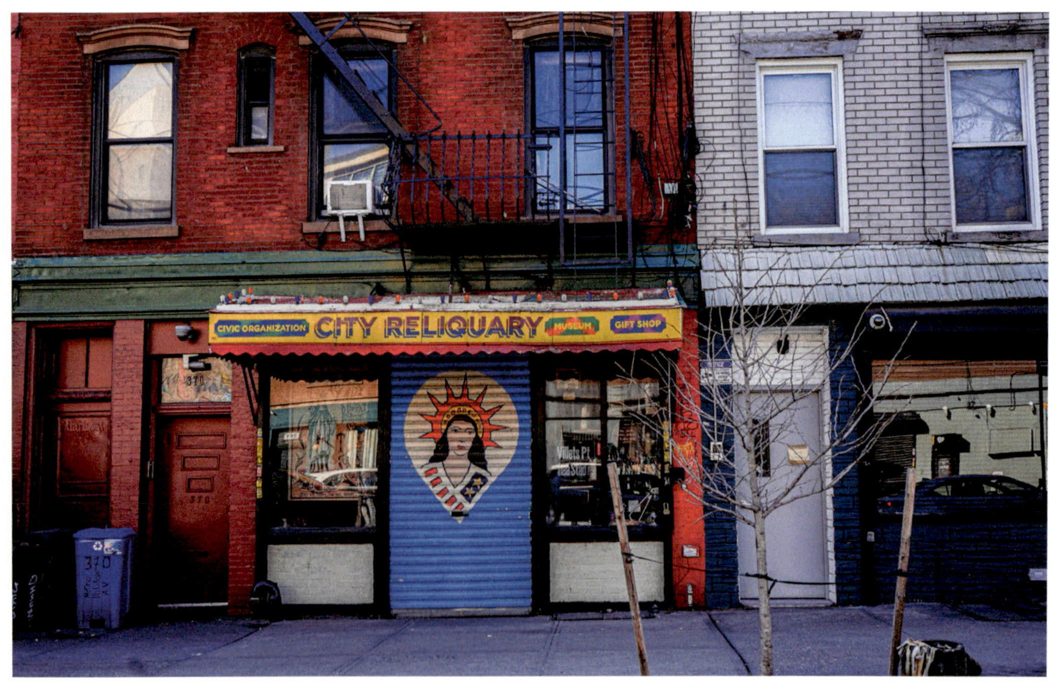

City Reliquary in Williamsburg is a museum, gift shop, and civic organization boasting a large collection of obscure objects and ephemera including rat bones and terra cotta fragments of landmark buildings. (*Photo: Liz Cooke*)

Right: The Williamsburg Savings Bank Building, once the tallest building in Brooklyn, went from a bank to dentists' offices to luxury condos. It is seen here towering over the Times Control House, a Flemish Revival-style kiosk that serves as the entrance to the Atlantic Avenue IRT train station. (*Photo: Liz Cooke*)

Below: Built atop the historic Dime Savings Bank building on Dekalb Avenue in Downtown Brooklyn, the Brooklyn Tower is Brooklyn's tallest structure and its first "supertall" skyscraper. (*Photo: Andy Milford*)

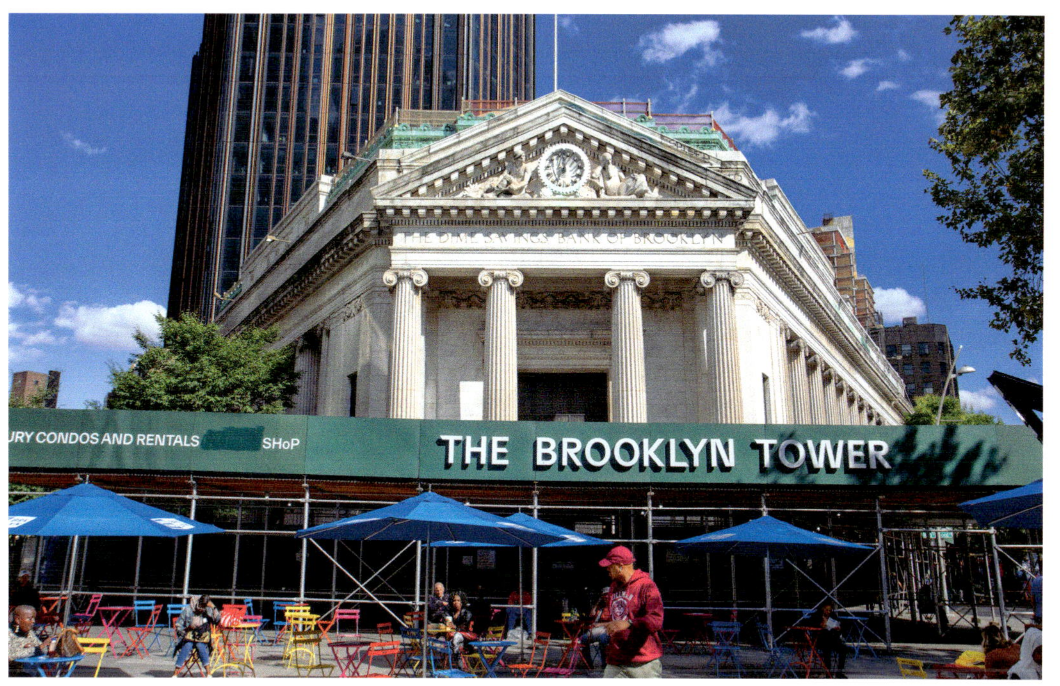

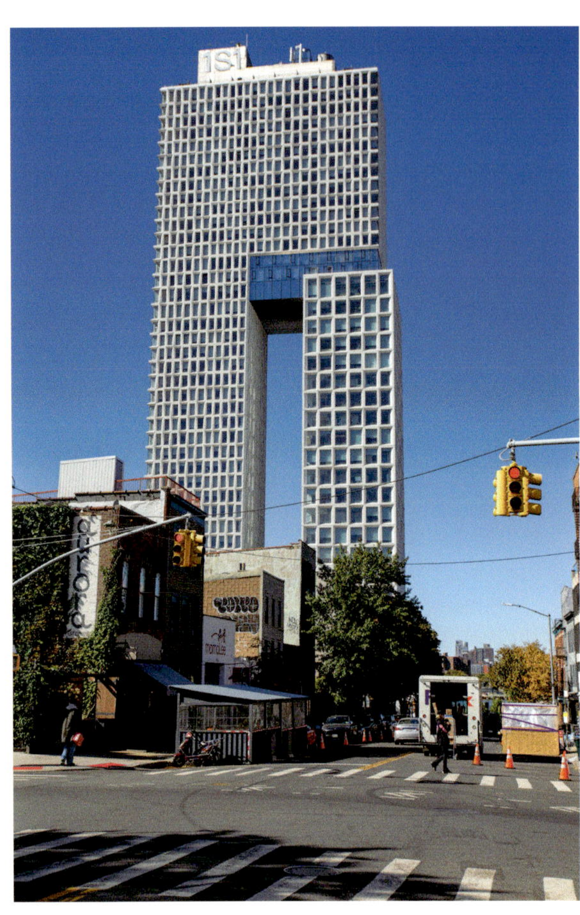

Left: One South First (1S1) is a "luxury waterfront rental" building on Williamsburg's Domino Park. (*Photo: Andy Milford*)

Below: The elaborate ornamentation on this 1920 building on Columbia Heights in Brooklyn Heights had fallen into disrepair before being restored in 2012. (*Photo: Liz Cooke*)

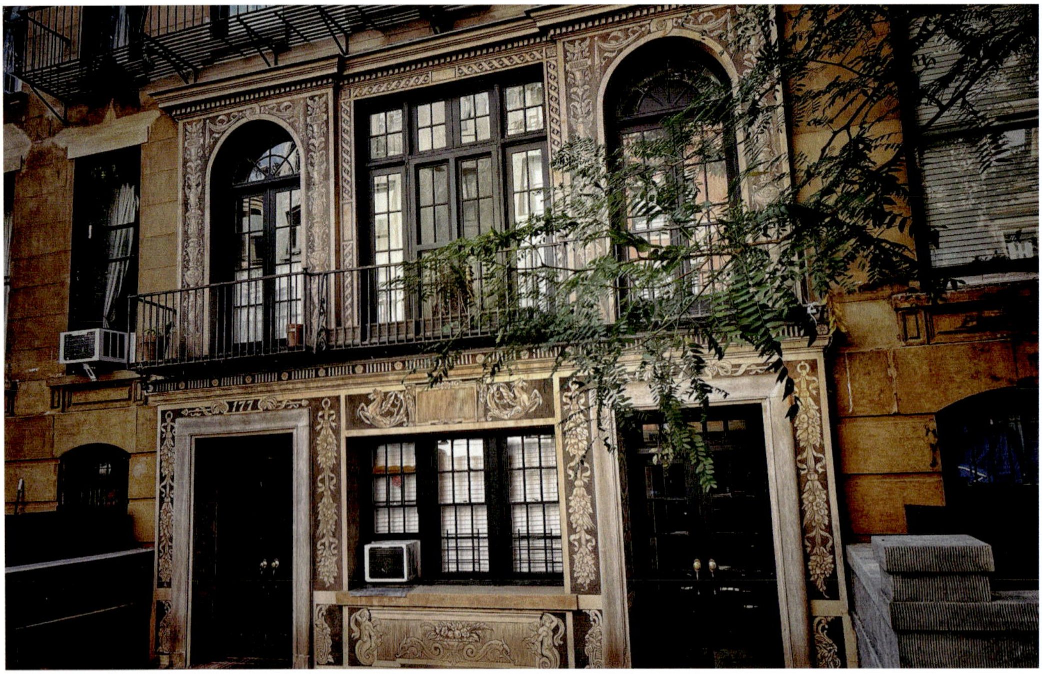

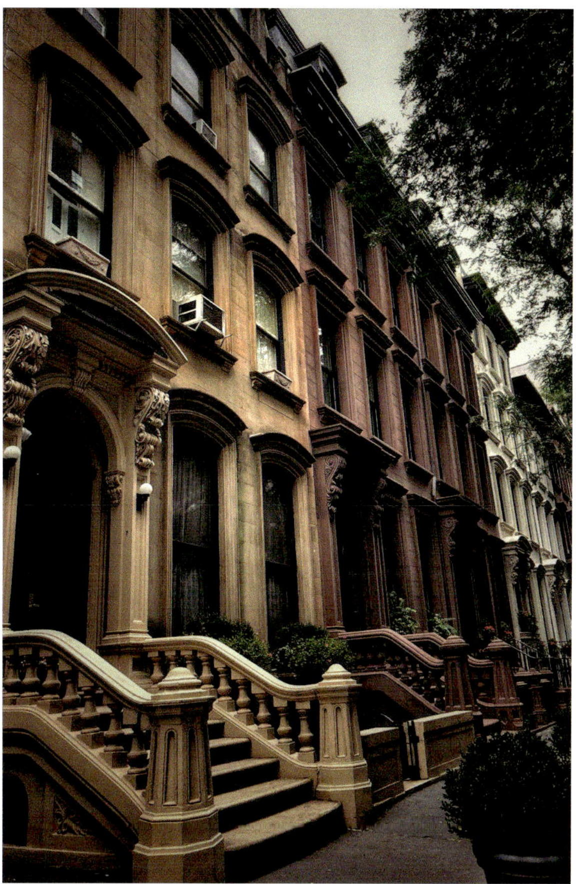

Right: With stunning views of the Lower Manhattan skyline and East River, these brownstones on Columbia Heights in Brooklyn Heights are among the most desirable properties in Brooklyn. (*Photo: Liz Cooke*)

Below: An entire book could (and should!) be written about the stoops of Brooklyn. Typically found on brownstones, limestone townhouses, and brick rowhouses like this one in Bed-Stuy, stoops were designed to protect homes from flooding and street debris. Over time, the stoop became a place to socialize in neighborhoods where apartments were small. (*Photo: Liz Cooke*)

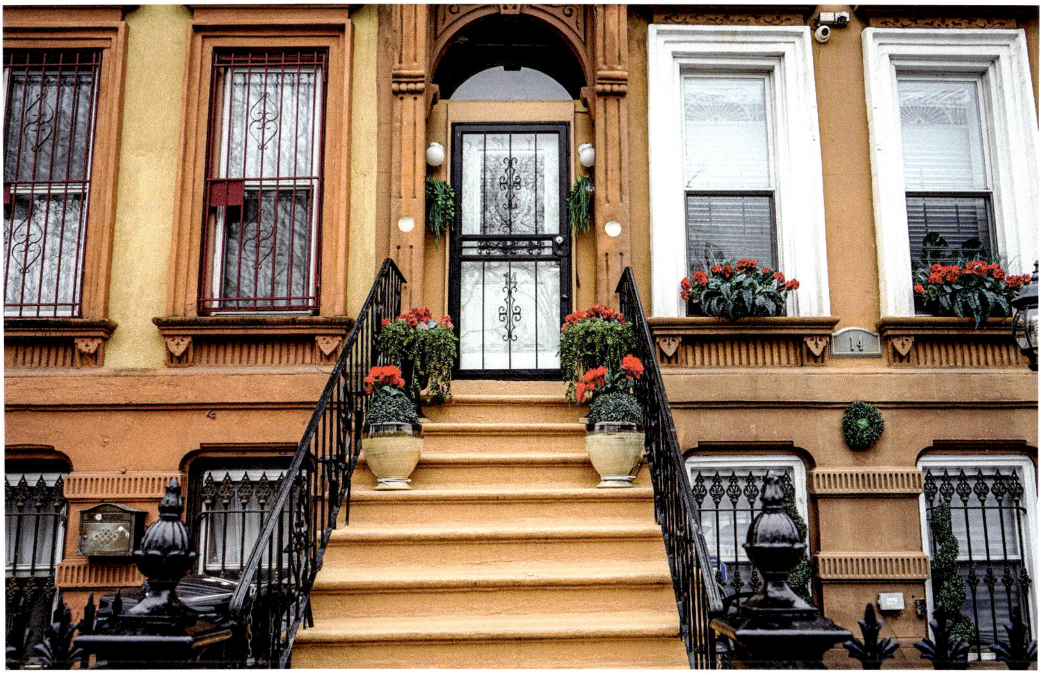

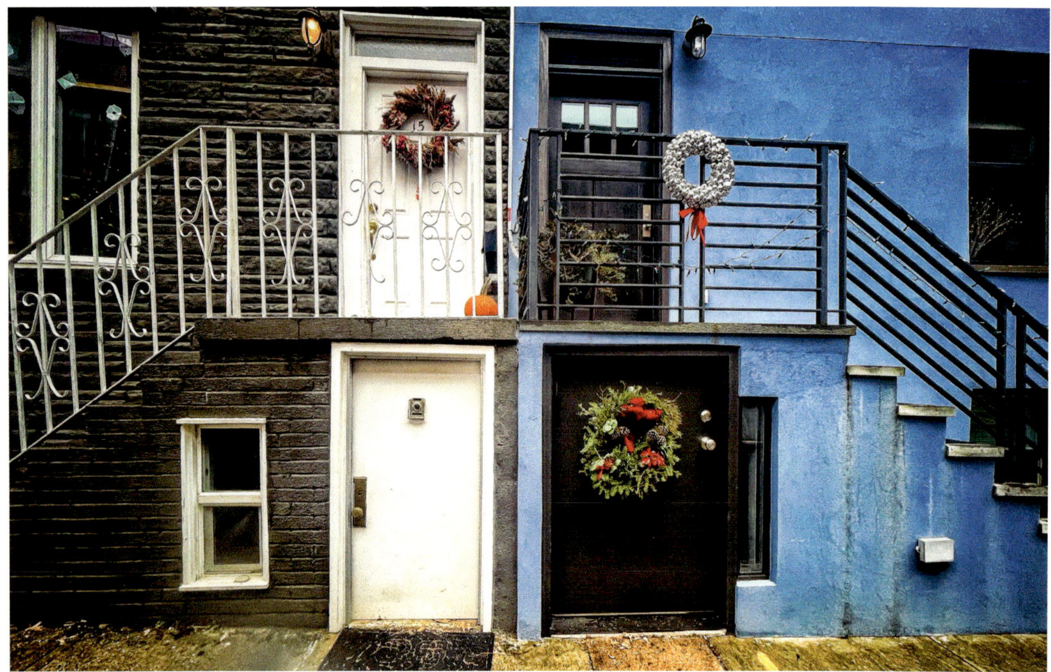

Dennett Place in Carroll Gardens is known for one of the borough's most curious architectural quirks—its tiny doors. Lining the row of brick townhouses, these knee-high doors, often just a few feet tall, have puzzled residents and visitors for generations. (*Photo: Liz Cooke*)

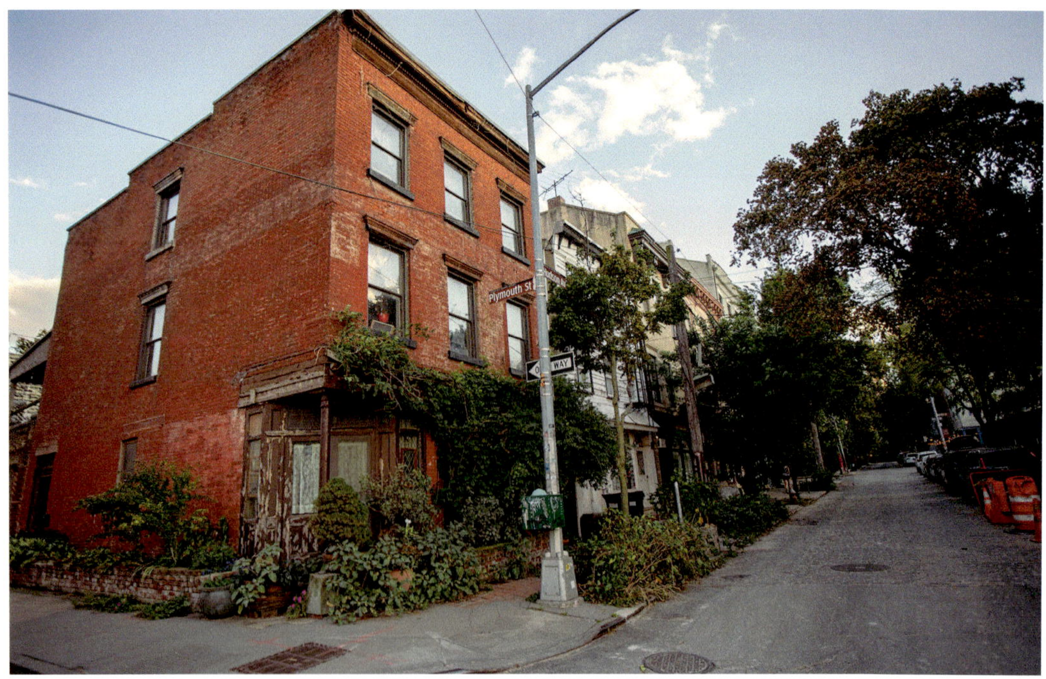

Unlike the developed streets of nearby Dumbo, Plymouth Street in Vinegar Hill retains its traditional charm, with cobblestone streets, low-rise brick warehouses, and historic Federal-style row houses. (*Photo: Andy Milford*)

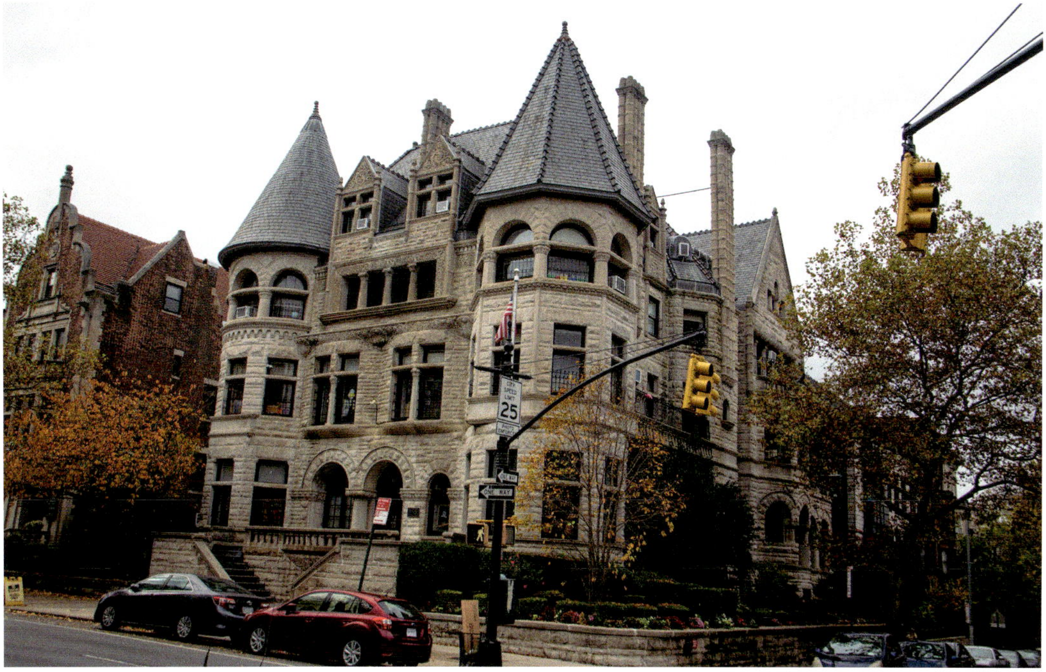

The Hulbert Mansion, a nineteenth-century Gilded Age gem on Prospect Park West, now serves as the home of the Poly Prep Lower School. (*Photo: Andy Milford*)

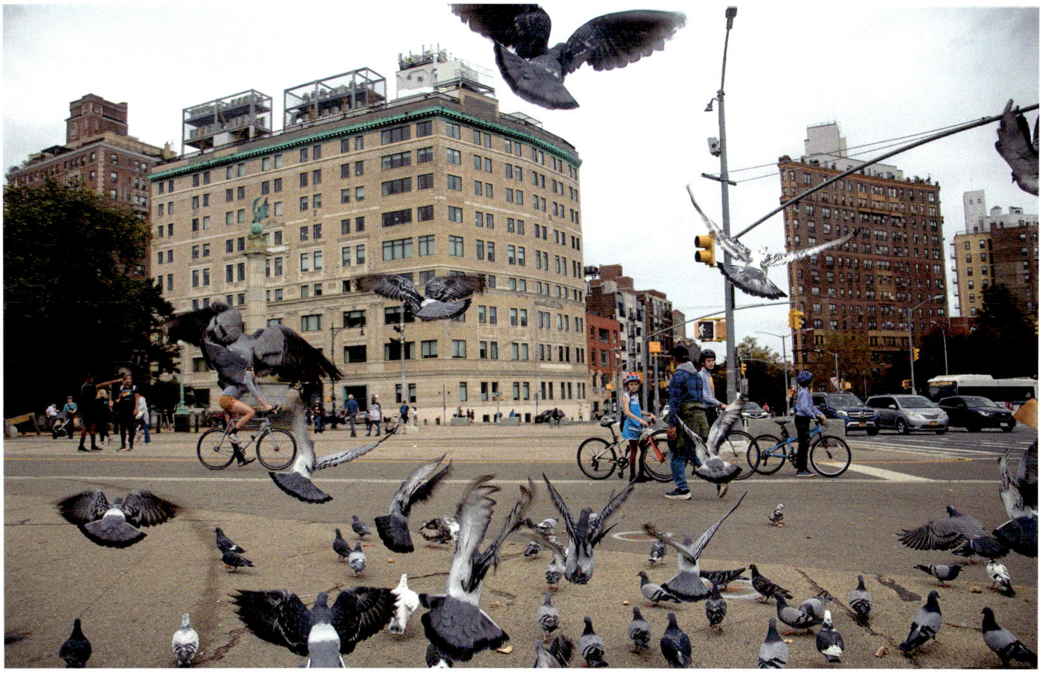

One Prospect Park West has an intriguing past. Once a lavish hotel for the Knights of Columbus and later a "scandal-plagued" senior residence, it is now—wait for it—luxury condos overlooking Grand Army Plaza. (*Photo: Andy Milford*)

Brooklyn has always been a mosaic of cultures, with neighborhoods like Greenpoint, Sunset Park, Flatbush, and Brighton Beach serving as gateways for immigrants from around the world. Gentrification often disrupts these communities, replacing mom-and-pop shops, ethnic restaurants, and cultural institutions with businesses that cater to wealthier newcomers. The changes can feel like a loss of identity, with the borough's rich cultural diversity giving way to a homogenized, less authentic version of itself.

But it's not all doom and gloom. Some argue that gentrification has brought much-needed investment to Brooklyn, improving infrastructure, schools, and public safety. Parks have been revitalized, new bike lanes have been added, and public spaces like the Brooklyn Navy Yard and Industry City have been transformed into vibrant creative and commercial destinations.

Ultimately, the story of gentrification in Brooklyn is still being written. It's a story of tension and transformation, of opportunity and loss. The borough that once symbolized affordability and grit is now a global lifestyle brand, but beneath the glossy condos and organic markets, Brooklyn's soul endures. Whether it's the aroma of fresh dumplings in Sunset Park, or the graffiti-covered walls of Bushwick, the essence of Brooklyn is alive and well.

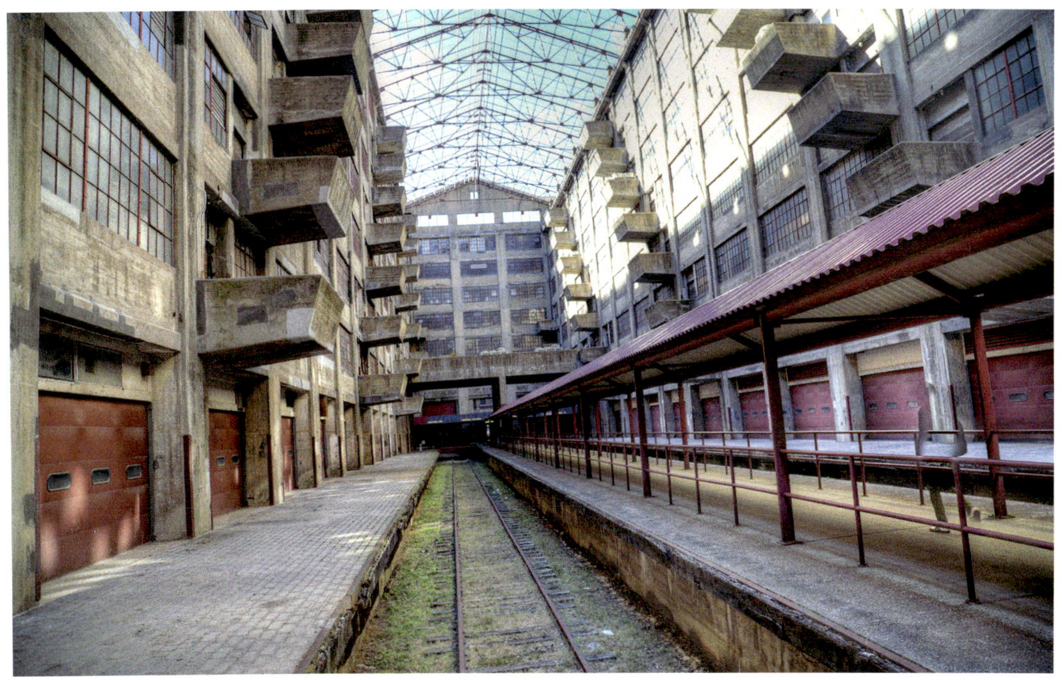

The atrium at the Brooklyn Army Terminal (BAT) in Sunset Park was designed by famed architect Cass Gilbert and completed in 1919. It served as a major logistics hub during World War II. While not open to the public, tours are occasionally offered through Open House New York. (*Photo: Andy Milford*)

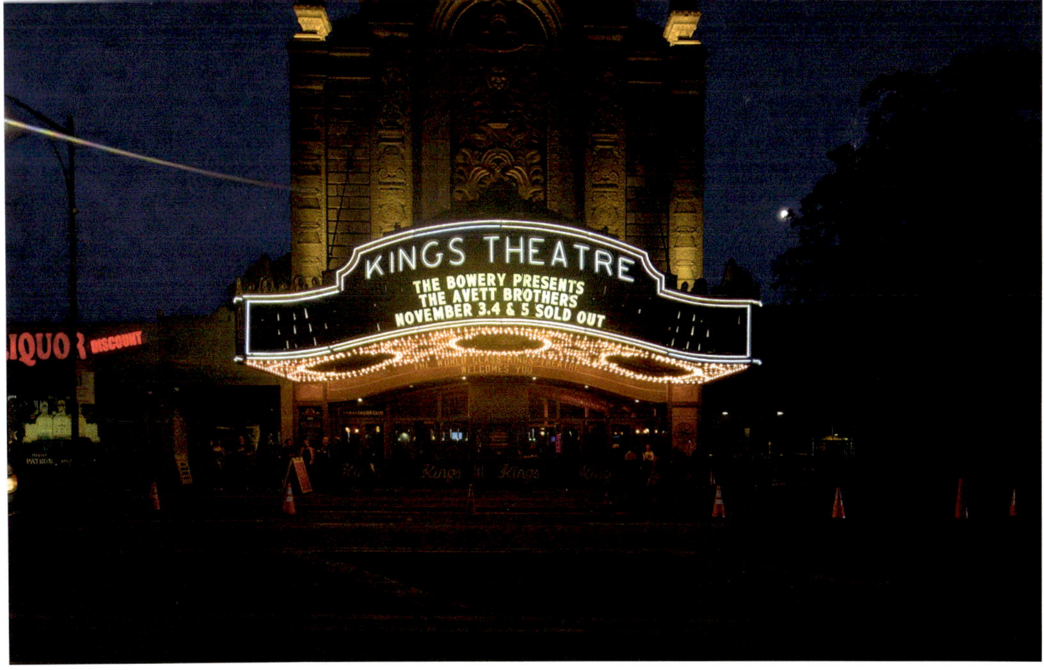

From living room concerts and DIY clubs to outdoor festivals and grand theaters, Brooklyn's music scene is nothing short of legendary. The Kings Theatre in Flatbush, a once-forgotten 1929 movie palace, is now a premier concert venue. (*Photo: Andy Milford*)

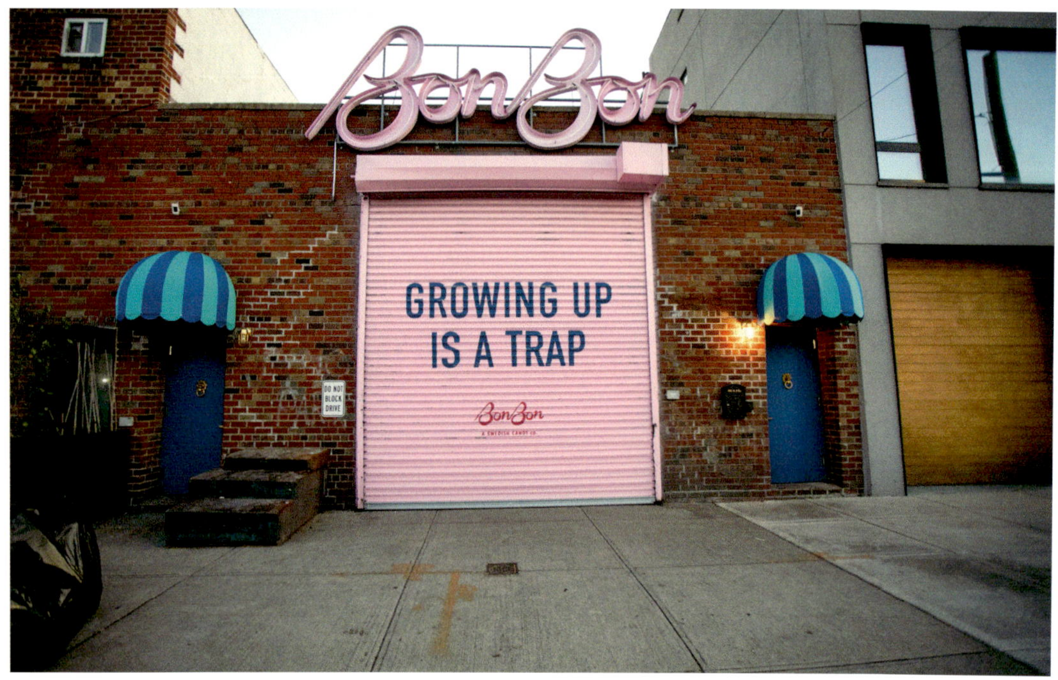

Located on Degraw Street in Red Hook, Bon Bon is a manufacturer of authentic Swedish candy. Upon entering, visitors are greeted with a "world of pure imagination." (*Photo: Andy Milford*)

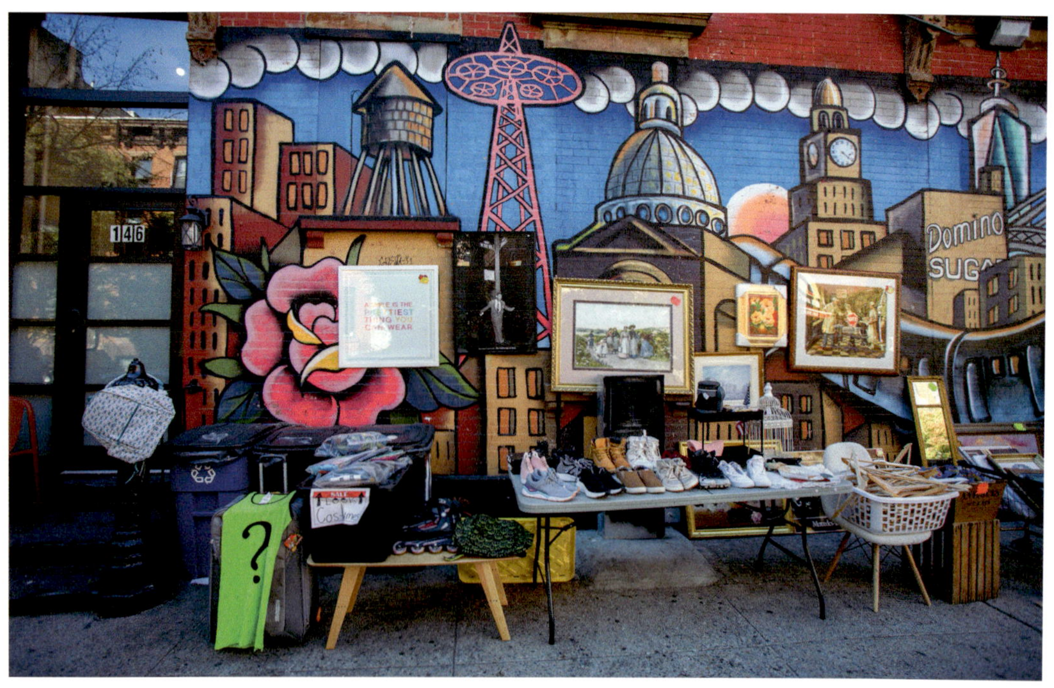

Collectors of vintage goods have abundant choices in Williamsburg. Seen here, a tempting array of art and sneakers. (*Photo: Andy Milford*)

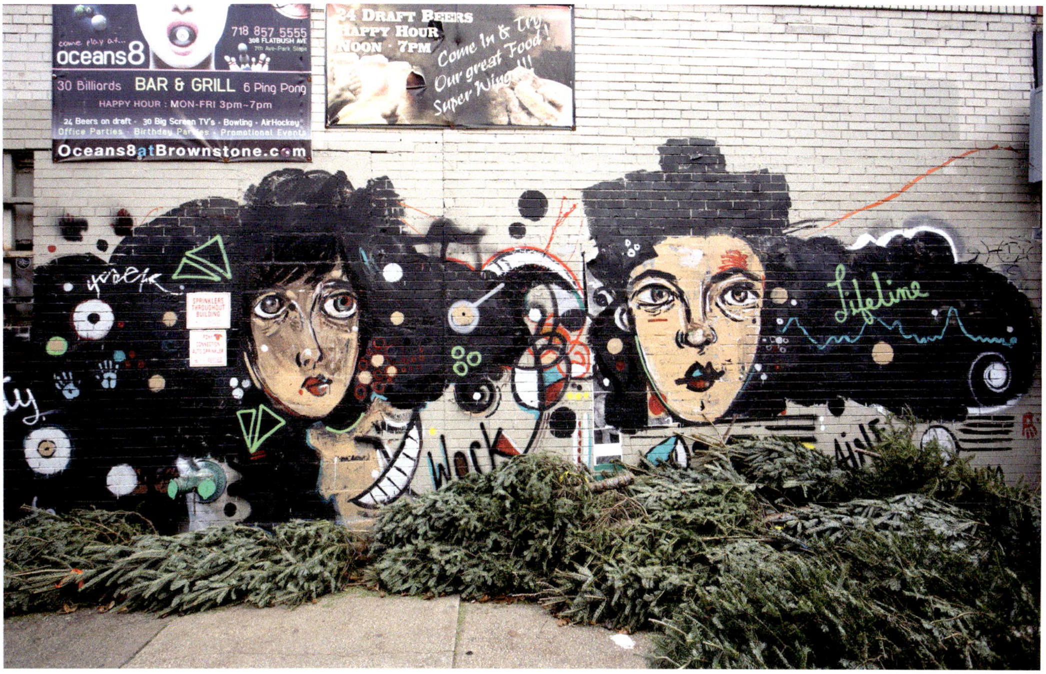

Above: Mural seen at Oceans 8 Bar and Billiards, a popular hangout in Prospect Heights. (*Photo: Andy Milford*)

Right: @Surface of Beauty mural in Bushwick by artist Adam Fujita. (*Photo: Andy Milford*)

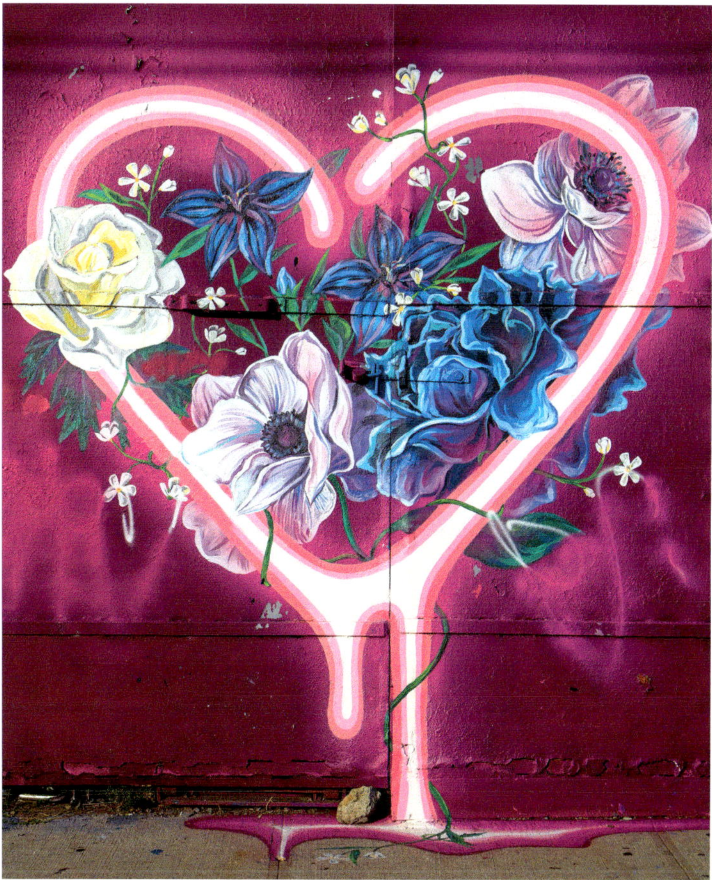

2

Immigrant Brooklyn

In the late nineteenth and early twentieth centuries, Brooklyn became a gateway for European immigrants. Irish immigrants fleeing the Great Famine established communities in neighborhoods like Vinegar Hill and Greenpoint, while Italians populated areas such as Bensonhurst and Carroll Gardens. Jewish immigrants from Eastern Europe created thriving communities in Williamsburg, Borough Park, and Brighton Beach. Because they are American citizens, Puerto Rican immigrants were able to enter the country with relative ease and many found well-paid factory work in the industrial neighborhoods of Williamsburg and Greenpoint. These early waves of immigrants brought with them not only labor but also vibrant traditions. Irish pubs, Italian bakeries, Puerto Rican bodegas, and Jewish delis became cornerstones of neighborhood life. Churches, synagogues, mosques, and temples provided spaces for spiritual enrichment, social gatherings, celebrations, and places of solace when times got tough.

Walk through any neighborhood in Brooklyn and you are bound to come across streets lined with shops bearing signs in unfamiliar languages. There might be Arabic, Turkish, and Farsi along Atlantic Avenue; Russian, Ukrainian, Armenian, and Bukharian in Brighton Beach; Mandarin in Sheepshead Bay; Pakistani in Midwood; Fujianese in Sunset Park; Cantonese in Bensonhurst; Spanish in Coney Island; Yiddish in Crown Heights; Creole in Flatbush's Little Haiti and all manner of Caribbean dialects throughout the borough. This profusion of languages, dialects, and alphabets can make Brooklyn seem like a gorgeous symphony or a blaring cacophony, and it is, of course, both.

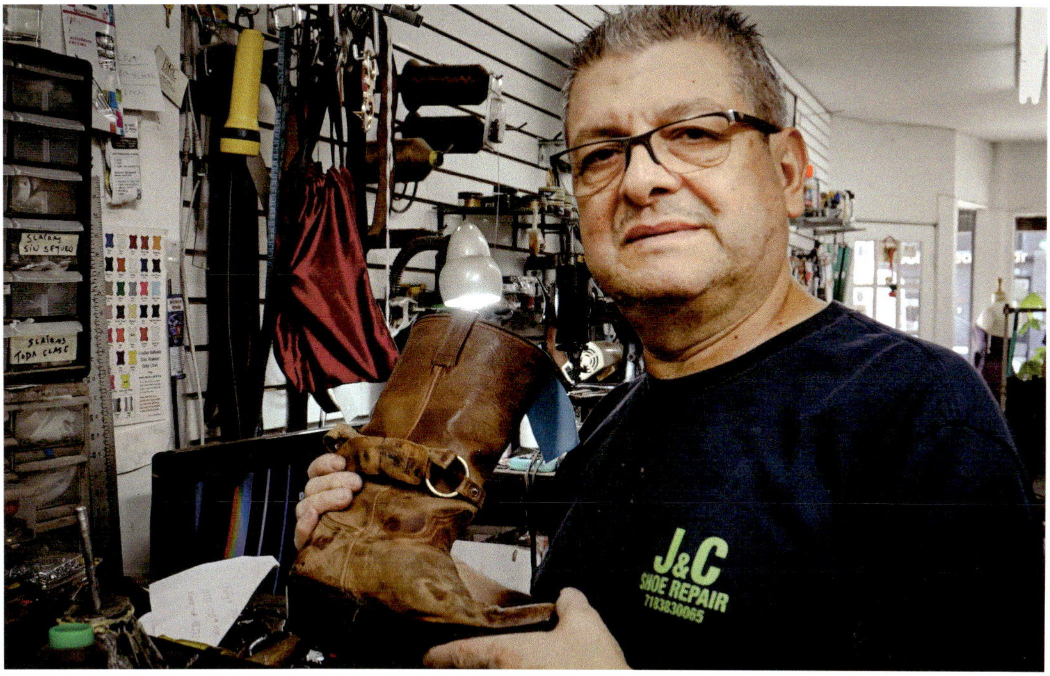

Jairo, owner of J & C Shoe Repair in Greenpoint, has more than thirty years' experience repairing shoes and boots. (*Photo: Liz Cooke*)

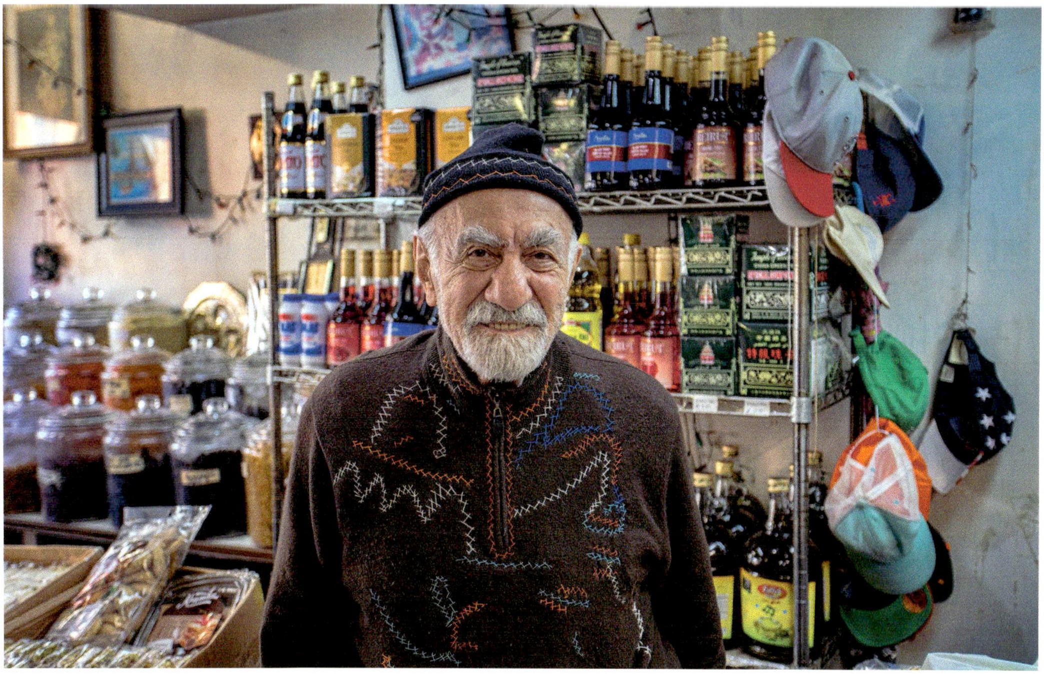

Abraham Karkanni, owner of Malko Karkanni Bros. importers of Middle Eastern groceries, sweets and supplies on Atlantic Avenue. (*Photo: Andy Milford*)

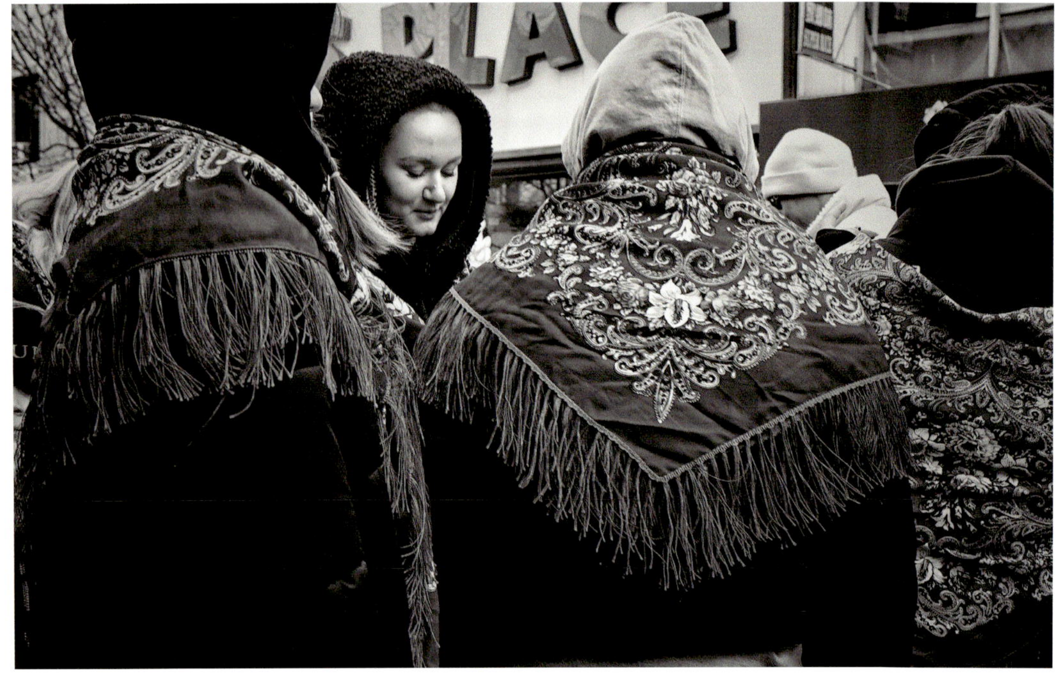

For generations, Bensonhurst has been an immigrant stronghold. These women joined the throngs at the Lunar New Year parade. (*Photo: Liz Cooke*)

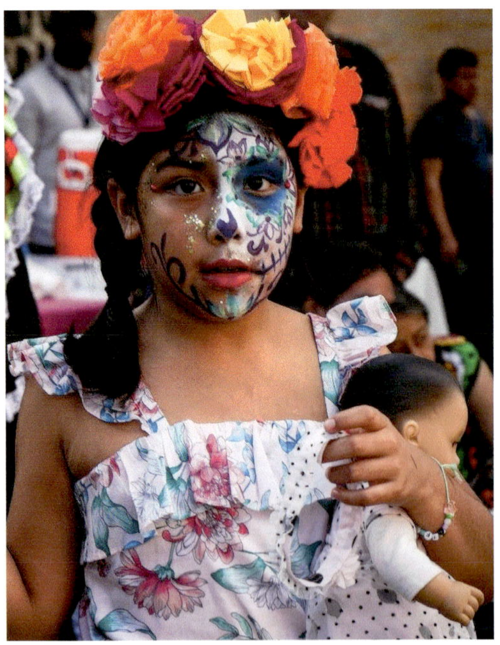

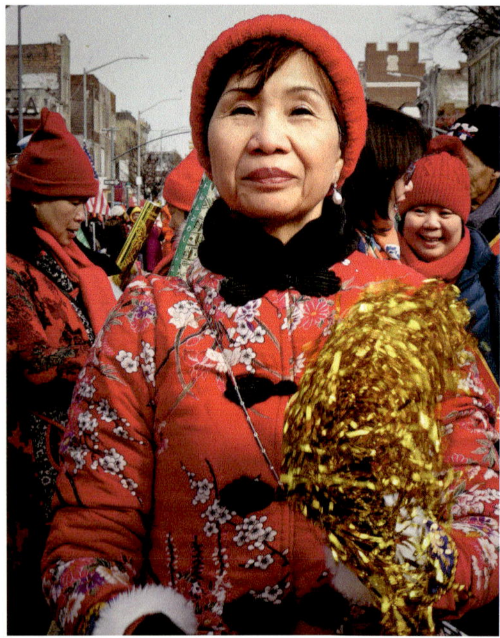

Above left: A painted face on a young girl at the Día de los Muertos (Day of the Dead) celebration, an important cultural event for members of Sunset Park's Mexican community. (*Photo: Liz Cooke*)

Above right: Thousands lined the streets in Bensonhurst to celebrate the Lunar Year, including this woman in traditional dress. (*Photo: Liz Cooke*)

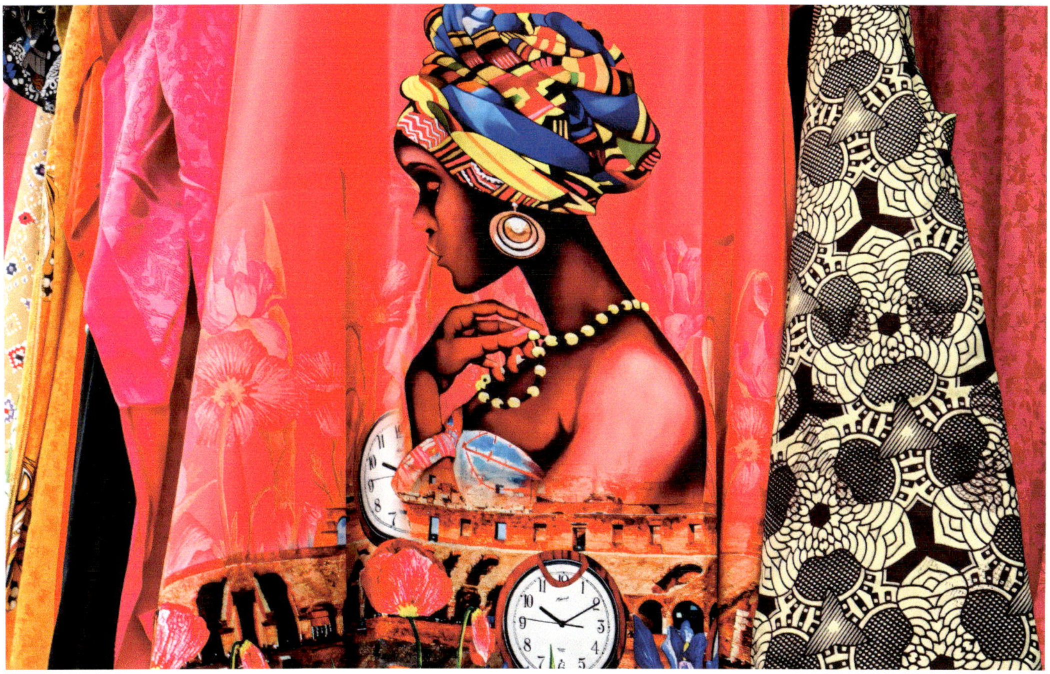

Bright fabrics celebrating Caribbean culture are plentiful in the Little Haiti section of Flatbush. (*Photo: Liz Cooke*)

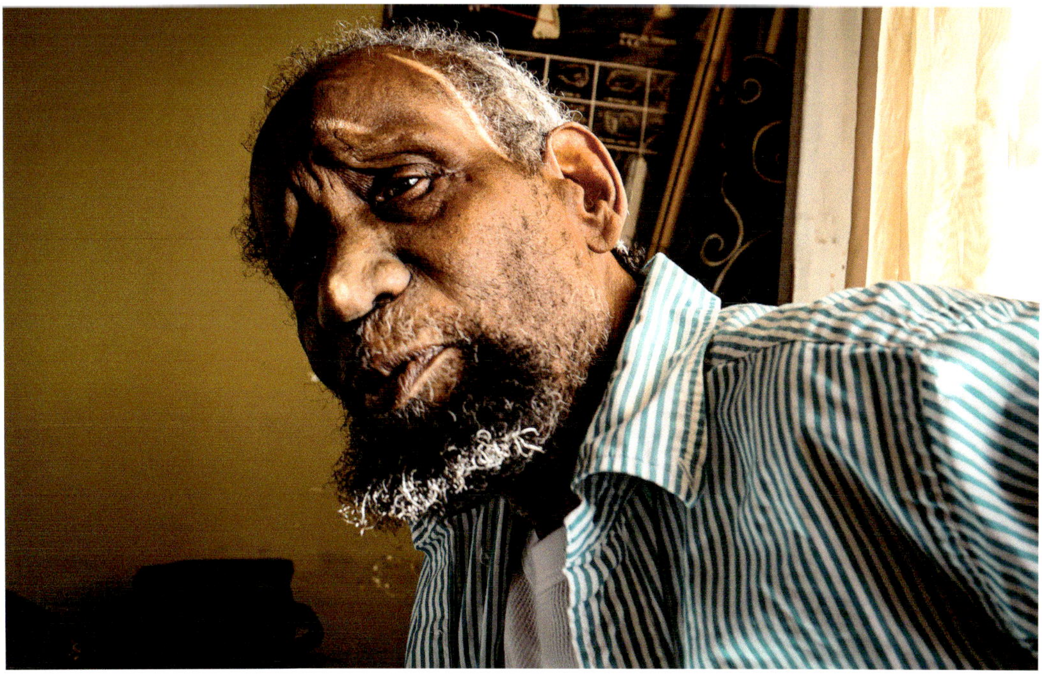

In Crown Heights, martial arts training within the Muslim community is seen as a way to build discipline, strength, and self-defense skills, aligning with the values of self-improvement and preparedness in Islam. The grandmaster of one Crown Heights center is pictured here. (*Photo: Liz Cooke*)

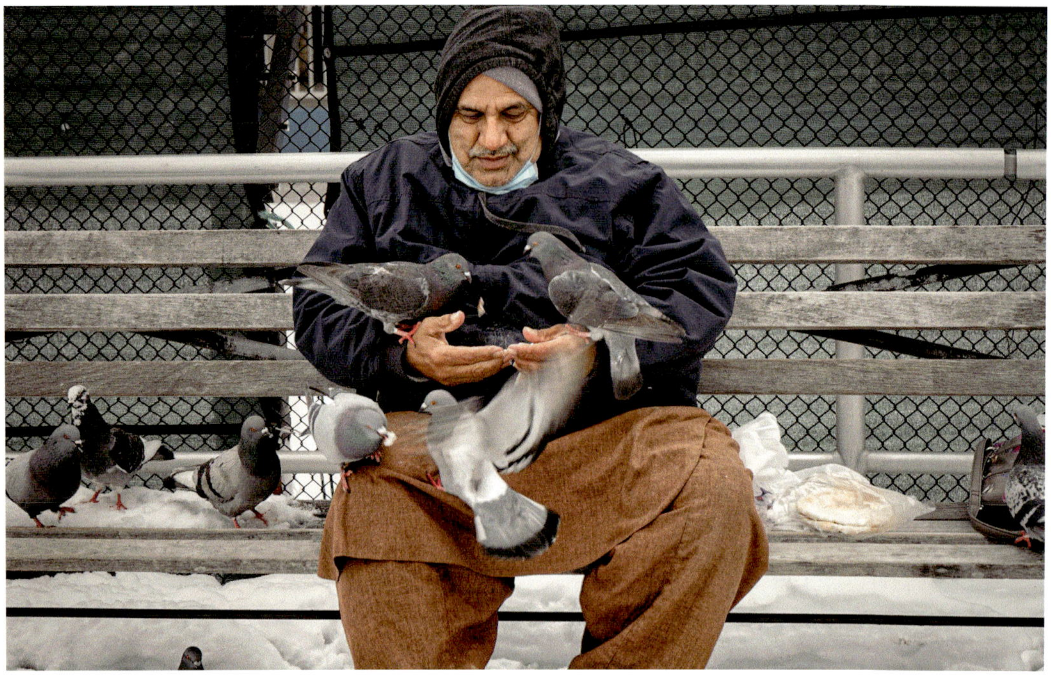

Feeding the pigeons on the boardwalk in Brighton Beach is a time-honored tradition. (*Photo: Liz Cooke*)

Sunset Park exemplifies Brooklyn's dynamic multiculturalism. In the early twentieth century, Scandinavian immigrants dominated the area, leaving behind landmarks like the Danish Athletic Club. Today, Sunset Park is home to one of New York City's largest Chinese communities, centered along 8th Avenue, and a thriving Latinx population, concentrated near 5th Avenue. Walk along 8th Avenue and spend some time in any of the numerous open-air markets, where the fish are so fresh they can be seen flapping and jumping in water-filled buckets. Along 5th Avenue, the demographic changes to a Latin flavor. Here hand-pulled noodle shops are side by side with Salvadoran pupuserias and Mexican taquerias.

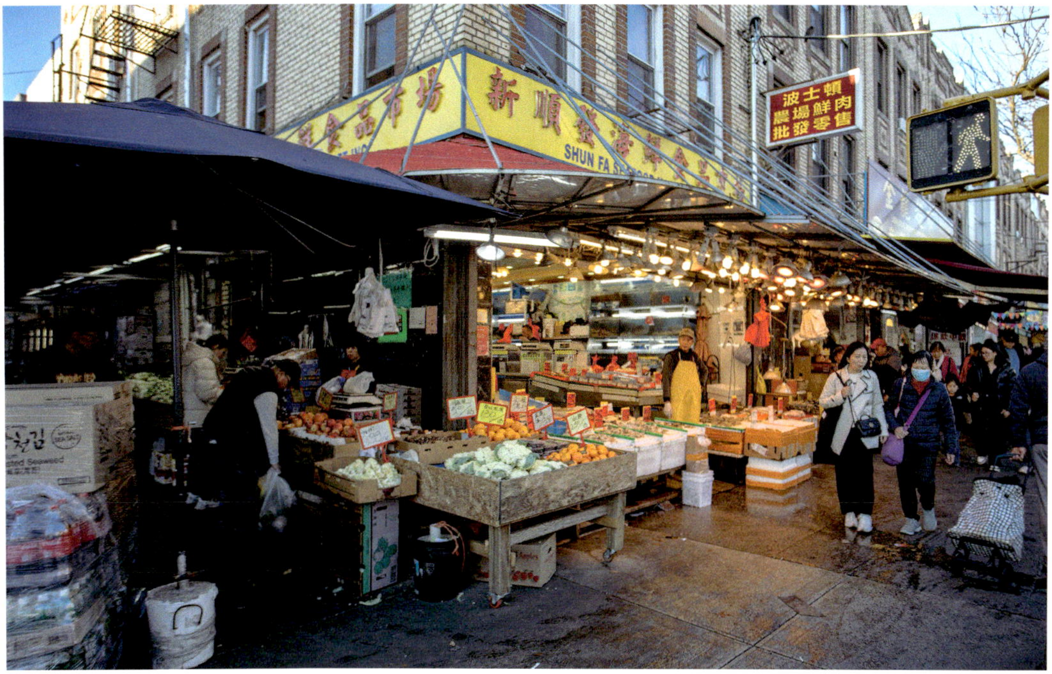

A busy market on 8th Avenue in the Chinese section of Sunset Park. (*Photo: Andy Milford*)

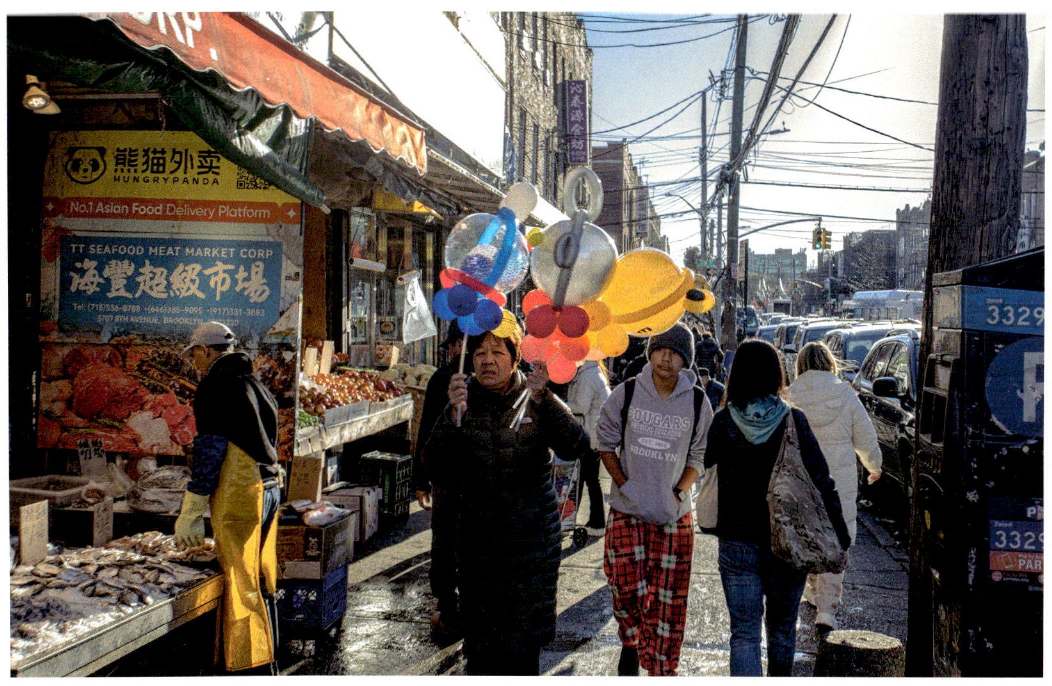

The streets of Sunset Park are crowded with businesses, people, traffic, and food. (*Photo: Andy Milford*)

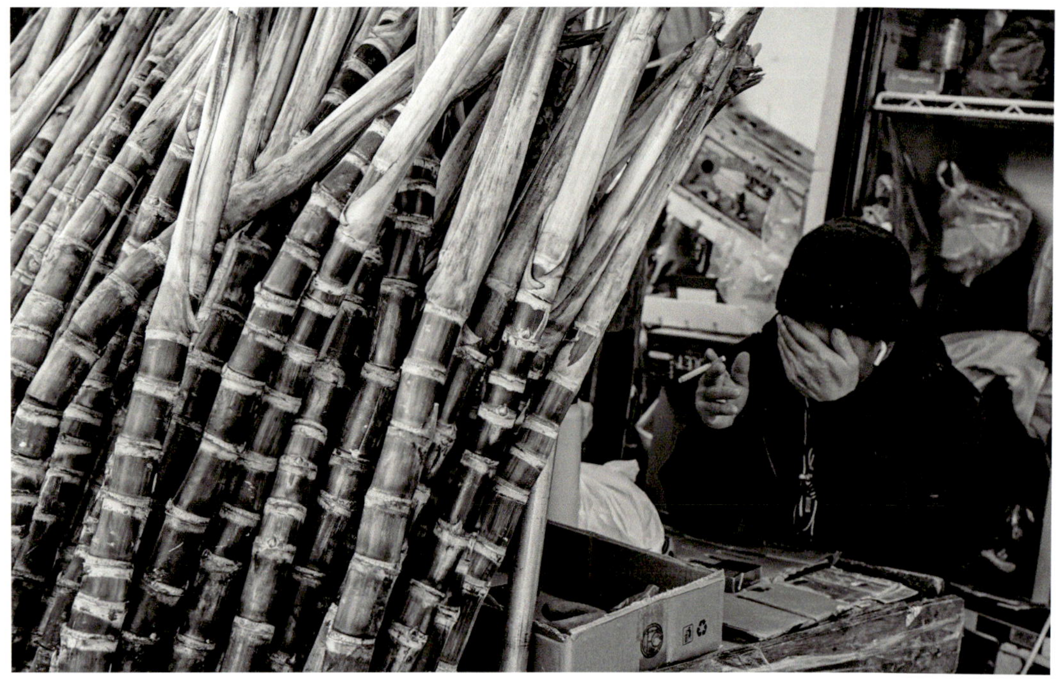

A vegetable vendor on 8th Avenue in Sunset Park after a long day. (*Photo: Liz Cooke*)

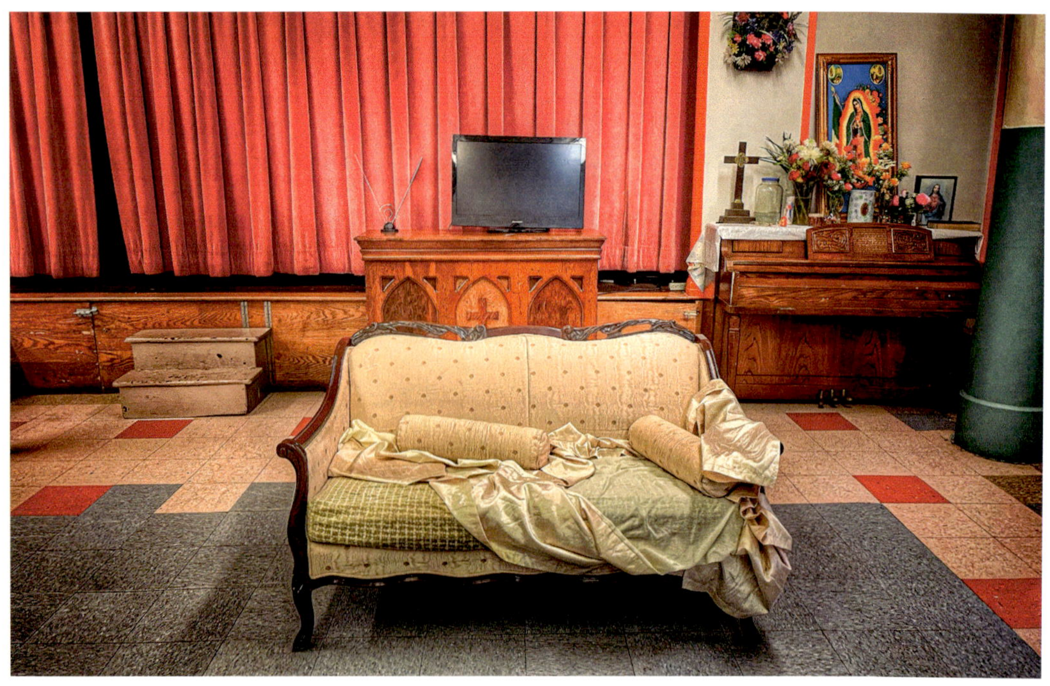

Community room in a Sunset Park church. (*Photo: Liz Cooke*)

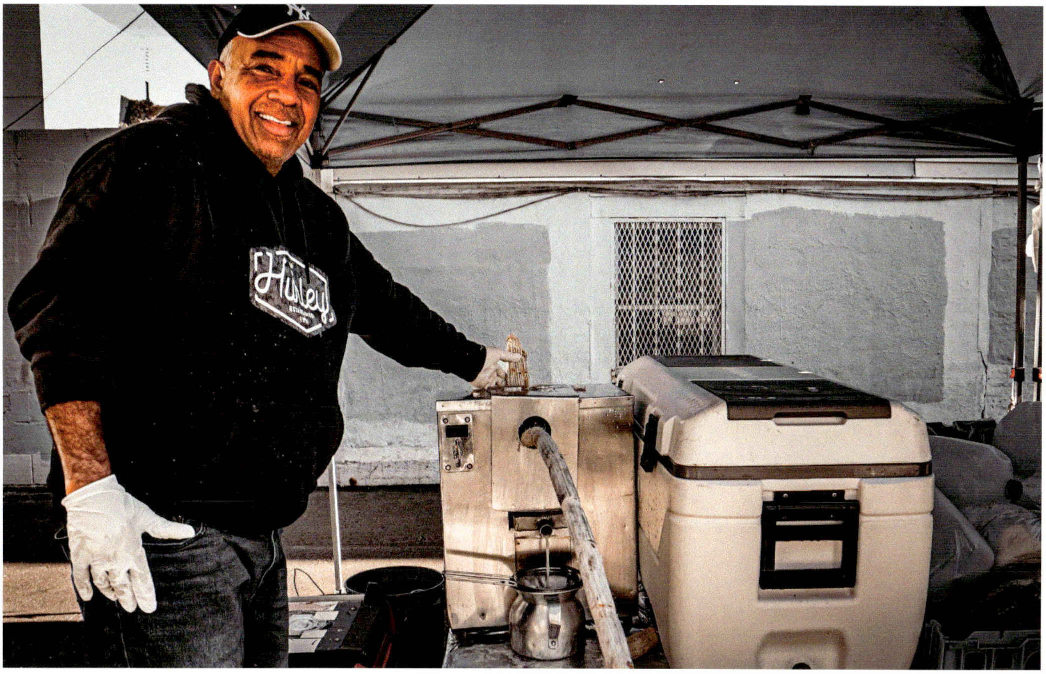

Sunset Park is home to a diverse mix of Spanish-speaking cultures. Along 5th Avenue, street vendors offer traditional treats, including fresh sugarcane juice, made by pressing the tough stalks through metal rollers. (*Photo: Liz Cooke*)

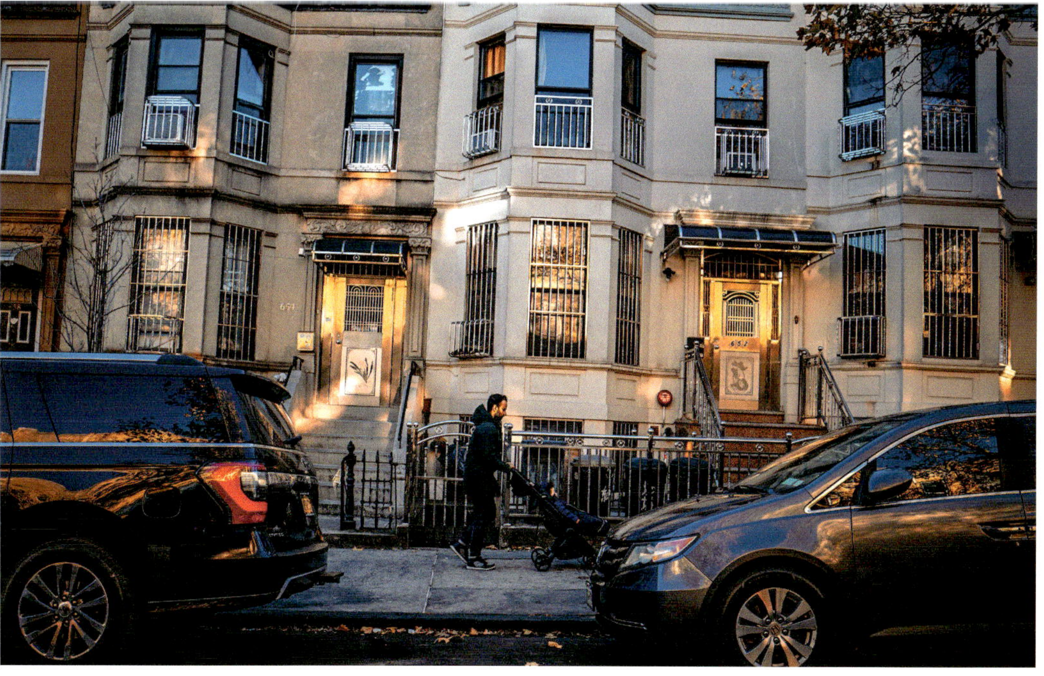

It was not that long ago that Sunset Park, like much of Brooklyn, was a grittier place. Today, the neighborhood is safer and more inviting, with new businesses and young families arriving every day. (*Photo: Liz Cooke*)

Brighton Beach, often referred to as "Little Odessa," is a hub for Russian-speaking immigrants, including Jews from Ukraine, Belarus, and Russia. The neighborhood's proximity to the ocean mirrors the Black Sea cities many residents left behind, and its boardwalk is a gathering place for elders who reminisce about their homelands while playing chess or sipping tea. While consistently a Jewish neighborhood for generations, there was a time before the arrival of Soviet Jews in the 1970s when Brighton was home to an earlier wave of immigrants: Jews fleeing pogroms and later the Holocaust in Eastern Europe. These Jews brought with them the Yiddish language and many religious and social traditions that struggle to survive in the more secular and assimilated culture of later arrivals.

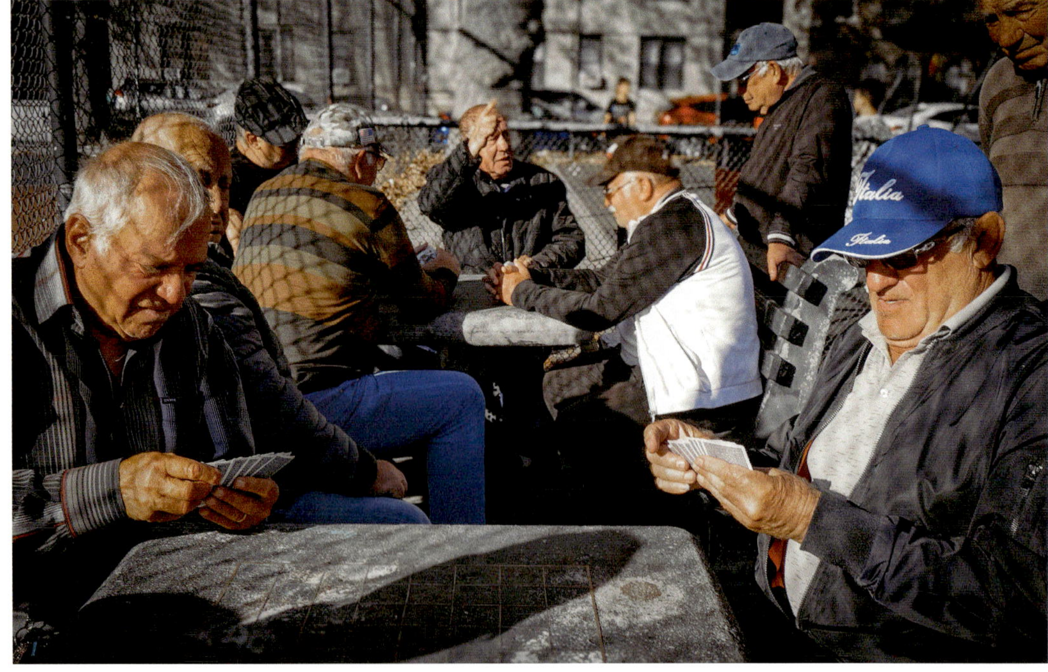

With rapid changes happening across the borough, it is comforting to see how little Brighton Beach has changed. In Second Street Park, Russian men play cards, chess and backgammon as they have for decades. (*Photo: Liz Cooke*)

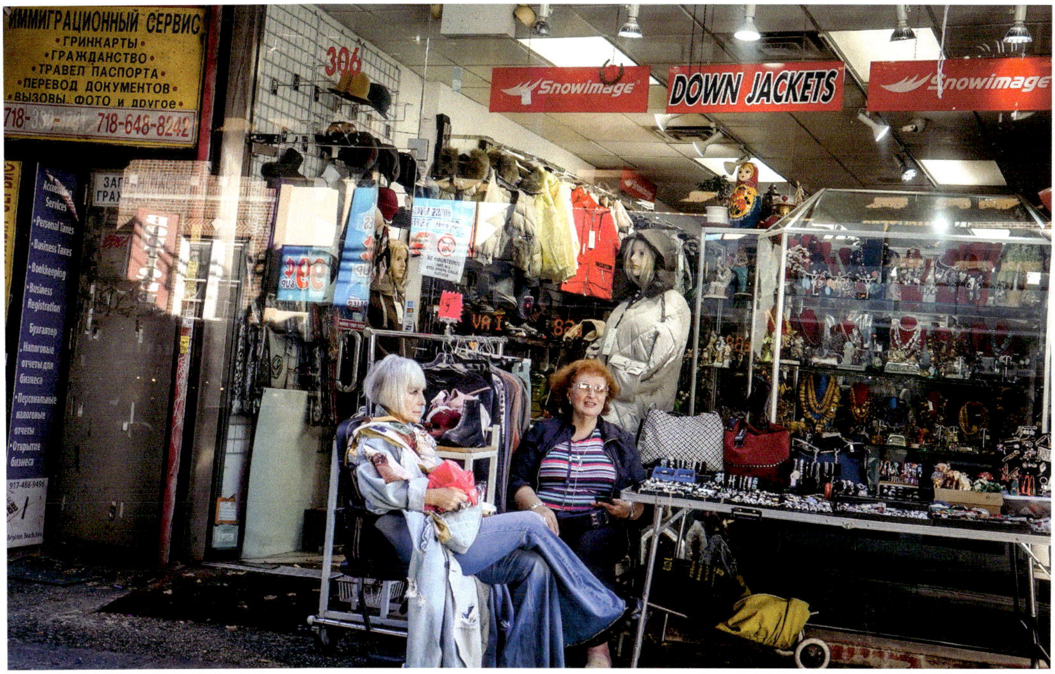

Two women enjoy the ever-changing street scene on Brighton Beach Avenue. (*Photo: Liz Cooke*)

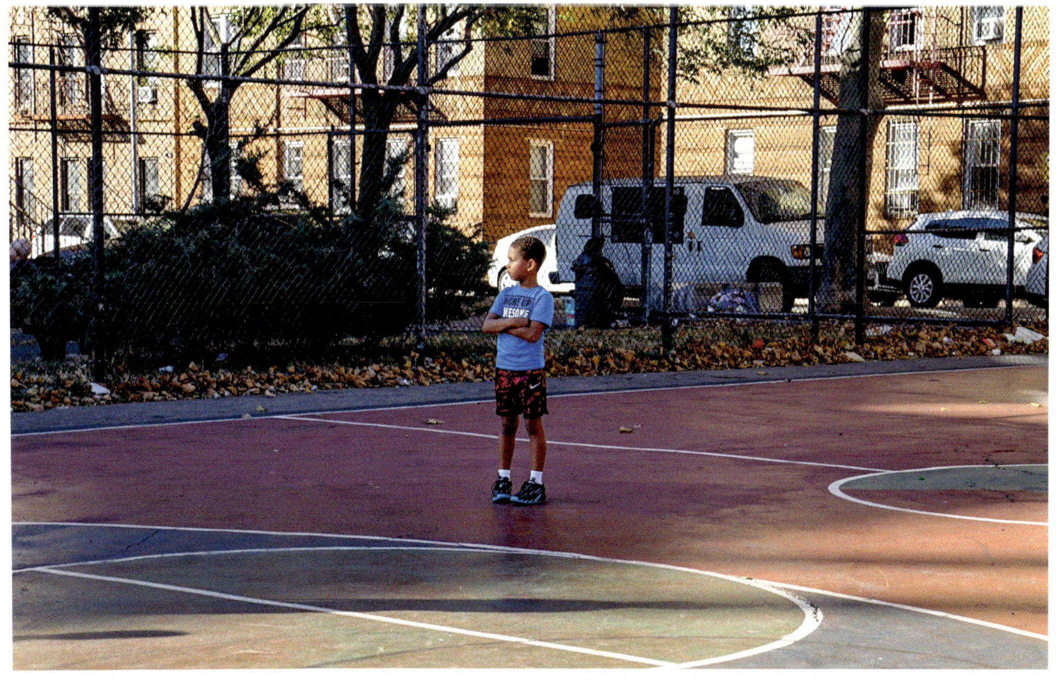

In many New York City playgrounds, there is a section for "little kids" with slides and swings and a section for "big kids" with basketball courts. This boy is hoping to shoot hoops with the "big kids." (*Photo: Liz Cooke*)

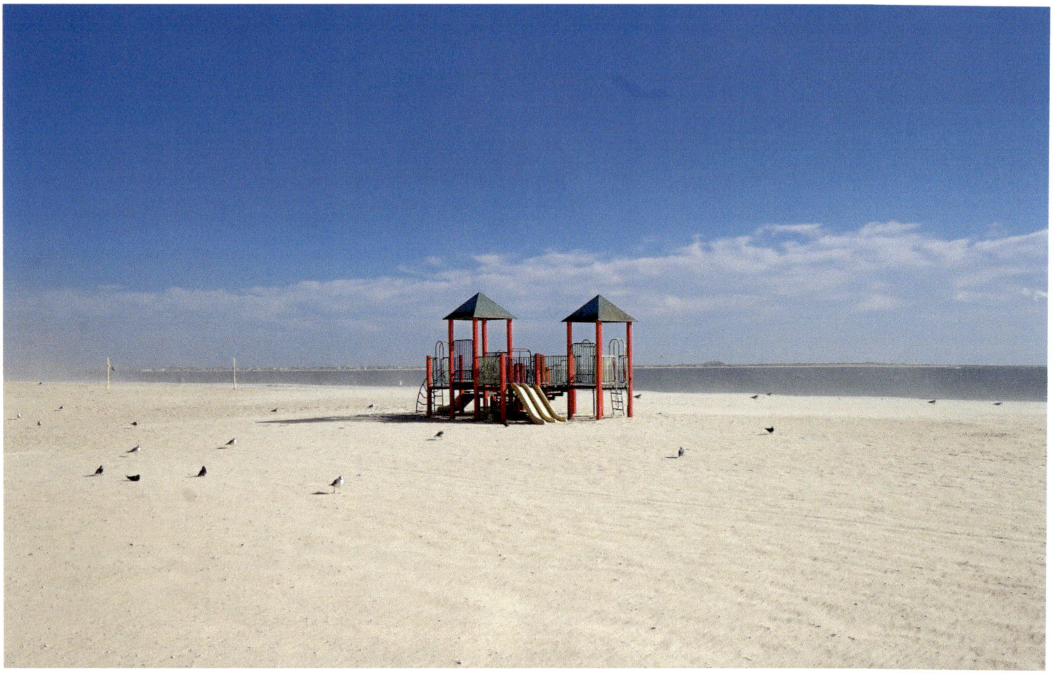

On a hot summer day, the Q train opens on the Brighton Beach stop and thousands of city dwellers pile out, heading for the sand and sea. Here, on a quiet mid-winter day, the beach is empty but for hungry seagulls. (*Photo: Liz Cooke*)

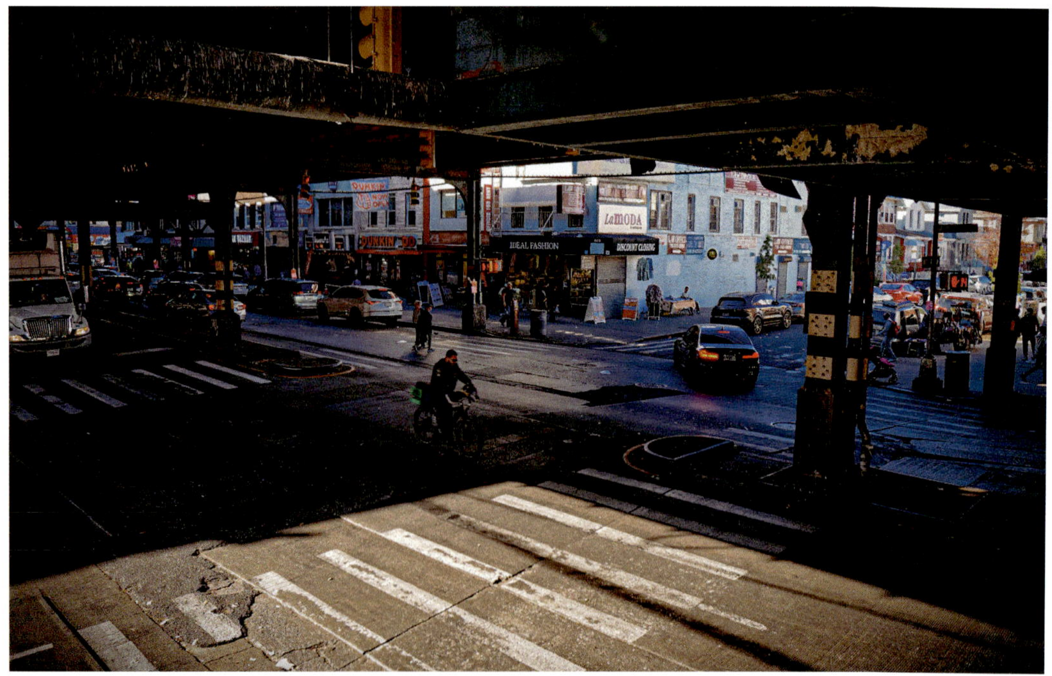

Brighton Beach Avenue is the heart of "Little Odessa," a busy commercial strip lined with Russian, Ukrainian, and Central Asian shops, all beneath the perpetual rumbling of the "el" overhead. (*Photo: Liz Cooke*)

Crown Heights is where you will find a rich tapestry of cultures. Immigrants from Jamaica, Trinidad, Haiti, and other Caribbean nations have shaped the neighborhood's identity, particularly along Nostrand Avenue, where Caribbean grocery stores and jerk chicken stands line the streets. Crown Heights is also home to one of Brooklyn's largest Hasidic Jewish communities. Shuls, yeshivas, mikvahs, bakeries, and other Jewish institutions line the streets. Most Jews here are of the Chabad-Lubavitch branch of Orthodox Judaism. The Lubavitch movement's headquarters at 770 Eastern Parkway is known familiarly as "770," and as part of the movement's outreach, visitors are welcome.

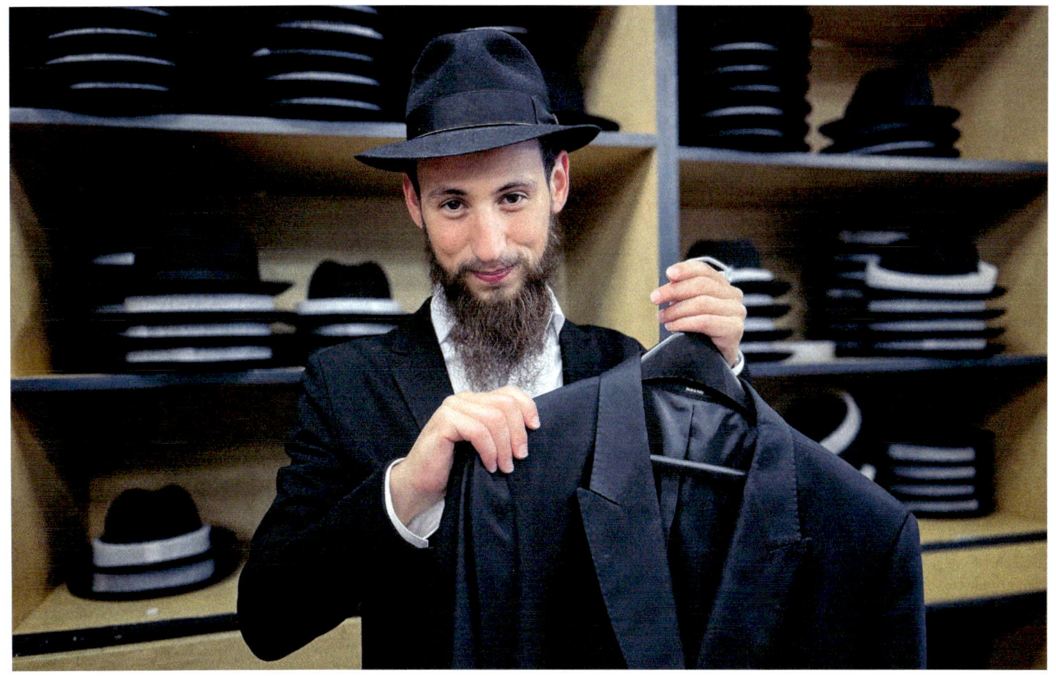

Mayer, a member of the Lubavitch sect, shows the suits and hats worn by observant Jews in his Crown Heights community. (*Photo: Liz Cooke*)

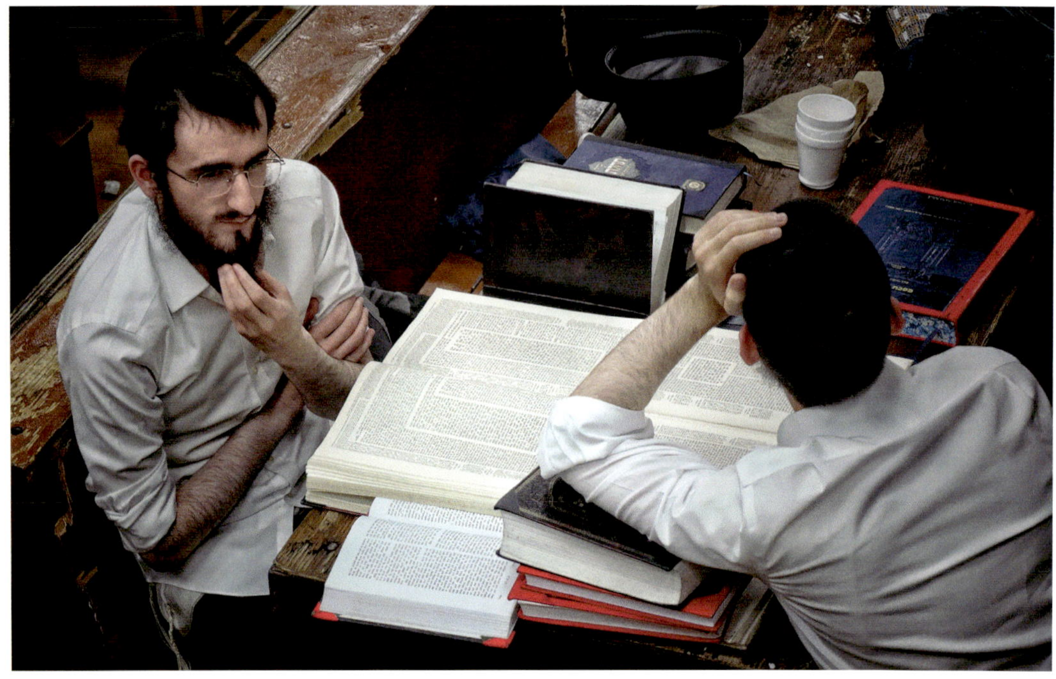

Inside 770 Eastern Parkway in Crown Heights, Lubavitch men engage in hours of study. Day and night, this study hall remains a center of learning, tradition, and connection for the Chabad-Lubavitch community. (*Photo: Liz Cooke*)

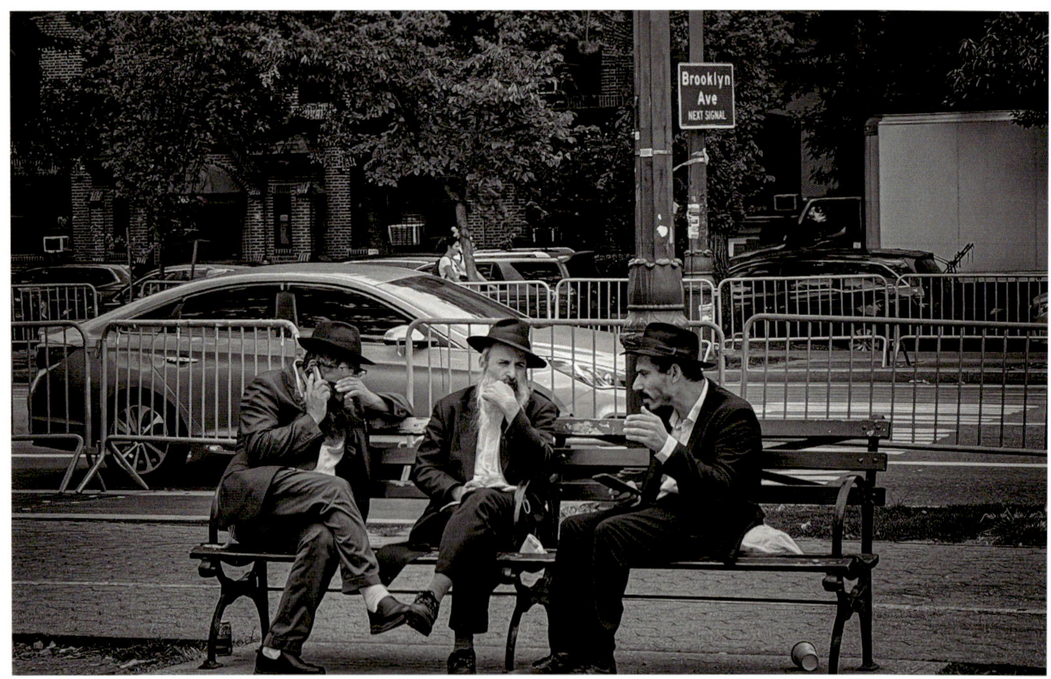

Three Orthodox men occupy a bench on Eastern Parkway in Crown Heights. (*Photo: Liz Cooke*)

Say the word "Williamsburg" and images come to mind of towering high-rises, tattooed hipsters, and overpriced coffee shops. This image—while somewhat accurate—misses the important fact that Williamsburg has, for generations, been a stronghold of Jewish life, largely due to the presence of the Satmar Hasidim—one of the largest Hasidic sects in the world. For years, Williamsburg was known as a Jewish "shtetl," a cohesive, if isolated, community offering everything an observant Jew could want or need—shuls, yeshivas, mikvahs, kosher shops—all within easy walking distance (a necessity since on the Sabbath, Orthodox Jews cannot drive or use modern technology). With the arrival of artists and investment bankers, tensions arose as rents soared, forcing many members of the Satmar Hasidim to consider other options. Working-class members of the Satmar sect are now expanding into traditionally Black neighborhoods like Clinton Hill and Bedford-Stuyvesant.

The south side of Williamsburg has a decidedly different flavor. Long a stronghold of Puerto Rican and Dominican culture, "Los Sures" manages to retain much of its Latinx heritage, despite the displacement of many families over the years. Tonita's (also known as the Caribbean Social Club) was opened in 1980 by Maria Antonio Cay who can still be found there, welcoming guests like Bad Bunny and Alexandria Ocasio-Cortez. Dominican families began arriving in the 1970s and are now Williamsburg's largest ethnic group.

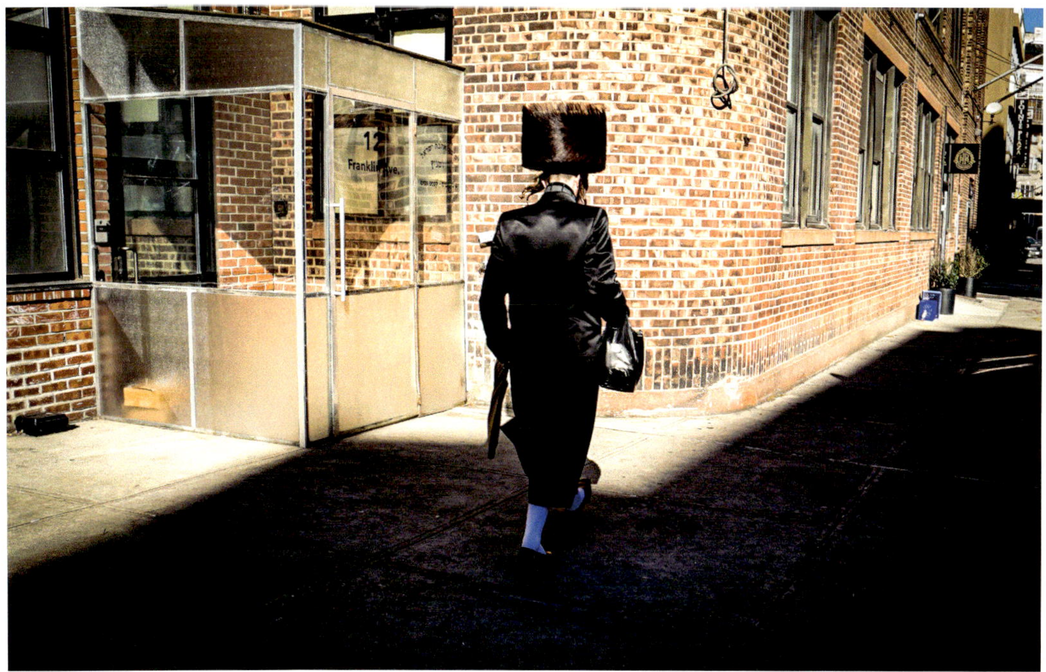

A member of the Satmar sect, seen walking to synagogue on the Jewish holiday of Sukkot. (*Photo: Liz Cooke*)

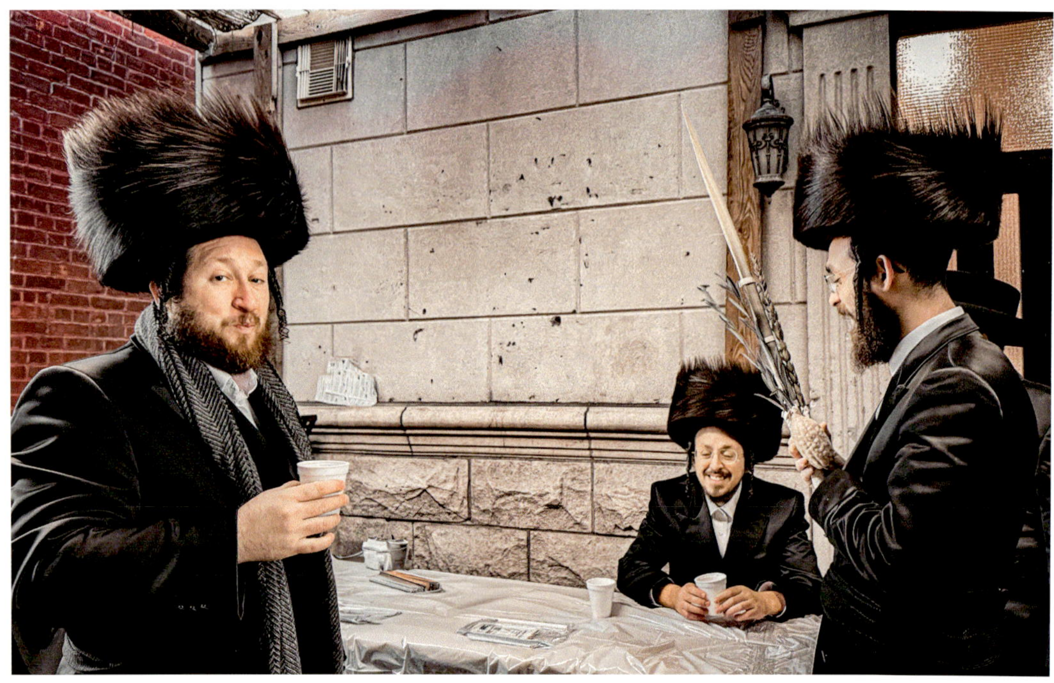

The Satmar sect in Williamsburg is one of the largest Hasidic communities in the world and is known for its strict religious observances, Yiddish-speaking homes, and deep-rooted customs. (*Photo: Liz Cooke*)

Once known as Brooklyn's "Little Italy," Bensonhurst was once packed with Italian bakeries, social clubs, and red sauce joints. Families who had moved out of Manhattan's Lower East Side in search of space and a better life settled here in the early to mid-twentieth century. By the 1950s and '60s, Bensonhurst was synonymous with Italian American culture—think feast processions, corner delis, and tight-knit communities where everyone knew everyone. But like all of Brooklyn, Bensonhurst kept evolving. By the 1980s and '90s, Chinese immigrants began moving in, opening restaurants, markets, and businesses along 18th Avenue and Bay Parkway. Over time, the neighborhood developed into one of the largest Chinese communities in New York, rivaling Sunset Park's Chinatown. Today, you'll see Cantonese and Fuzhounese signage alongside old Italian bakeries and pizzerias.

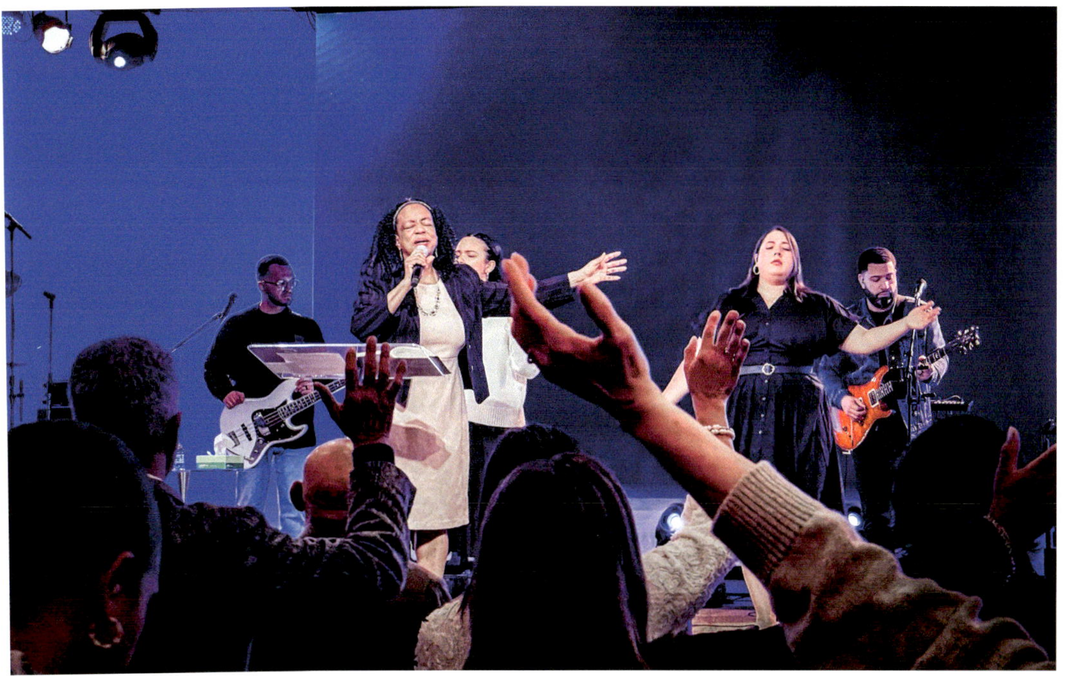

Dominican churches, like the Spirit of Brotherhood in Williamsburg, serve as spiritual and cultural hubs, blending faith with traditions from the Caribbean. Many churches offer services in Spanish and English and host lively worship, community gatherings, and outreach programs. (*Photo: Liz Cooke*)

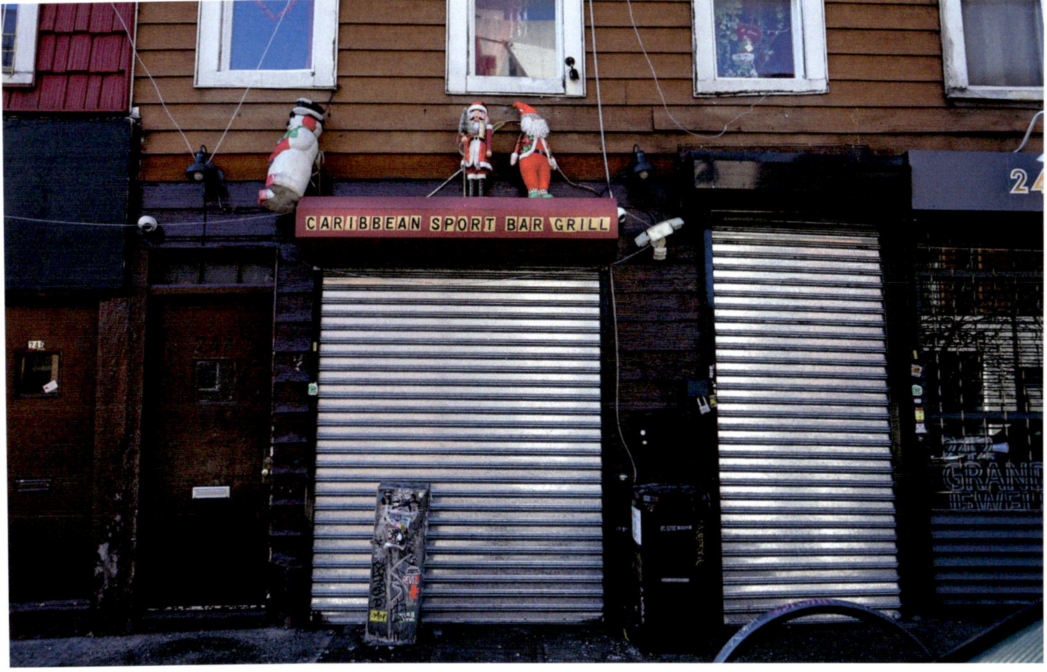

This innocuous gated storefront is home to Tonita's, also known as the Caribbean Social Club, the longest-running and last-remaining Latinx social club in South Williamsburg. (*Photo: Liz Cooke*)

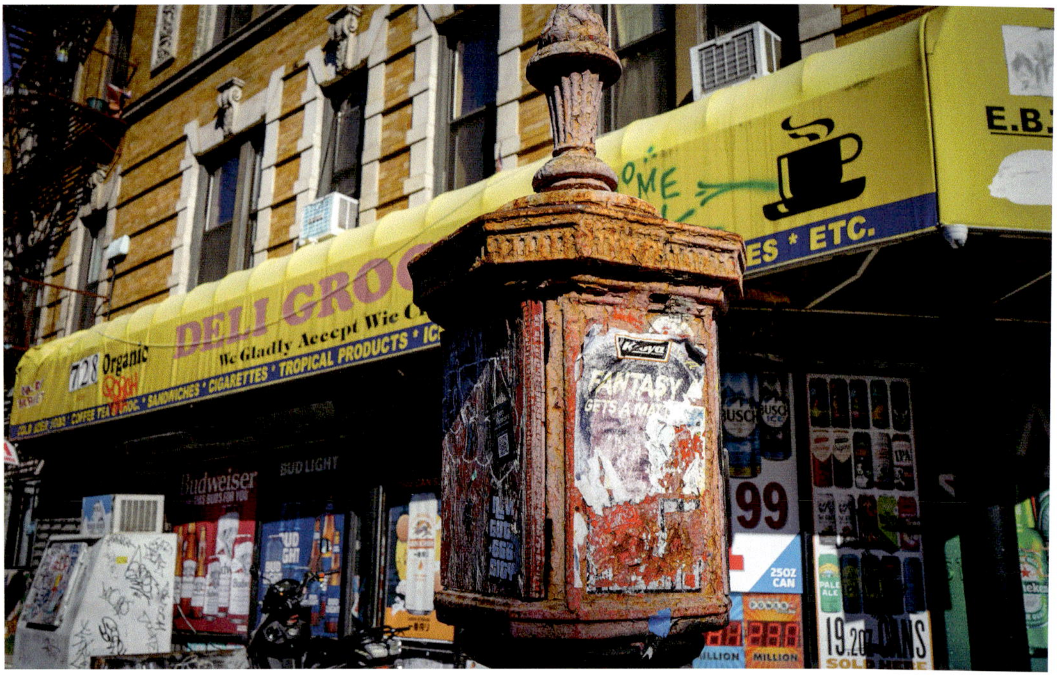

Bodegas in Los Sures, the Southside of Williamsburg, have long been neighborhood staples, offering everything from café con leche to everyday essentials. (*Photo: Liz Cooke*)

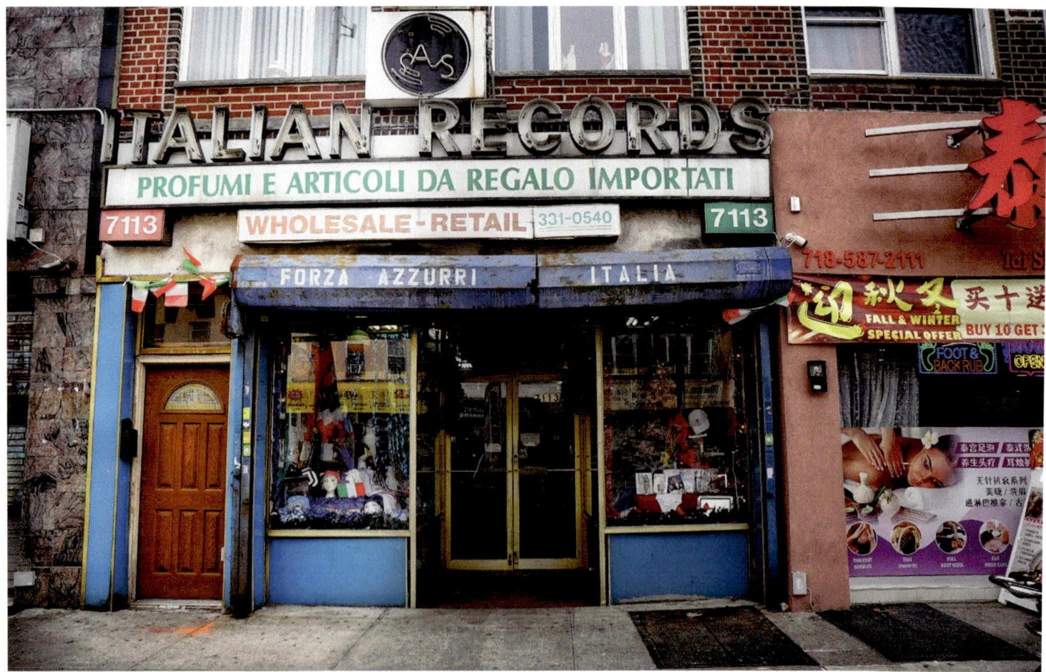

Bensonhurst has seen a shift in its demographics over the years, evolving from a predominantly Italian-American neighborhood to one that includes large Chinese, Russian, Mexican, and Arab communities. SAS Italian Records is the last Italian record store in the neighborhood. (*Photo: Liz Cooke*)

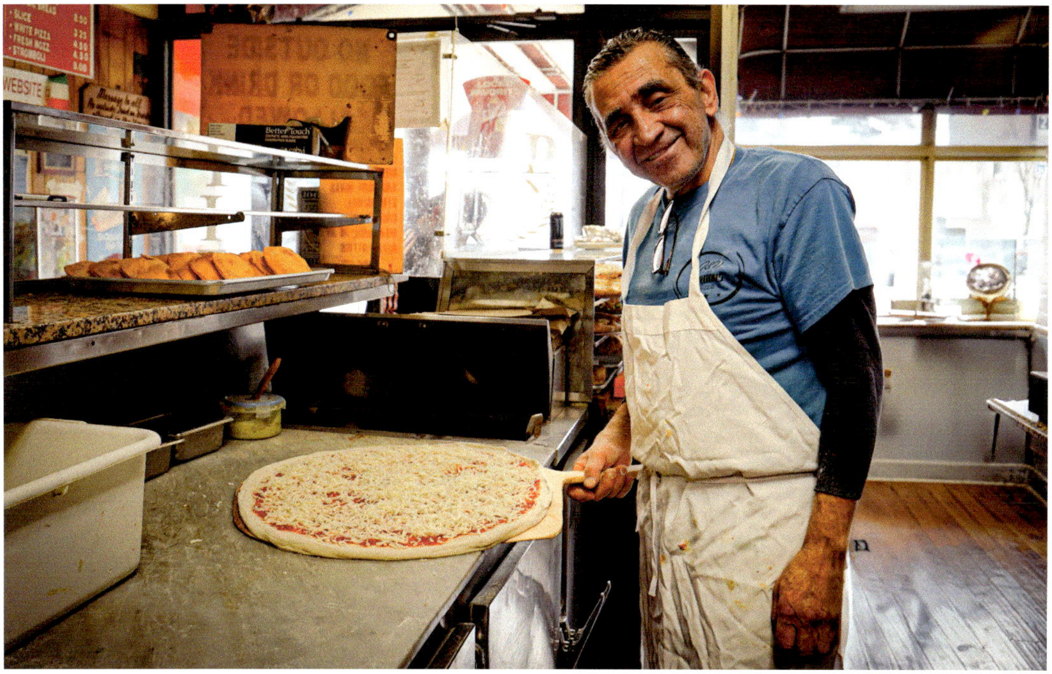

Pizza making at J&V Pizzeria in Bensonhurst. (*Photo: Liz Cooke*)

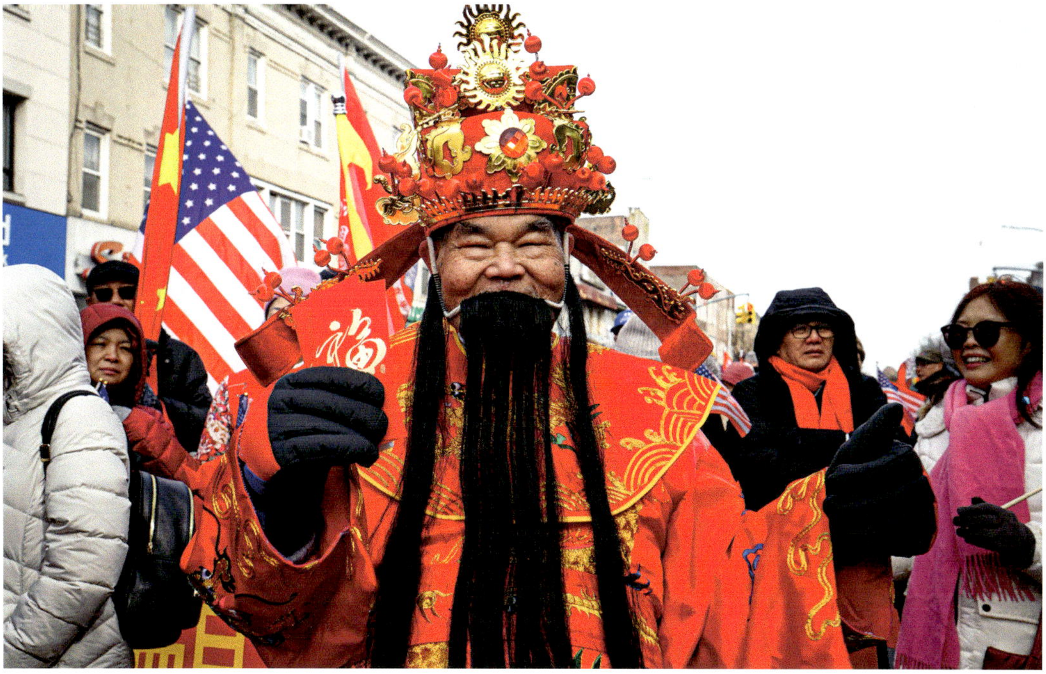

The Lunar New Year is a time of joy and celebration for the Chinese community in Bensonhurst. (*Photo: Liz Cooke*)

Food is a powerful marker of cultural identity in Brooklyn. Immigrant-owned restaurants, bakeries, and markets are integral to neighborhood life. Whether it's a bowl of borscht in Brighton Beach, a slice of Sicilian pizza in Bensonhurst, or a steaming bowl of noodles in Sunset Park, these culinary offerings reflect the diversity of the borough's population. And while no two people seem to be able to agree on who makes Brooklyn's best pizza (or bagels, or babka, or beef patties), food has always been a bridge between cultures. In Brooklyn, everyone is welcome at the table.

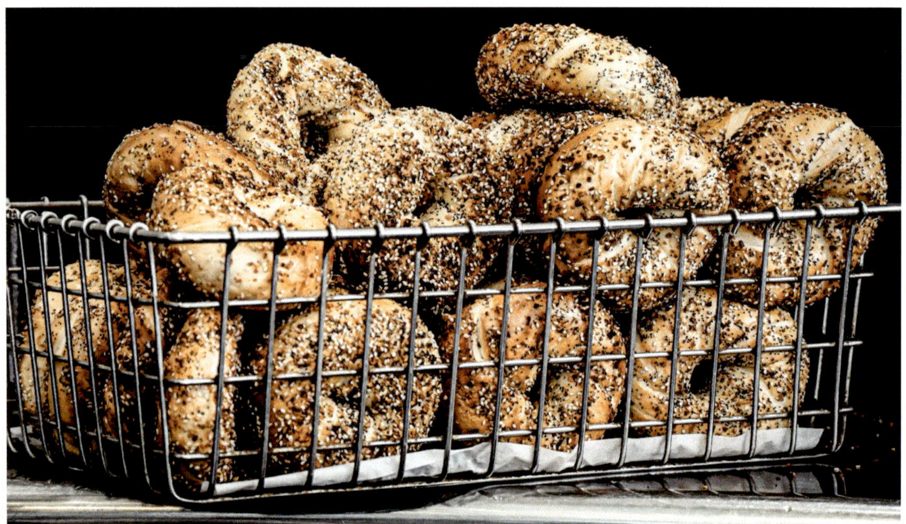

Brooklynites have very strong opinions about what makes a quality bagel. These are from the Bagel Point in Greenpoint. (*Photo: Liz Cooke*)

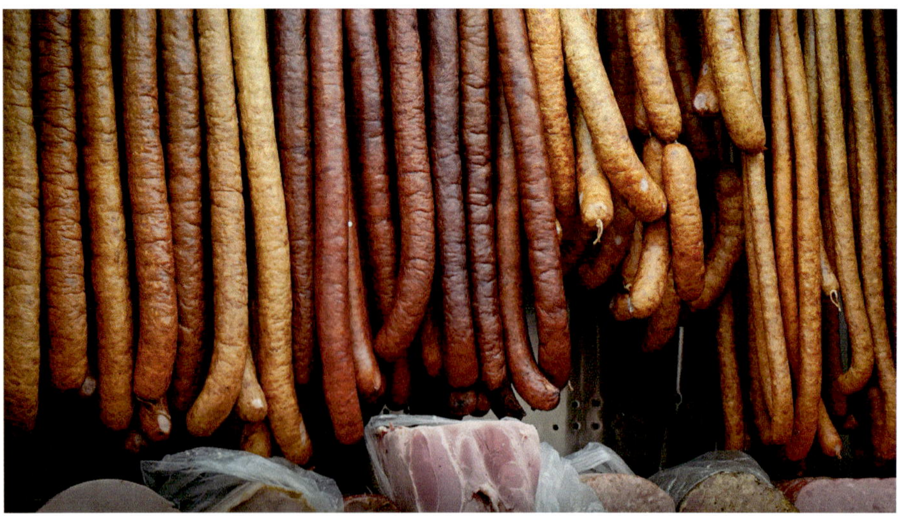

Greenpoint, once the heart of Brooklyn's Polish community, is still home to a few traditional kielbasa shops. (*Photo: Liz Cooke*)

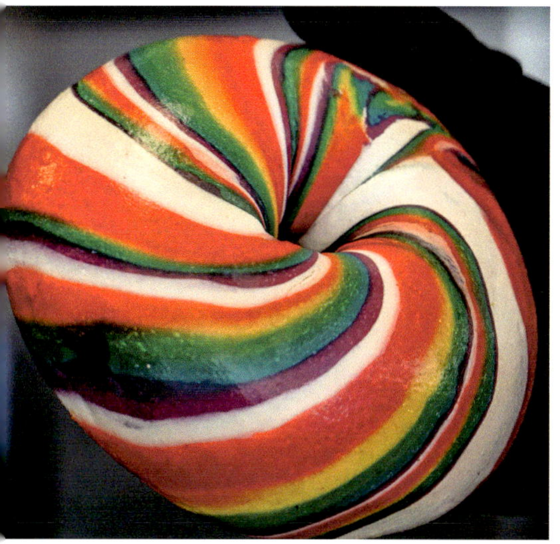

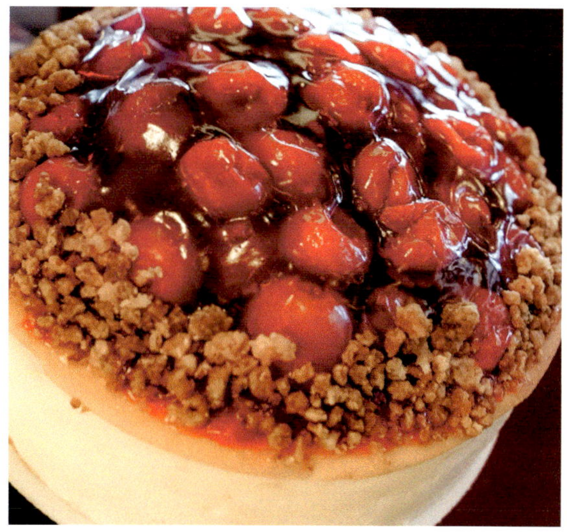

Above left: To a true Brooklynite, a multi-colored bagel could be sacrilegious, but this one passes the test, at Bagel Point in Greenpoint. (*Photo: Liz Cooke*)

Above right: Junior's, founded in 1950 by Harry Rosen, is a Downtown Brooklyn staple, famous for its rich, creamy cheesecake, made using a family recipe. (*Photo: Liz Cooke*)

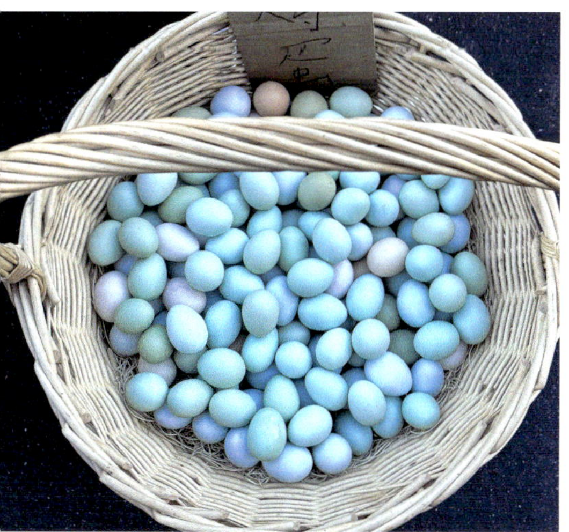

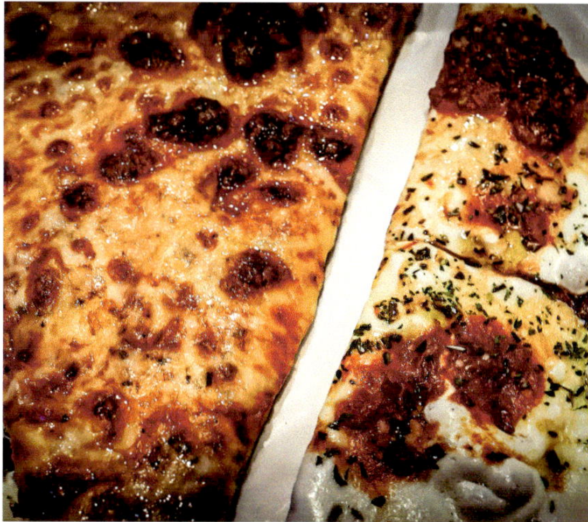

Above left: Bright blue eggs line a basket outside a Chinese market in Sunset Park. (*Photo: Liz Cooke*)

Above right: Pizza may very well be at the center of Brooklyn's food culture. From thin-crust slices to Sicilian squares, Brooklyn's pizza scene reflects the borough's love for quality, no-frills food. (*Photo: Liz Cooke*)

3

Lost Brooklyn

If new Brooklyn is a place of change and transformation, old Brooklyn was a place of permanence and tradition. It was a place where kids played stickball in the street, neighbors knew each other by name, and the smell of home cooking permeated the hallways of crowded apartment buildings. My childhood neighborhood of Brighton Beach fit the image perfectly. It was a neighborhood of old people pushing shopping carts, young people running the streets, kosher bakeries and delis, egg creams, knishes, black and white cookies, and even Diamond's, the clothing store owned by Neil Diamond's parents. Almost everyone was Jewish, and many of the elders bore concentration camp numbers tattooed on their forearms.

Brighton Beach in the 1970s and 1980s was experiencing a radical transformation from an Eastern European Jewish stronghold to a home for recent Soviet emigres. Tastes and traditions were not the same and over time, as the older Jewish population died out, the Brighton of my youth became "Little Odessa." These photographs, taken in 1979 and 1980, captured that pivotal moment.

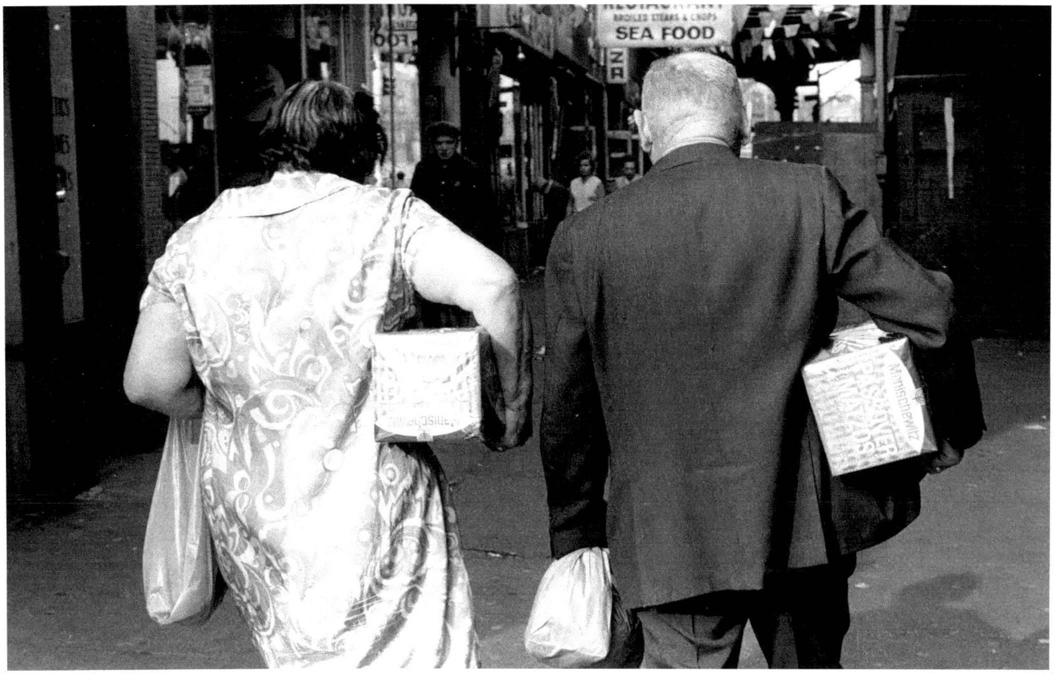

A husband and wife prepare for Passover with large boxes of matzoh purchased on Brighton Beach Avenue. (*Photo: Liz Cooke*)

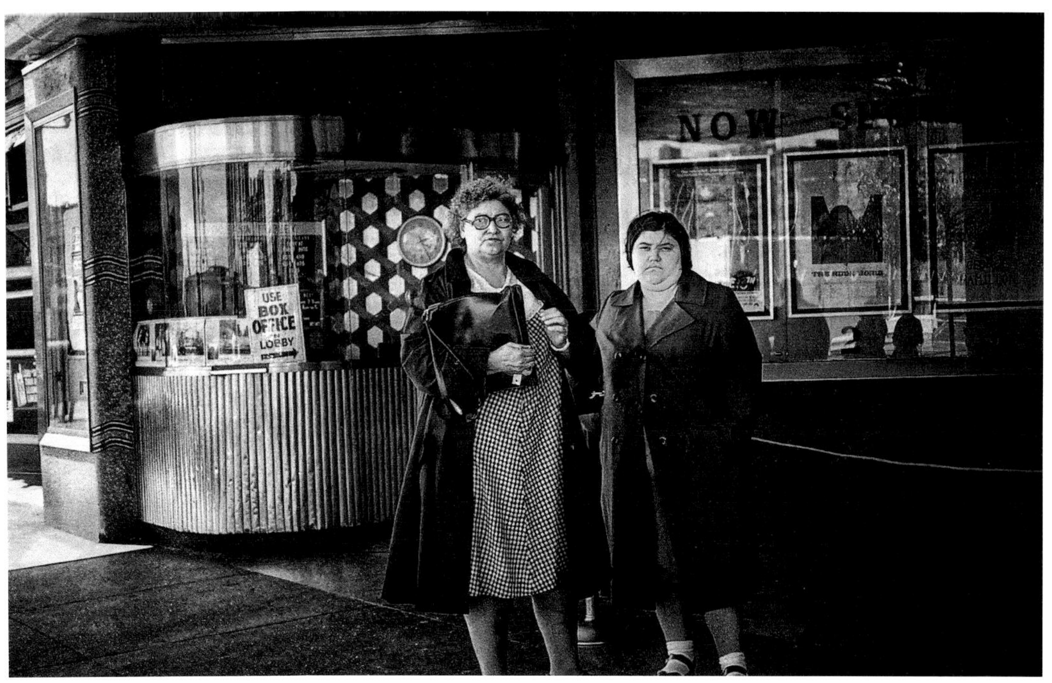

The Oceana movie theatre was once the entertainment hub of Brighton Beach. As movie attendance declined, the theater became a Russian night club. It is now home to Netcost Market, a Russian grocery store. (*Photo: Liz Cooke*)

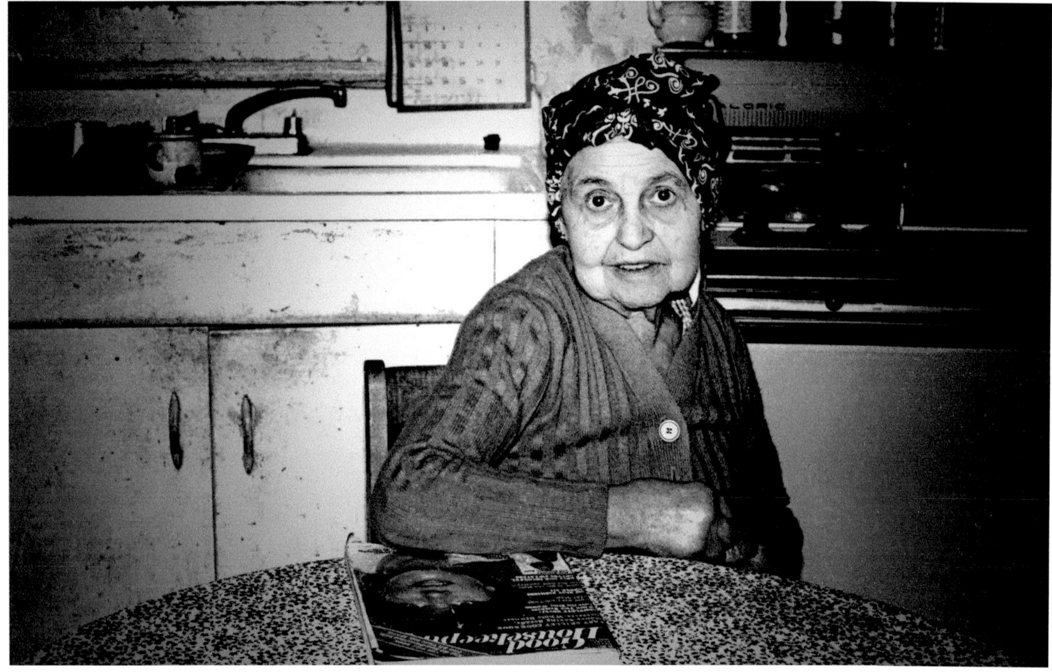

Rebbitzen Rivka, seen at her kitchen table in the family section of the Beth Hamedrosh Hagodol Shul on Neptune Avenue in Brighton Beach. (*Photo: Liz Cooke*)

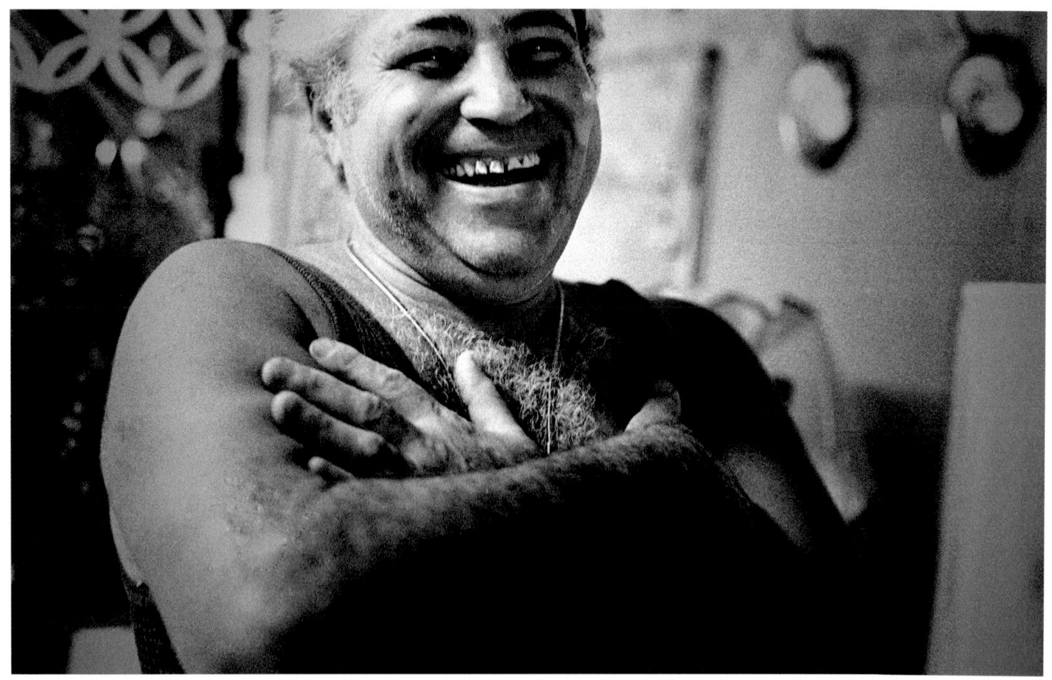

Big smiles from this Soviet emigre in Brighton Beach. (*Photo: Liz Cooke*)

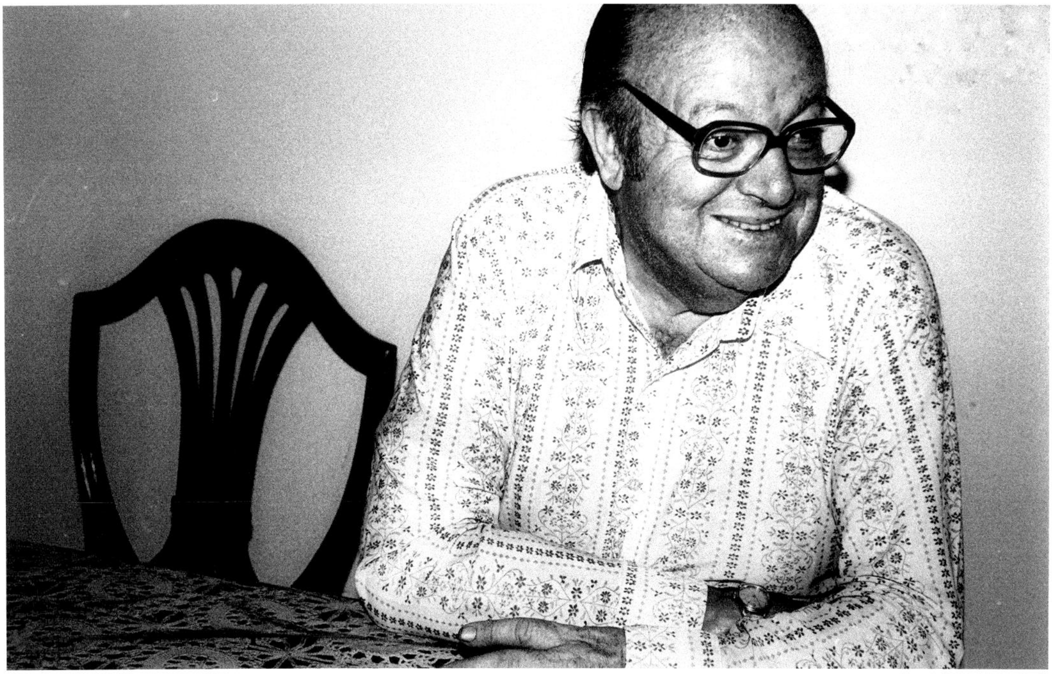

Solomon Wieder was born in Czechoslovakia in 1926. After enduring the horrors of Auschwitz and Bergen-Belsen, he emigrated to the United States where he started a family and became an active voice in Holocaust education and remembrance. (*Photo: Liz Cooke*)

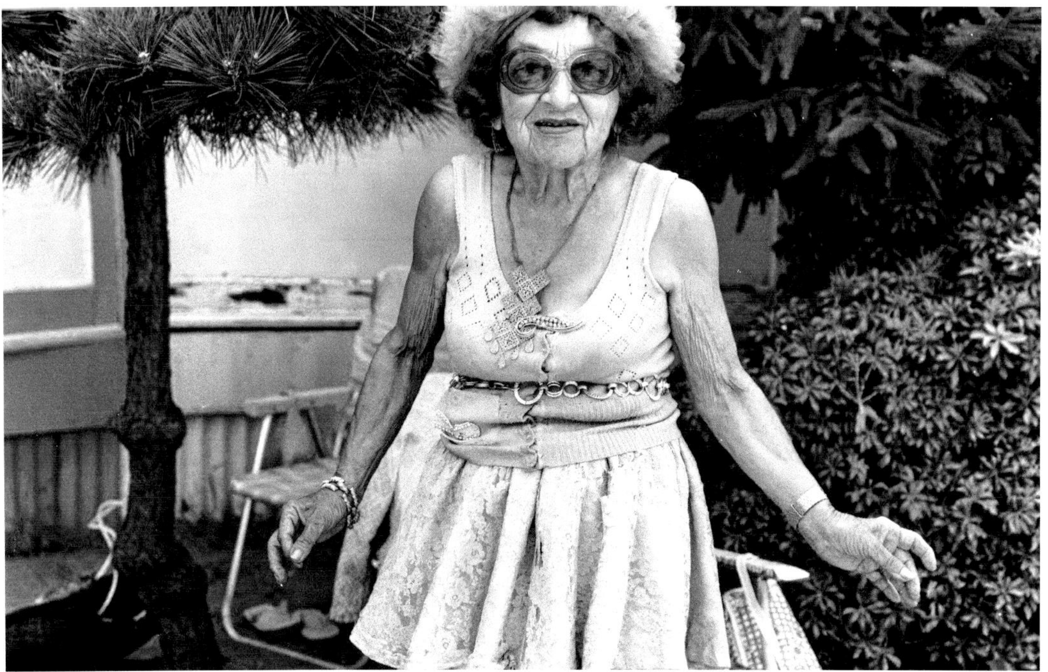

Elsie—a Holocaust survivor—was one of many older people who came to the Brighton Beach Baths during the summer season to enjoy dancing, swimming, handball and mahjong. (*Photo: Liz Cooke*)

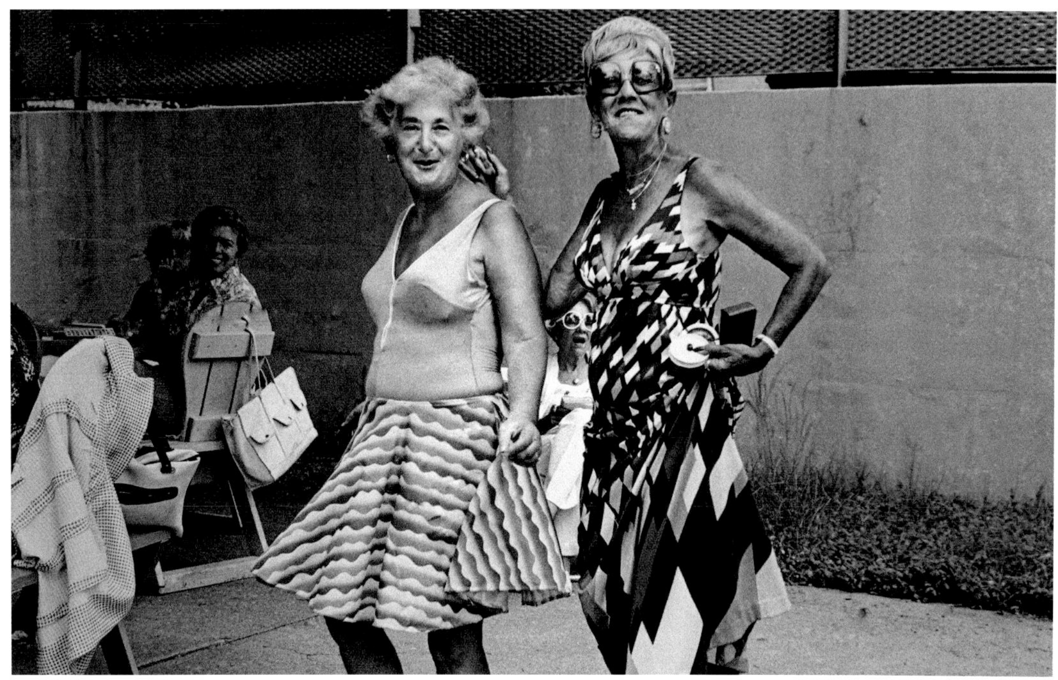

The Brighton Beach Baths closed in 1970 after many years as a popular summer spot. "The Baths"—once famous for its large outdoor swimming pool and bathhouse—was demolished to make way for new developments. (*Photo: Liz Cooke*)

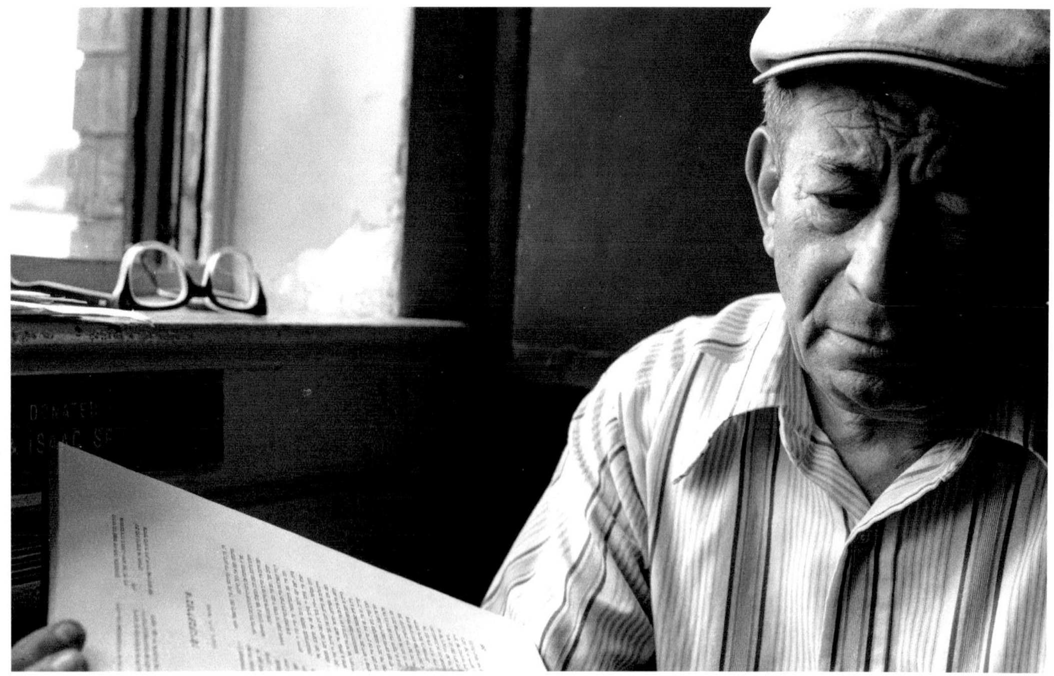

A survivor of the concentration camps, Samuel Glanz is seen here reading from his Yizkor book—a memorial book published by Jewish communities to honor and remember those who perished during the Holocaust. (*Photo: Liz Cooke*)

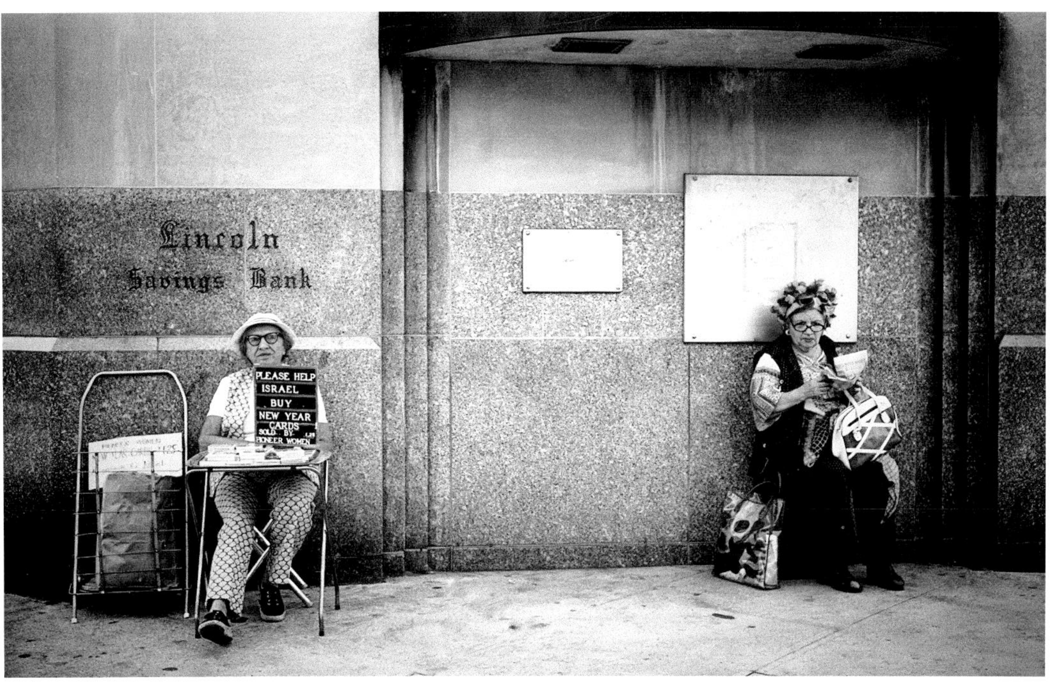

"Pishka ladies" in front of the Lincoln Savings Bank Building on Brighton Beach Avenue collected donations for Jewish charitable organizations. The term "pishka" comes from the Yiddish word for a small charity box. (*Photo: Liz Cooke*)

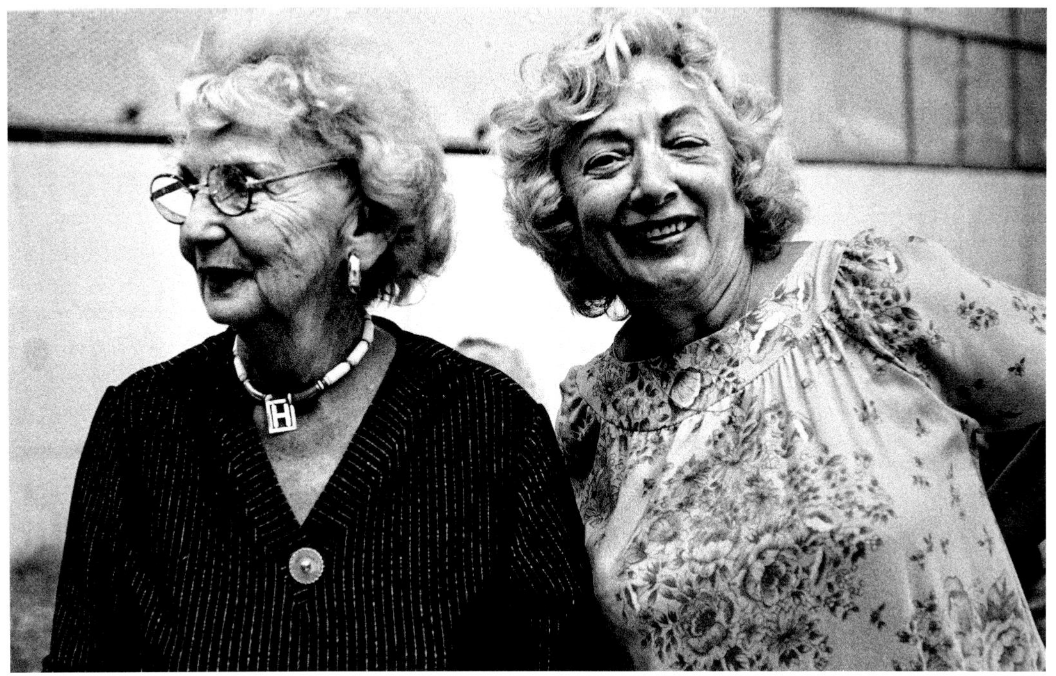

In a neighborhood that has seen more than its share of suffering, Brighton Beach was also a place of joy and togetherness. These women share a laugh at a luncheon at the Shorefront YM-YWHA. (*Photo: Liz Cooke*)

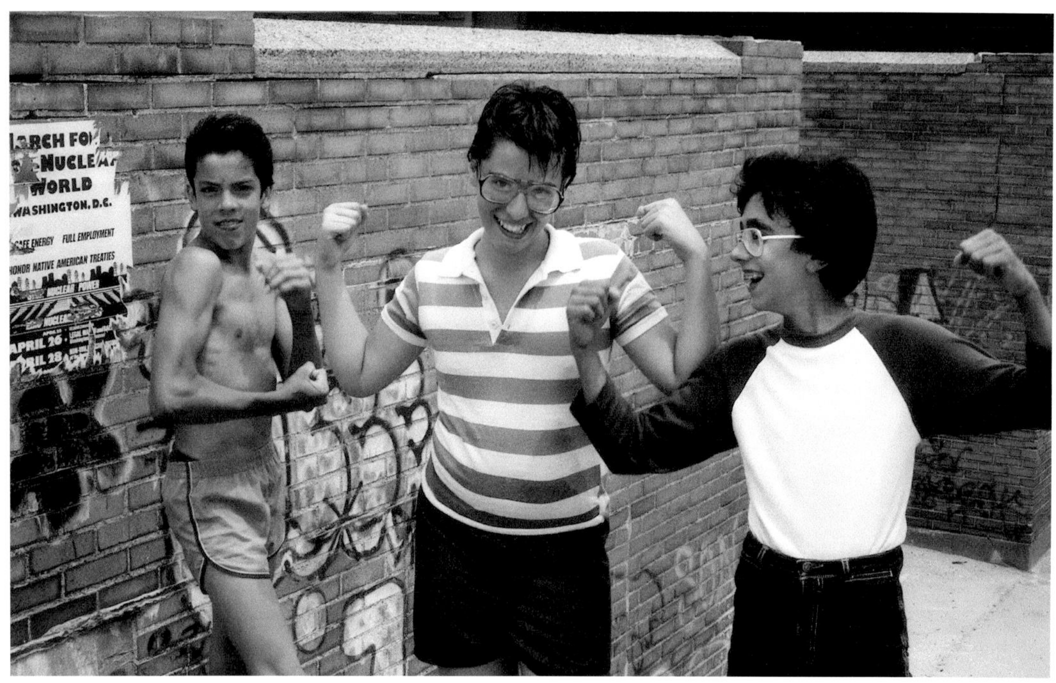

Three young boys playfully flex their muscles at the entrance to the beach in Brighton Beach. (*Photo: Liz Cooke*)

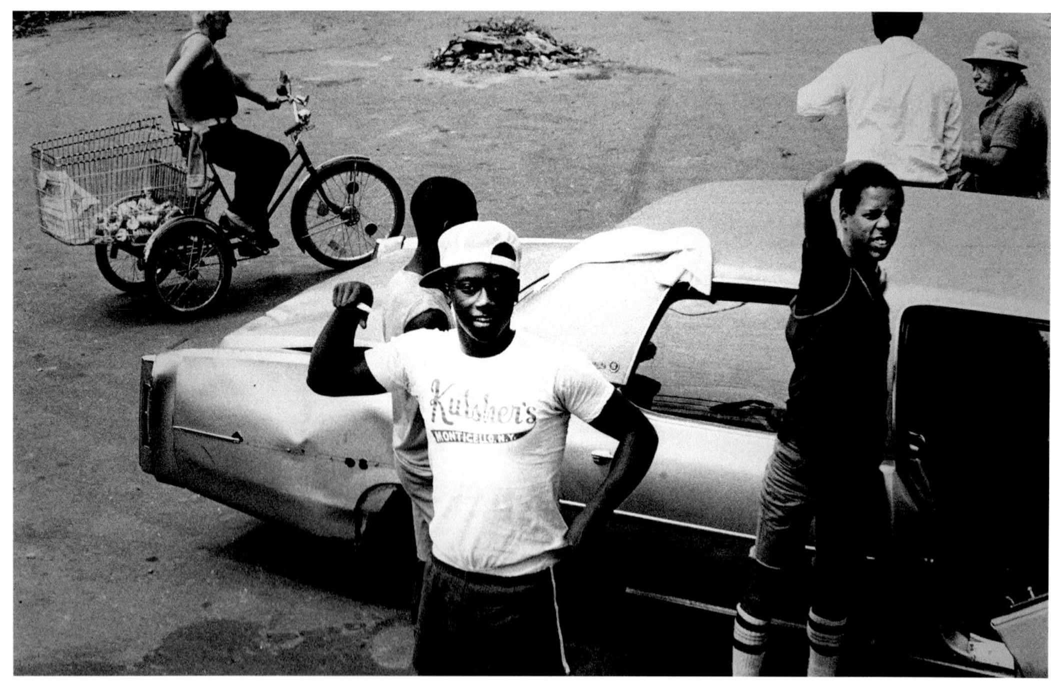

Even with the beach mere steps away, the allure of an abandoned lot was irresistible to these young men (and this writer). Despite being a predominantly Jewish neighborhood, Brighton Beach was also home to many African American, Puerto Rican, and Asian families. (*Photo: Liz Cooke*)

4

Forever Brooklyn

The story of Brooklyn is written on every stoop, in every luncheonette and in every overcrowded apartment. It's written on the basketball courts in neighborhood playgrounds and in former dive bars transformed into trendy watering holes. The story of Brooklyn is etched in the faces of elders and in the exuberant energy of creative newcomers. It's written in the early works of rap legends like the Notorious B.I.G. and Lil' Kim—both products of Bed-Stuy and pioneers in Brooklyn's rap and hip-hop scene. It's written in storefront churches and backyard barbecues and spontaneous dance parties on summer nights in Coney Island. It's written in 9/11 remembrances and street-side memorials. It's written in stories of surviving the impacts of Superstorm Sandy and COVID-19. When you know where to look, the story of Brooklyn is everywhere.

One of the most frequently told stories is about the experience of walking across the Brooklyn Bridge. On any day of the week, some 30,000 people will walk across the historic structure. Some may be commuting from Brooklyn to Wall Street, others may be out for a run, but anyone who has ever crossed the East River on the Brooklyn Bridge knows this: the Brooklyn Bridge isn't just a means of getting from one borough to another, it's a step back in time.

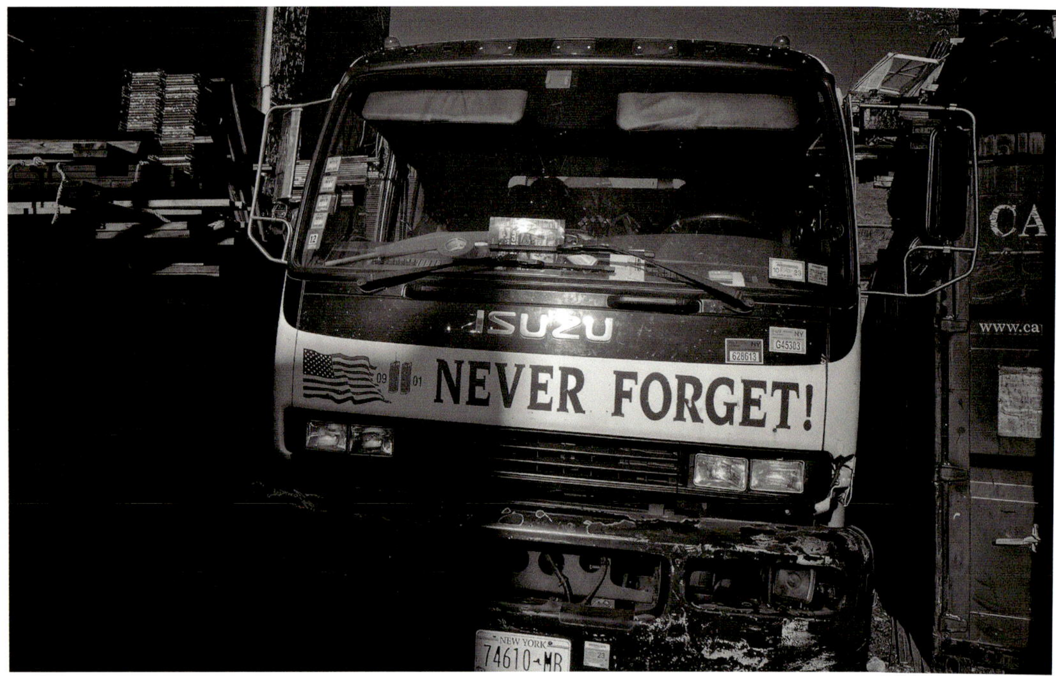

A warehouse truck in Sunset Park bears the reminder to "Never Forget." In a somewhat strange twist, the pallets stacked in the upper left corner bear an eerie resemblance to the Twin Towers. (*Photo: Liz Cooke*)

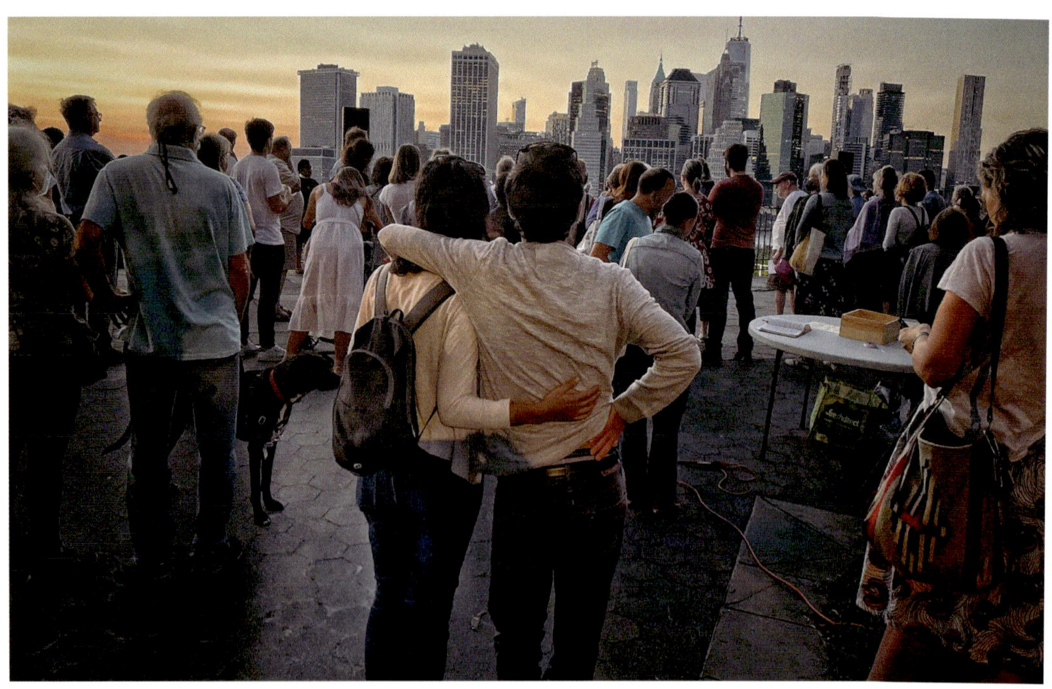

Gathering on the Brooklyn Heights Promenade on the twentieth anniversary of September 11, 2001. (*Photo: Liz Cooke*)

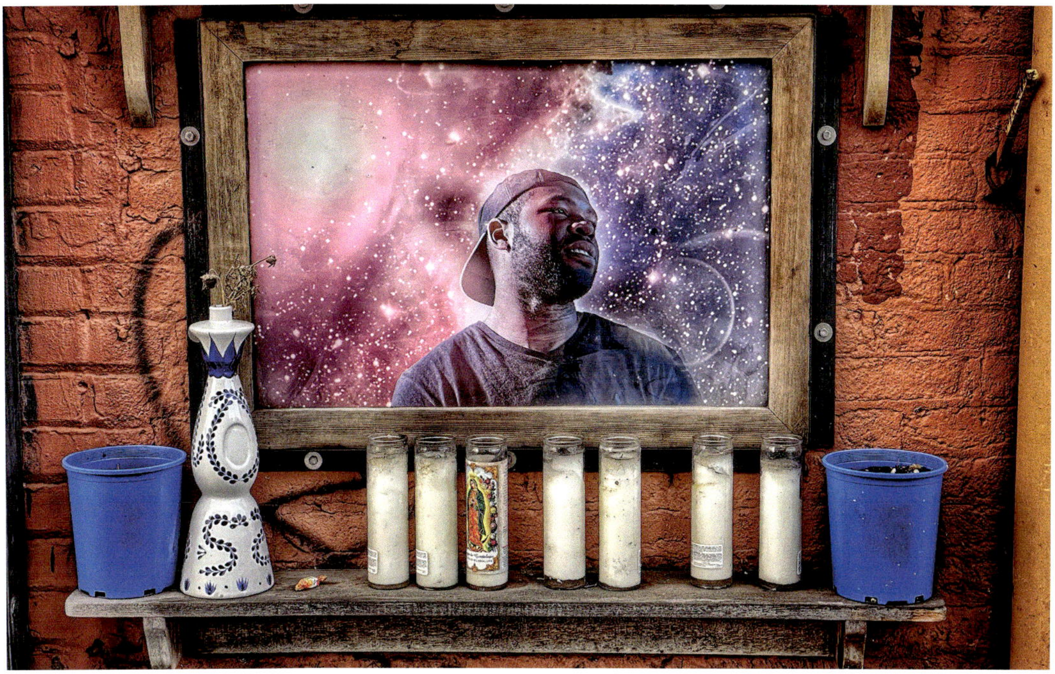

A street-side memorial in Red Hook commemorates the life of someone gone too soon. (*Photo: Liz Cooke*)

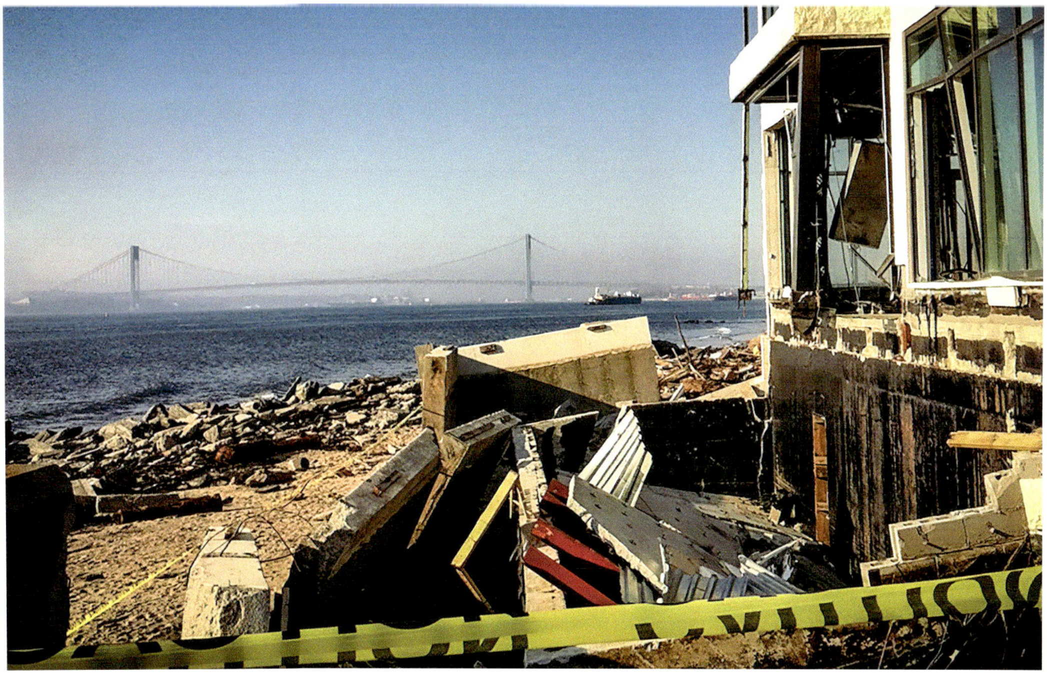

Sea Gate, a private gated community at the western tip of Coney Island, suffered severe damage from Superstorm Sandy on October 29, 2012. The recovery process was long and complex, taking several years to rebuild homes, infrastructure, and the seawall that was heavily damaged by the storm surge. (*Photo: Liz Cooke*)

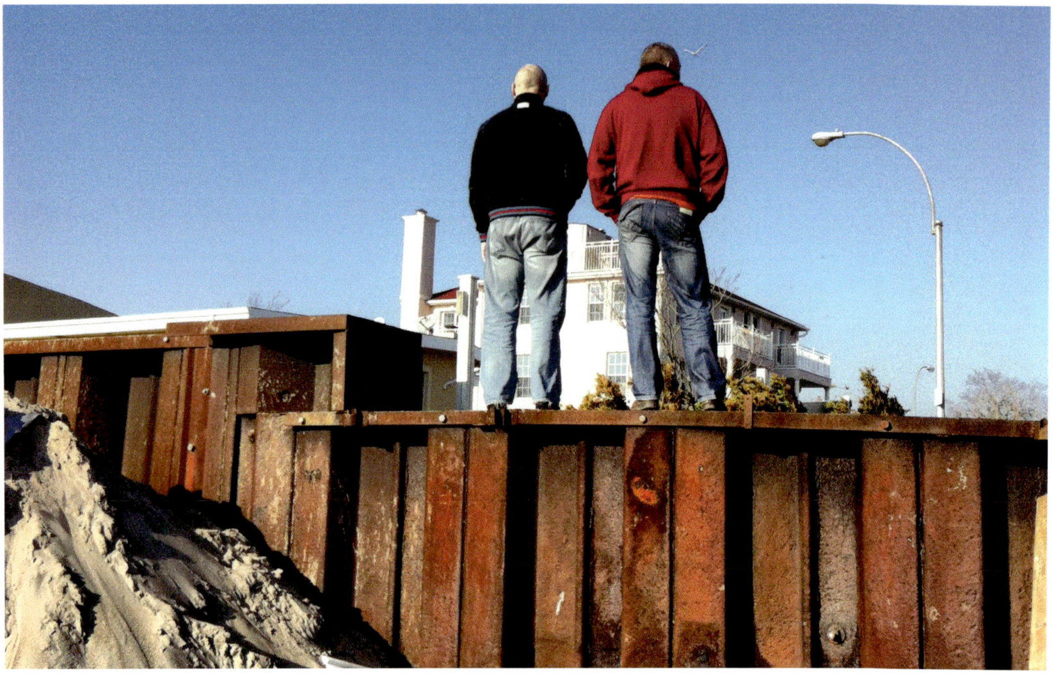

The coastal community of Sea Gate was hit hard by Superstorm Sandy on October 29, 2012. These men are seen surveying the damage and destruction. (*Photo: Liz Cooke*)

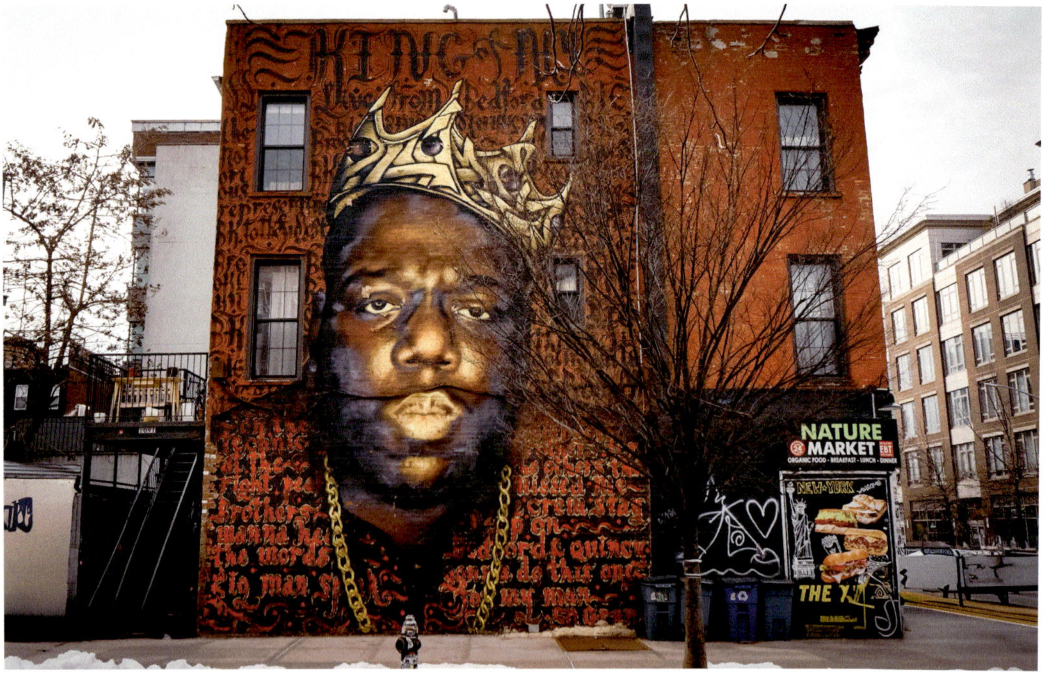

The "King of New York" mural of the Notorious B.I.G. in Bed-Stuy, has become a landmark in the neighborhood where Biggie grew up. (*Photo: Liz Cooke*)

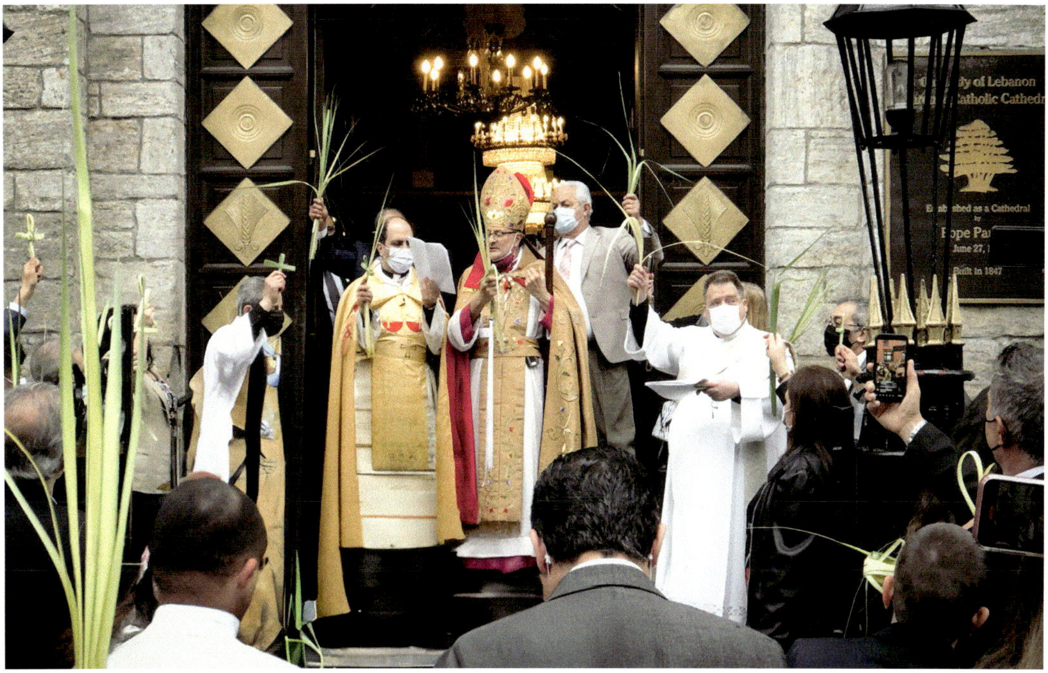

Our Lady of Lebanon Maronite Cathedral in Brooklyn Heights adapted to the demands of the COVID-19 pandemic in 2020 by hosting outdoor services. (*Photo: Liz Cooke*)

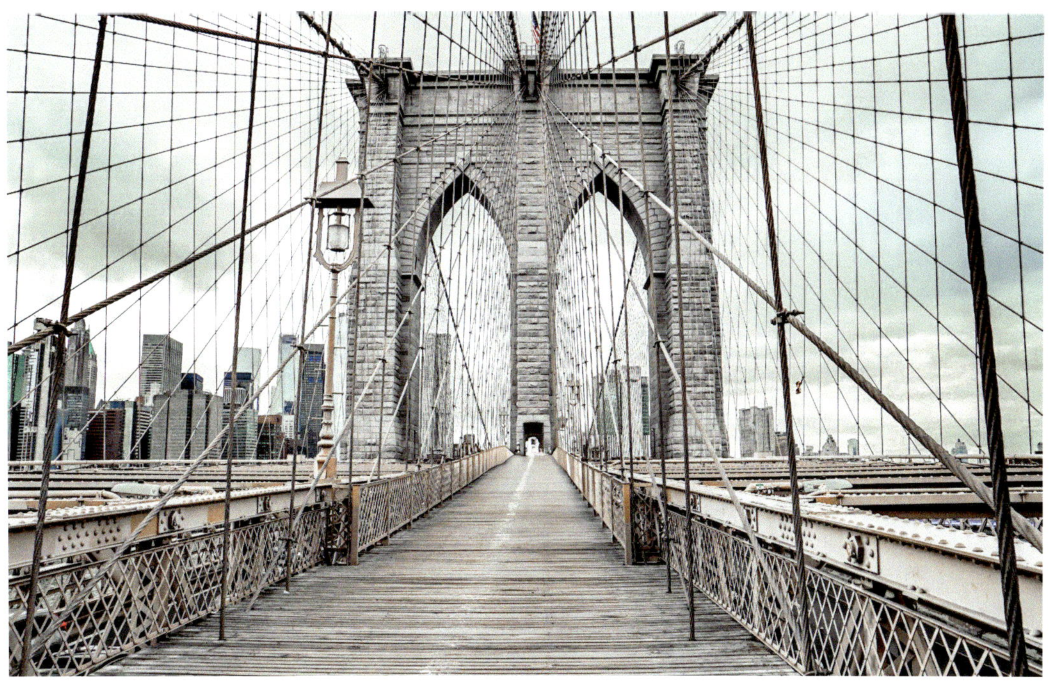

When it opened in 1883, the Brooklyn Bridge was the first to use steel cables instead of iron. In 1884, P. T. Barnum marched twenty-one elephants (including the famous Jumbo) across the bridge to prove its safety to skeptical New Yorkers. (*Photo: Liz Cooke*)

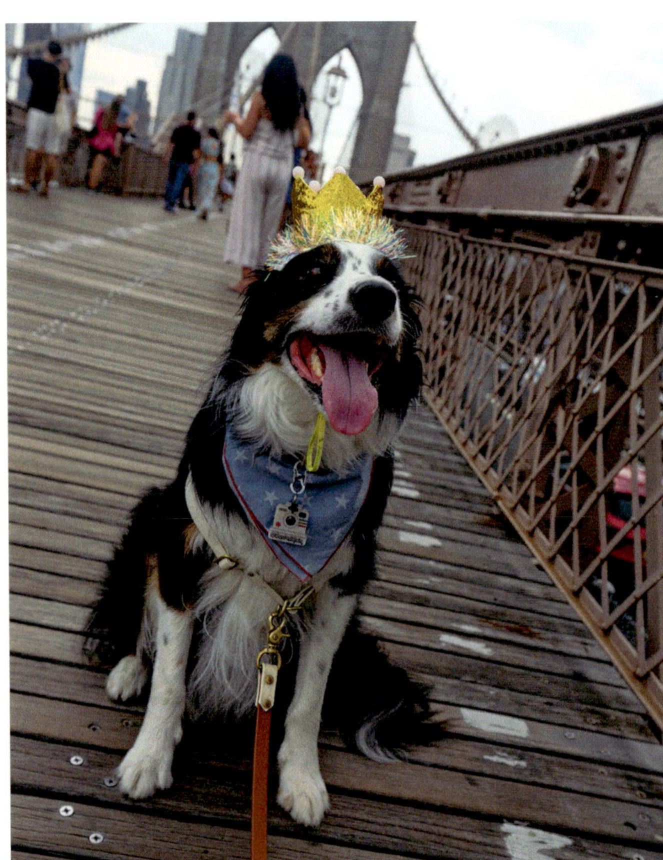

On busy weekend days, the Brooklyn Bridge can see over 30,000 pedestrians. On typical weekdays, the bridge accommodates approximately 10,000 pedestrians, 3,500 cyclists, and an unknown number of dogs. Alvin, an Instagram influencer, is celebrating his birthday with a walk across the bridge. (*Photo: Andy Milford*)

In Brooklyn, nostalgia runs deep. Here you can still get a thrill in Coney Island by taking a ride on the Cyclone, the wooden coaster built in 1927. For a taste of old Brooklyn, head to the corner of Flatbush and DeKalb Avenues for cherry cheesecake at Juniors, a Downtown Brooklyn institution since 1950, or Peter Luger's in Williamsburg, one of the country's oldest steakhouses. DiFara's Pizza on Avenue J was discovered long ago (and has the long lines to prove it) but is worth the trek to Midwood. (Sadly, owner and pizza icon Domenico DeMarco died in 2022.) For a real immersion in old-time Brooklyn, pay a visit to Montero's on Atlantic Avenue and feel transported to a time when longshoremen worked the docks of the busy Red Hook waterfront.

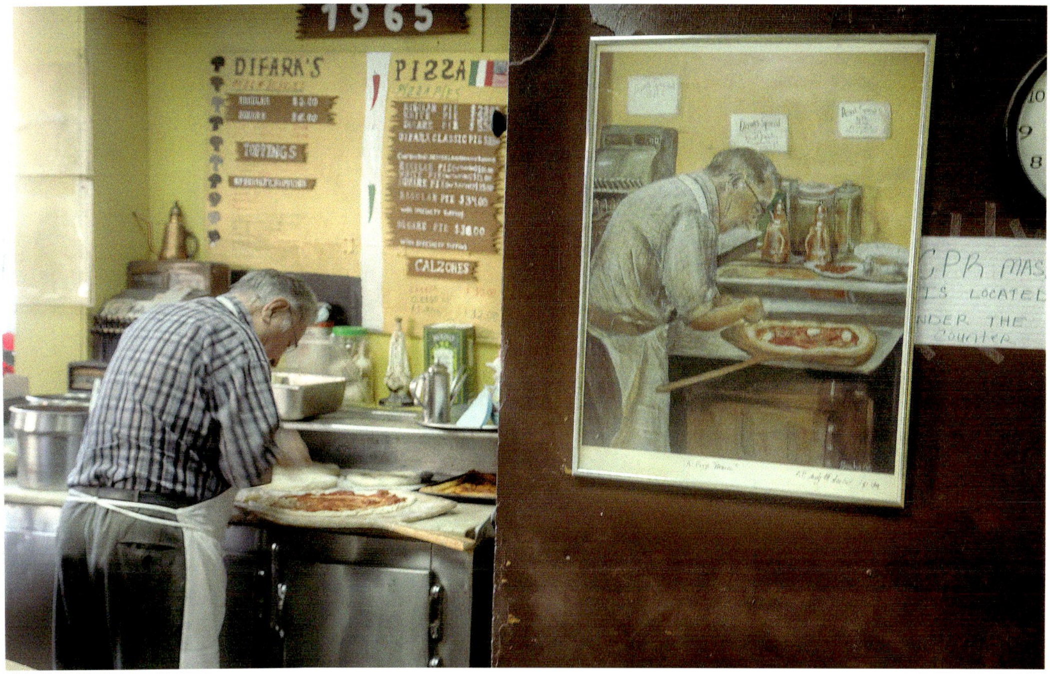

Legendary pizza-purveyor Domenico DeMarco at work. A slice of pizza at DiFara's would include a snip of fresh-grown basil, cut by Dom with a pair of scissors. (*Photo: Andy Milford*)

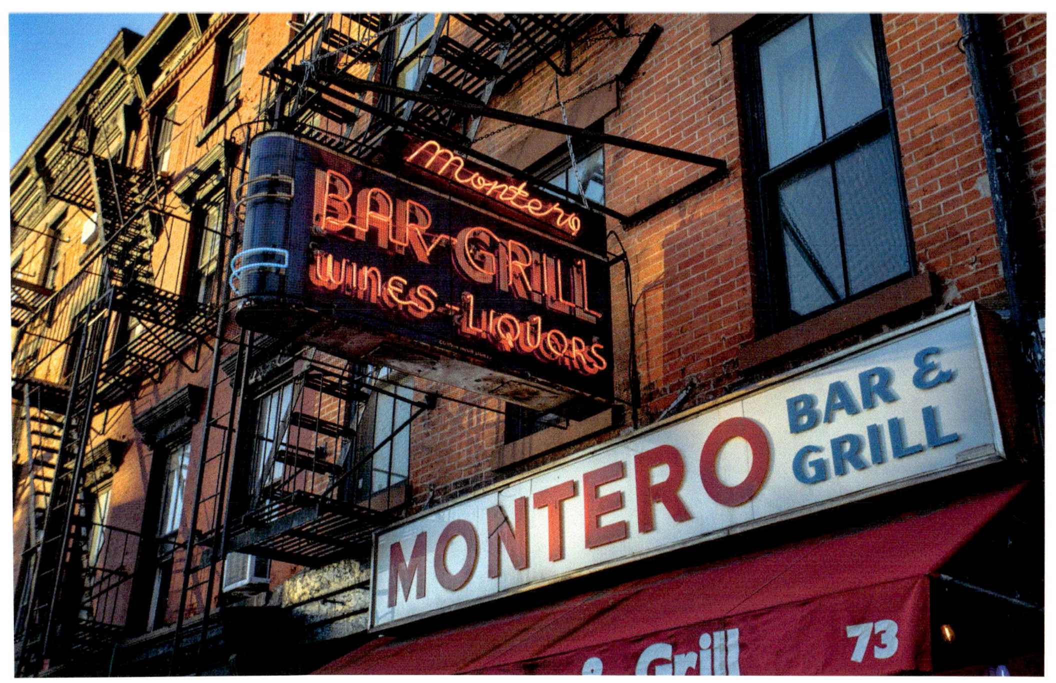

Montero's Bar & Grill on Atlantic Avenue is one of Brooklyn's last old-school waterfront bars. Opened in 1947, it was a longtime haunt for dockworkers, sailors, and locals. Today, it is a popular dive bar offering no-frills cocktails and karaoke. (*Photo: Andy Milford*)

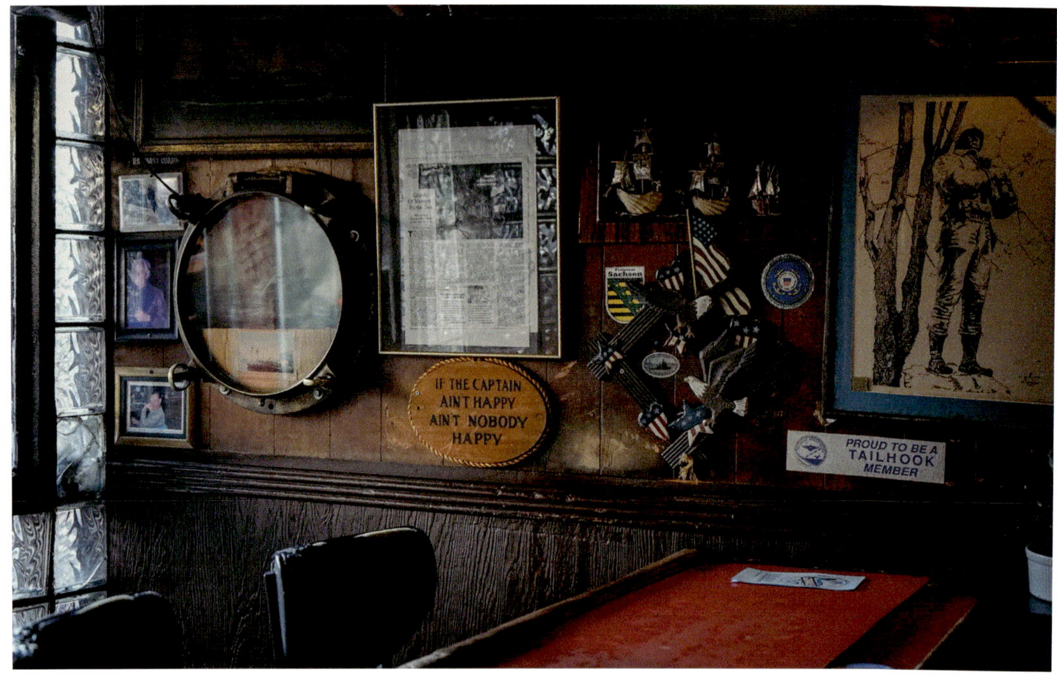

Nautical memorabilia line the walls at Montero's Bar & Grill on Atlantic Avenue. (*Photo: Liz Cooke*)

Travel further into the southern part of Brooklyn and you'll arrive in Sheepshead Bay, a waterfront neighborhood that was once a busy fishing village. Today, "the Bay" is still a prime destination for those looking to fish the waters of the Atlantic. Charter boats welcome visitors for angling and whale watching, while Emmons Avenue, the neighborhood's main street, offers a wide variety of seafood restaurants (locals swear by the calamari at Randazzo's).

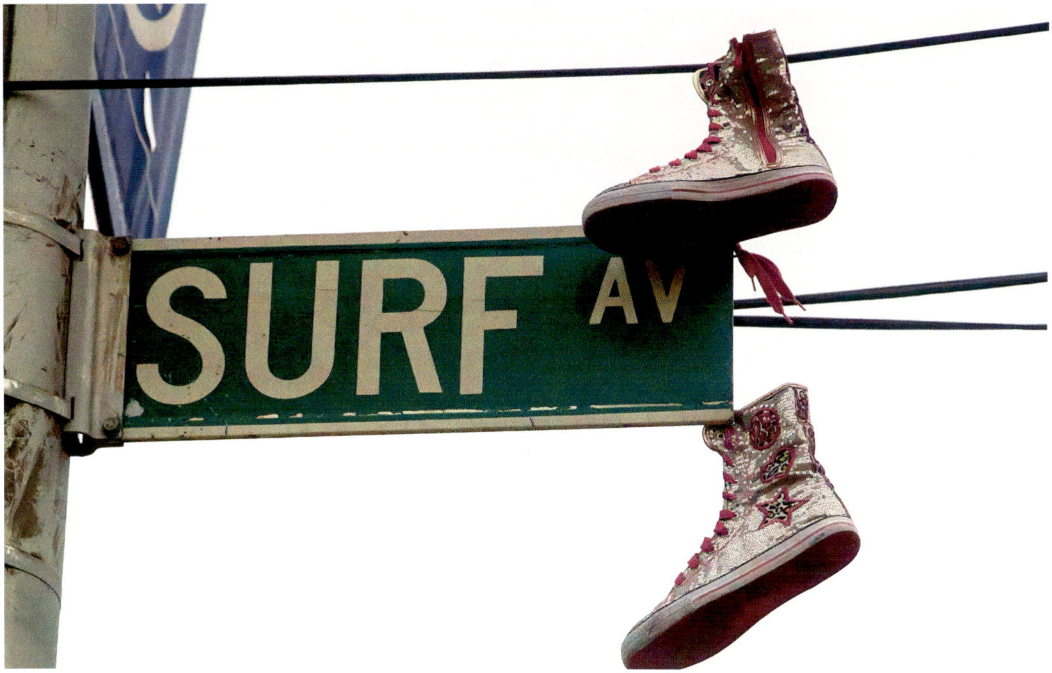

Sneakers hanging from a tree or telephone wire are a timeless symbol of old Brooklyn. This pair was seen on Surf Avenue in Coney Island. (*Photo: Andy Milford*)

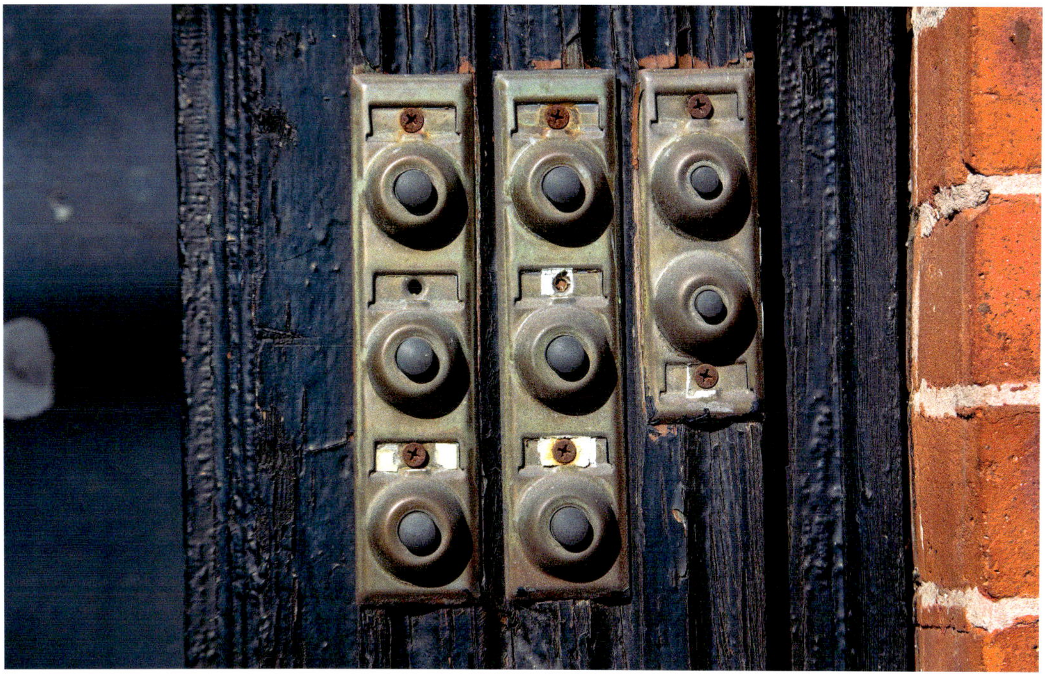

For all the recent luxury developments crowding the streets of Brooklyn, there are still artifacts of old Brooklyn, like this set of buzzers. (*Photo: Andy Milford*)

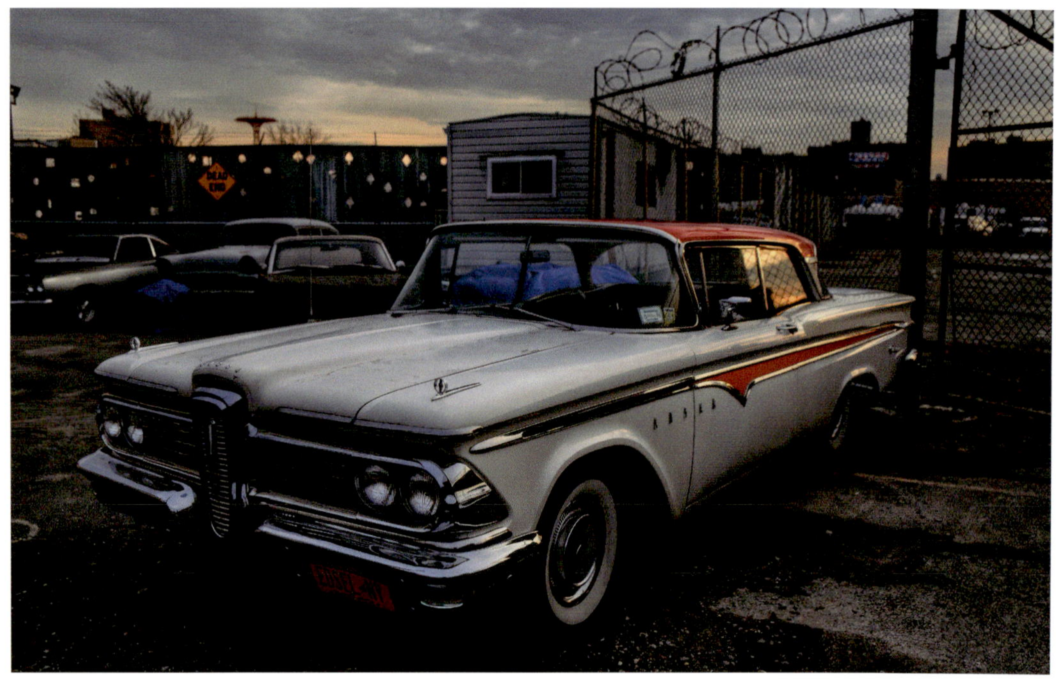

A 1959 Ford in the foreground with the 1939 Parachute Jump in the background, seen on Stillwell Avenue in Coney Island. (*Photo: Liz Cooke*)

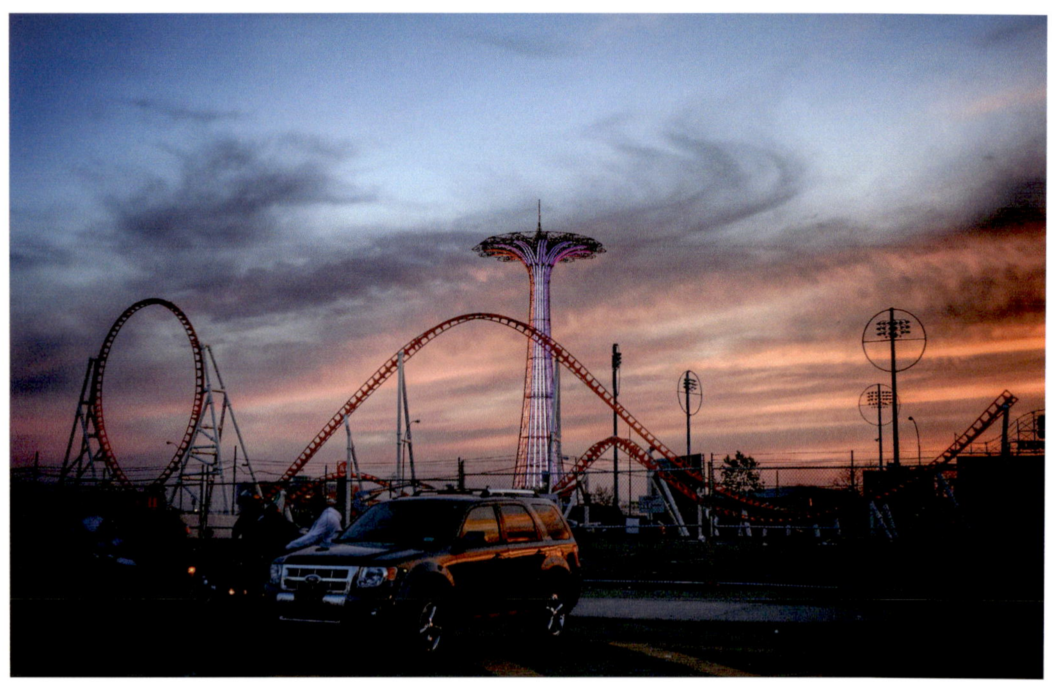

Built in 1939 for the New York World's Fair in Queens, the Parachute Jump was a Coney Island institution until it ceased operating in 1968. It remains a Brooklyn landmark. (*Photo: Liz Cooke*)

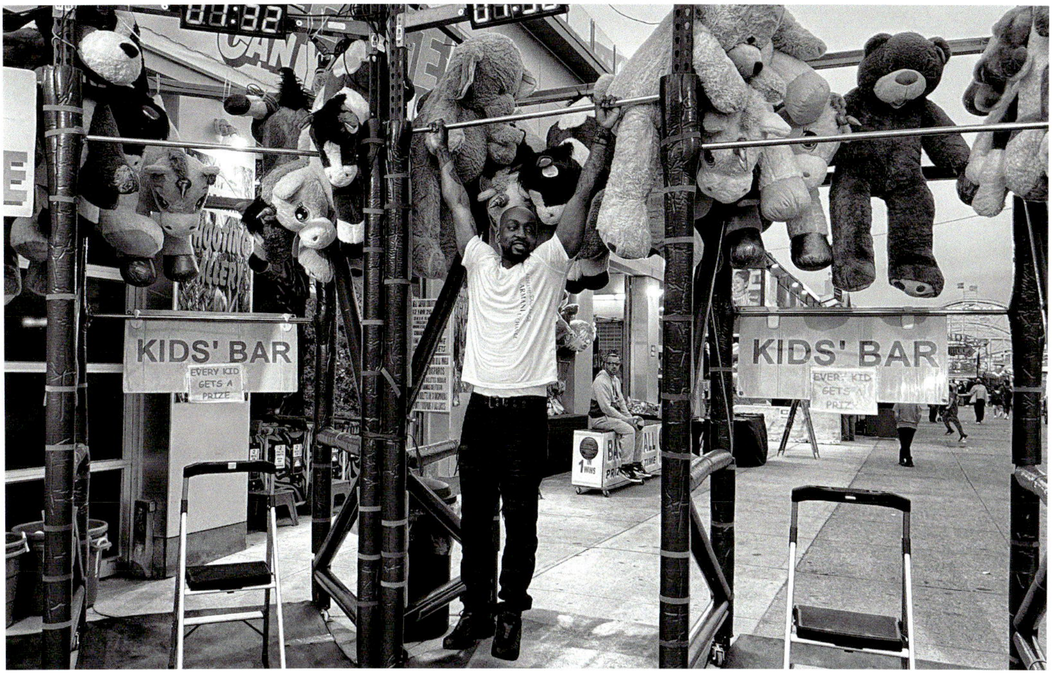

A man proves his strength on a Coney Island amusement. (*Photo: Liz Cooke*)

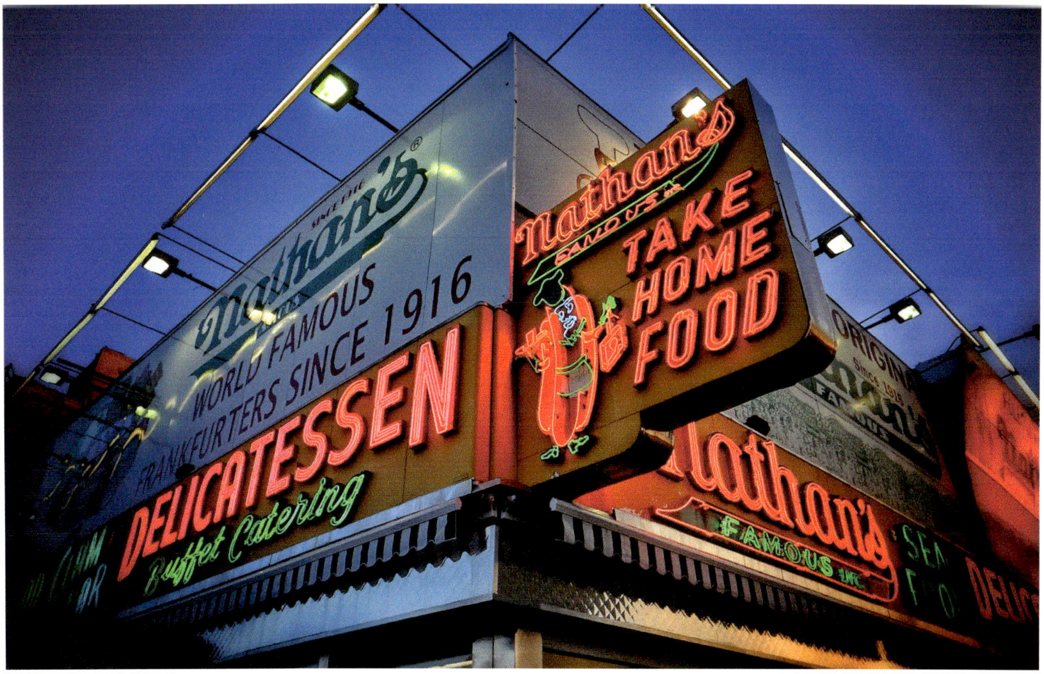

Nathan's Famous in Coney Island has been serving hot dogs since 1916. The bright neon signs glow over Surf Avenue, with the iconic "Frankster" hot dog logo grinning as it holds a fork. (*Photo: Liz Cooke*)

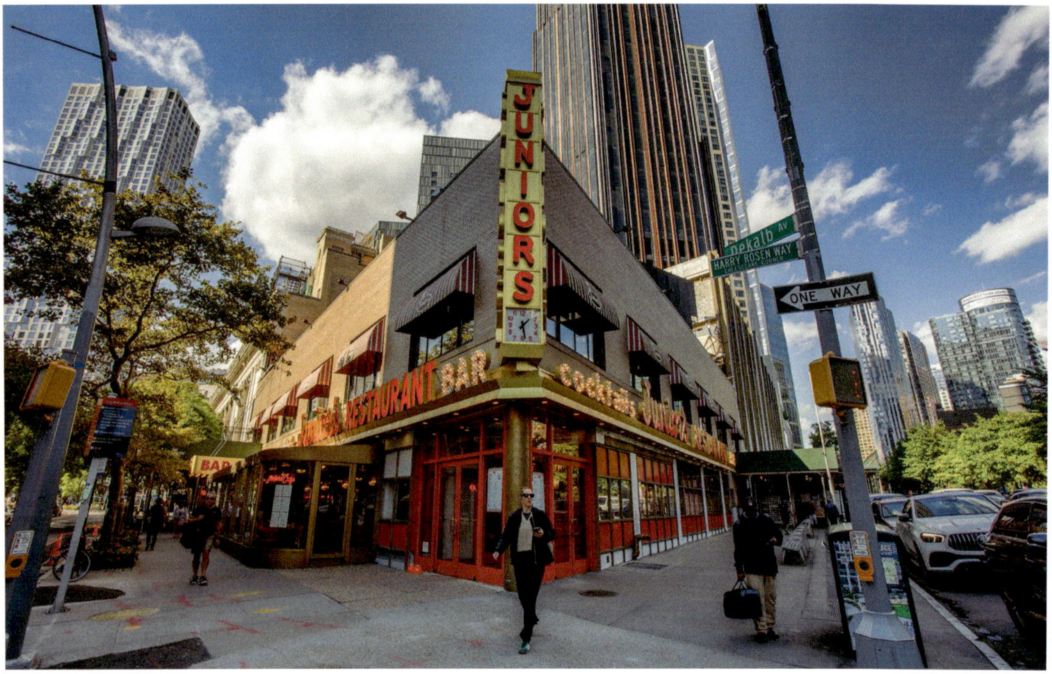

Junior's on Dekalb Avenue—a Brooklyn institution since 1950—is famous for its rich, creamy New York-style cheesecake and full menu of comfort foods. (*Photo: Andy Milford*)

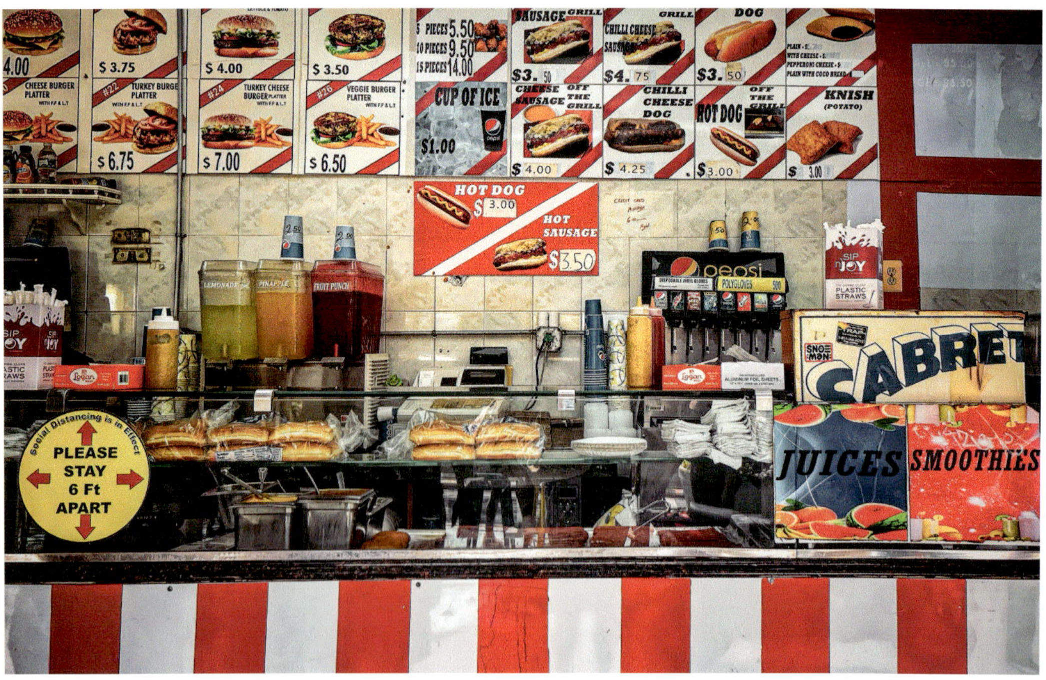

With its retro vibe and simple menu, Fulton Hot Dog in Downtown Brooklyn is a no-frills spot that has been serving quick bites to locals for years. (*Photo: Liz Cooke*)

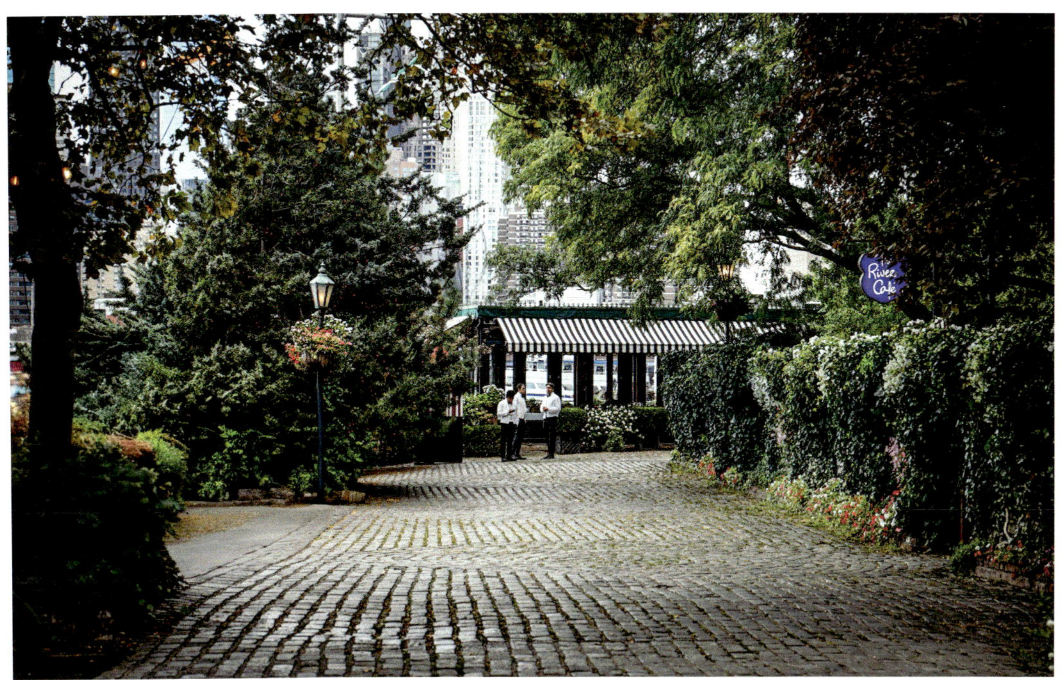

Above: In 1977 when the River Cafe opened, its location beneath the Brooklyn Bridge was abandoned and far from desirable. Today, the River Cafe is a premier dining destination, offering stunning skyline views and an upscale menu. (*Photo: Liz Cooke*)

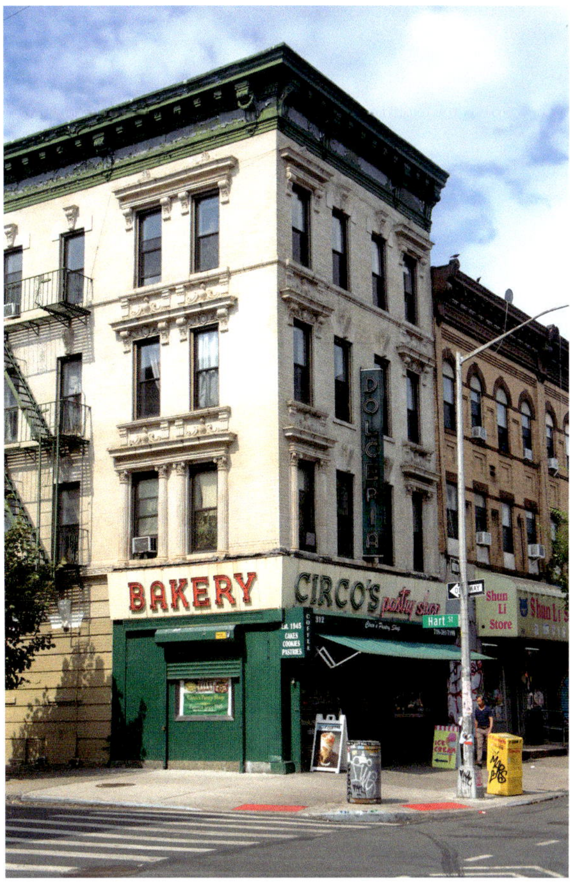

Right: Circo's Bakery in Bushwick has been serving the neighborhood for over fifty years. Along the way it gained a reputation for its authentic Italian pastries including cannoli and sfogliatella. (*Photo: Andy Milford*)

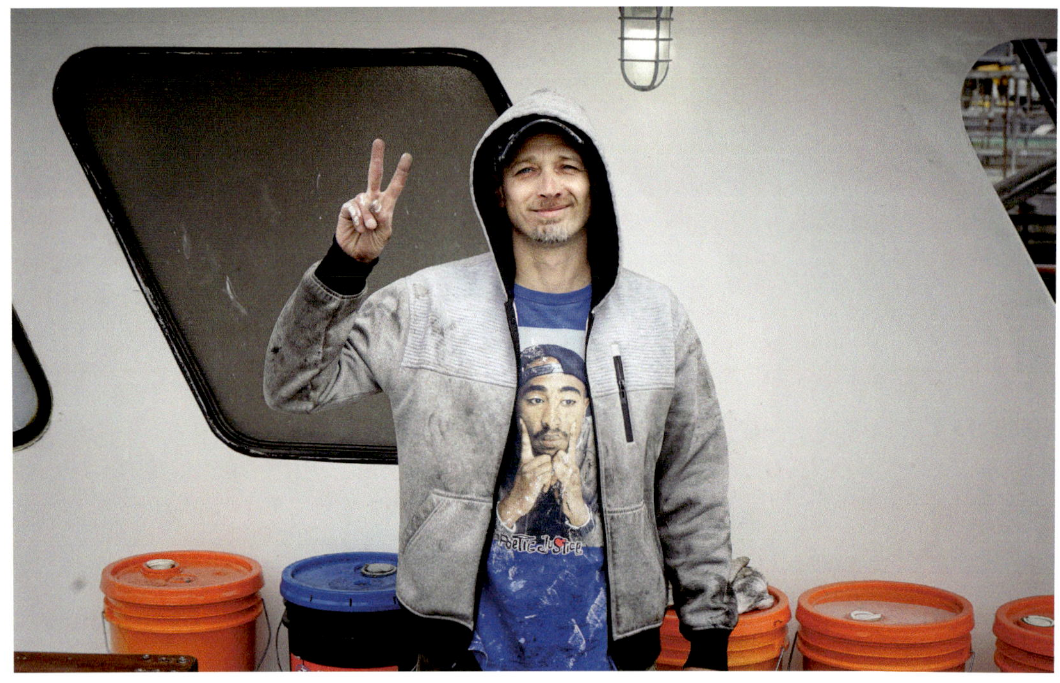

Flashing a peace sign and wearing a Tupac T-shirt, this fisherman just returned from the sea to home port in Sheepshead Bay. (*Photo: Liz Cooke*)

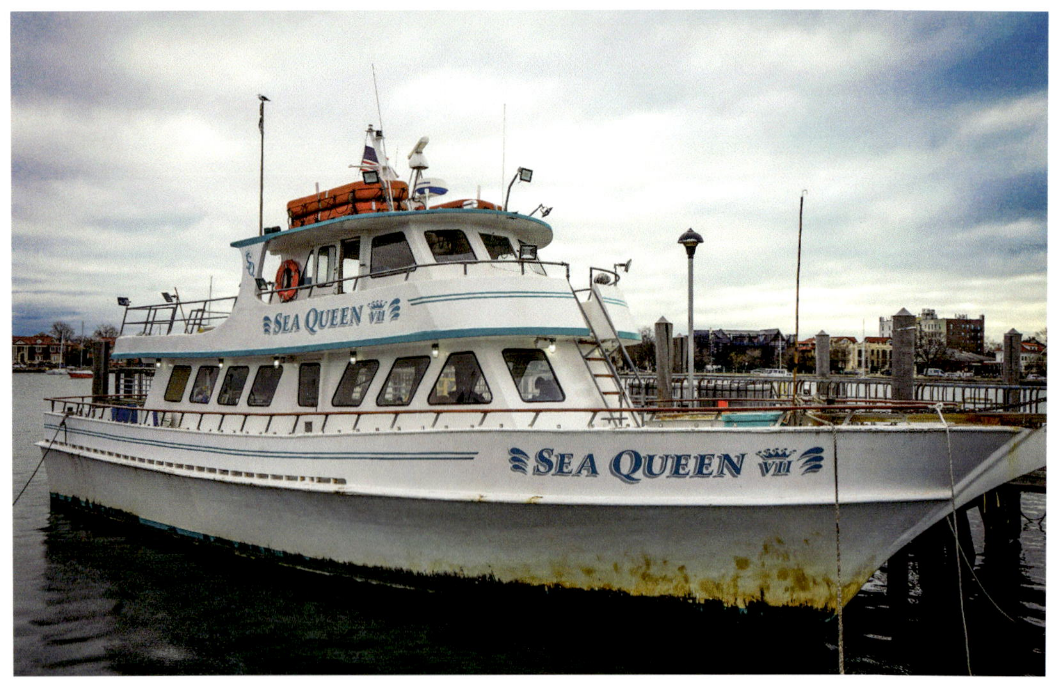

The Sea Queen in Sheepshead Bay is a historic boat and popular venue for events and cruises around the bay. (*Photo: Liz Cooke*)

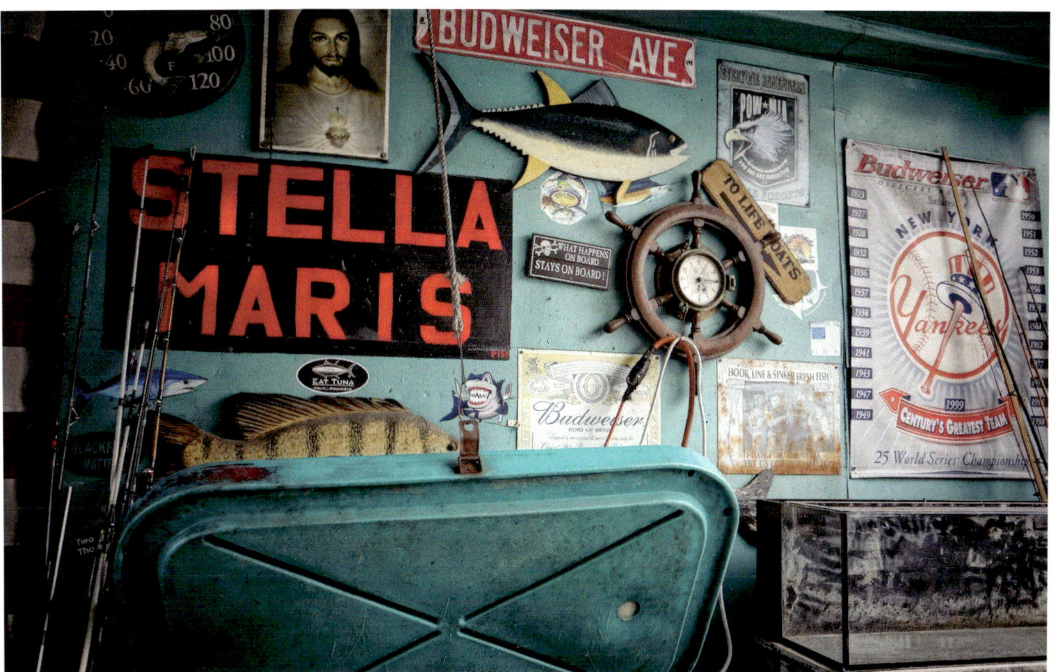

Stella Maris in Sheepshead Bay was a beloved institution since 1947, selling everything from fishing supplies to fresh bait. It closed permanently in 2024. (*Photo: Liz Cooke*)

What keeps Brooklyn going year after year, generation after generation? In a word—energy. In September, Eastern Parkway comes alive with hundreds of thousands of revelers at the West Indian Day Parade. On the Lunar New Year, thousands throng to Sunset Park and Bensonhurst to join in colorful parades. In November, the New York City Marathon passes through all five boroughs, with Brooklyn the first stop after the start on the Verrazzano Bridge in Staten Island. In June, thousands of costumed revelers throng to the boardwalk in Coney Island for the Mermaid Parade, a beloved tradition since 1983.

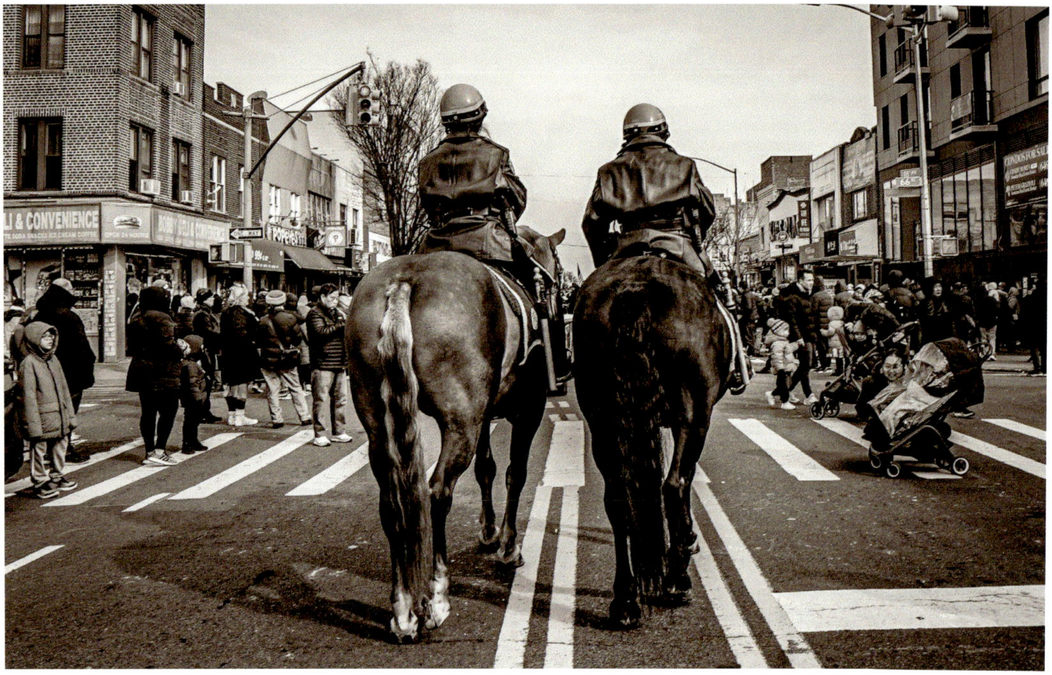

Mounted police officers attend the Lunar New Year celebration in Bensonhurst. (*Photo: Liz Cooke*)

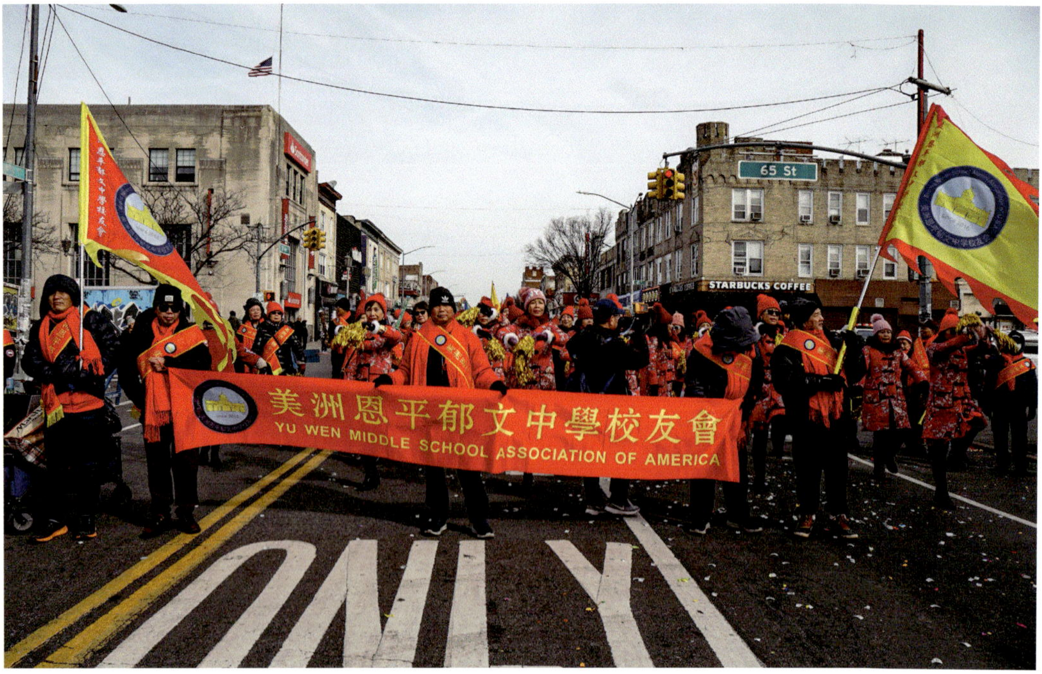

A wide variety of civic and social groups march in the Lunar New Year parade in Bensonhurst. (*Photo: Liz Cooke*)

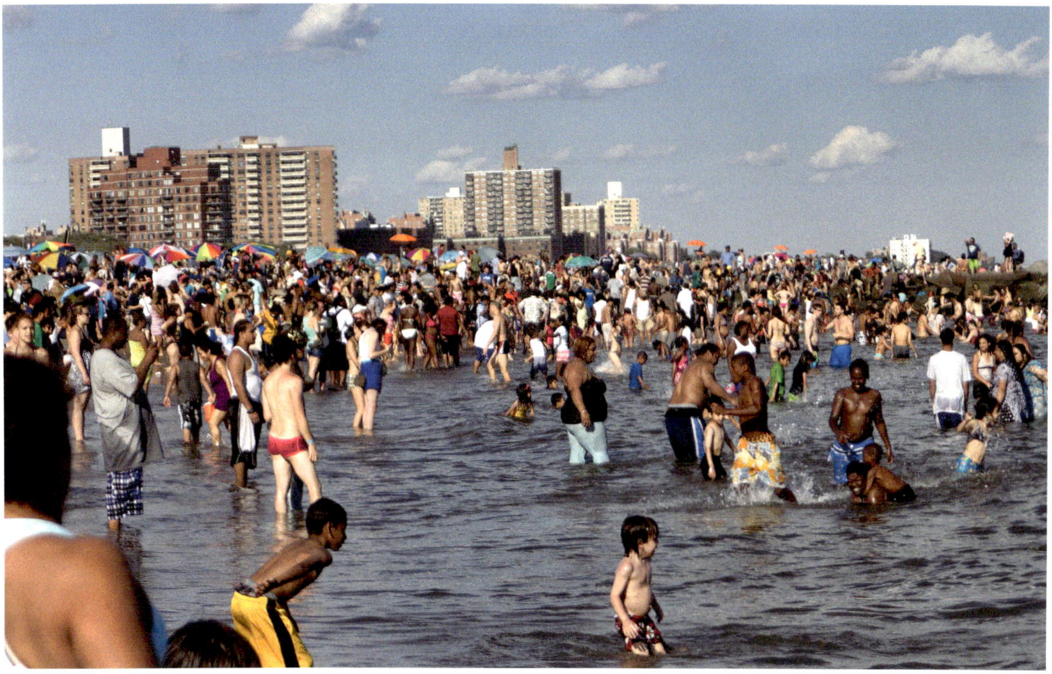

On a hot summer's day, the beach at Coney Island can attract more than 100,000 people. (*Photo: Andy Milford*)

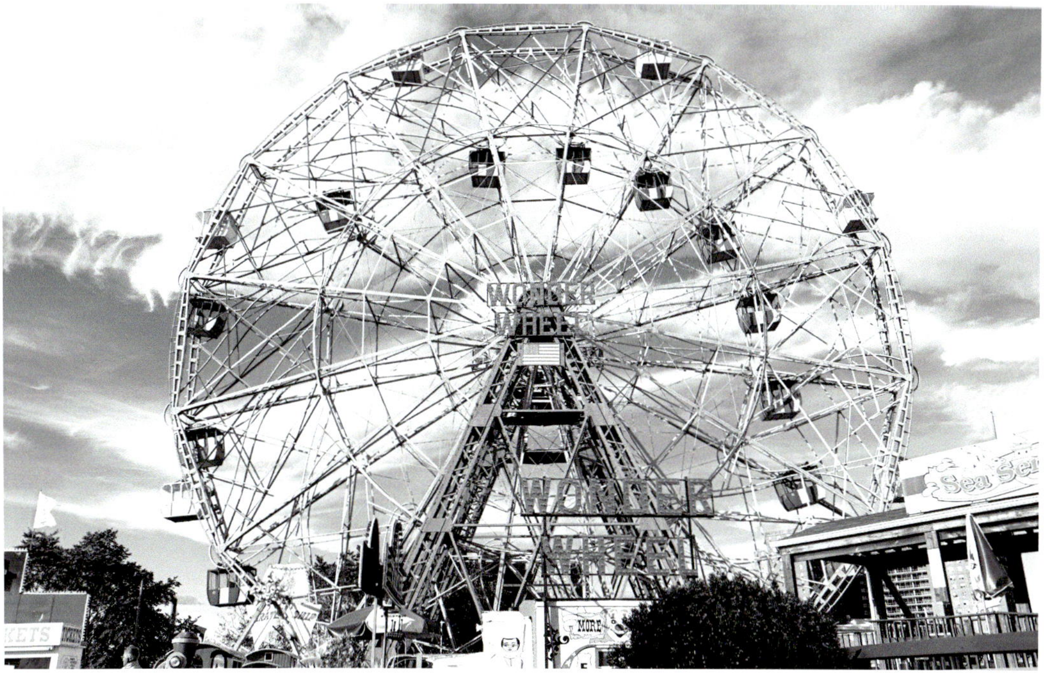

With its mix of stationary and swinging cars, the Wonder Wheel has been terrifying riders since 1920. While other rides have come and gone, the Wonder Wheel powers on and was designated a New York City Landmark in 1989. (*Photo: Andy Milford*)

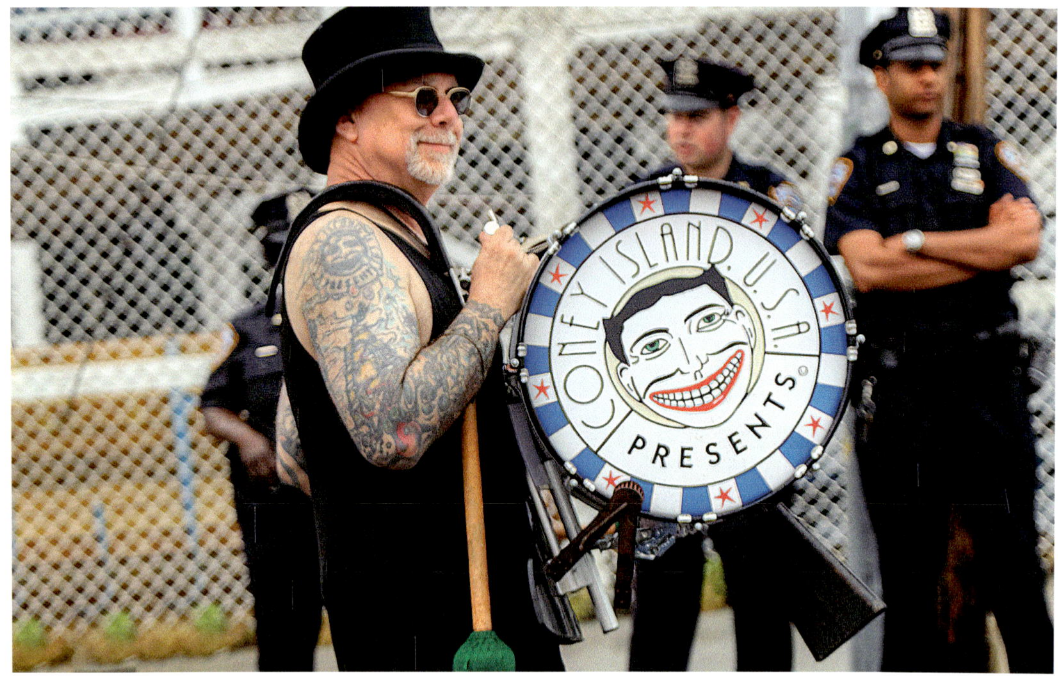

Coney Island's Mermaid Parade was founded in 1983 to bring the community together in celebration of the summer solstice. The parade features elaborate floats, marching bands and street performers. (*Photo: Andy Milford*)

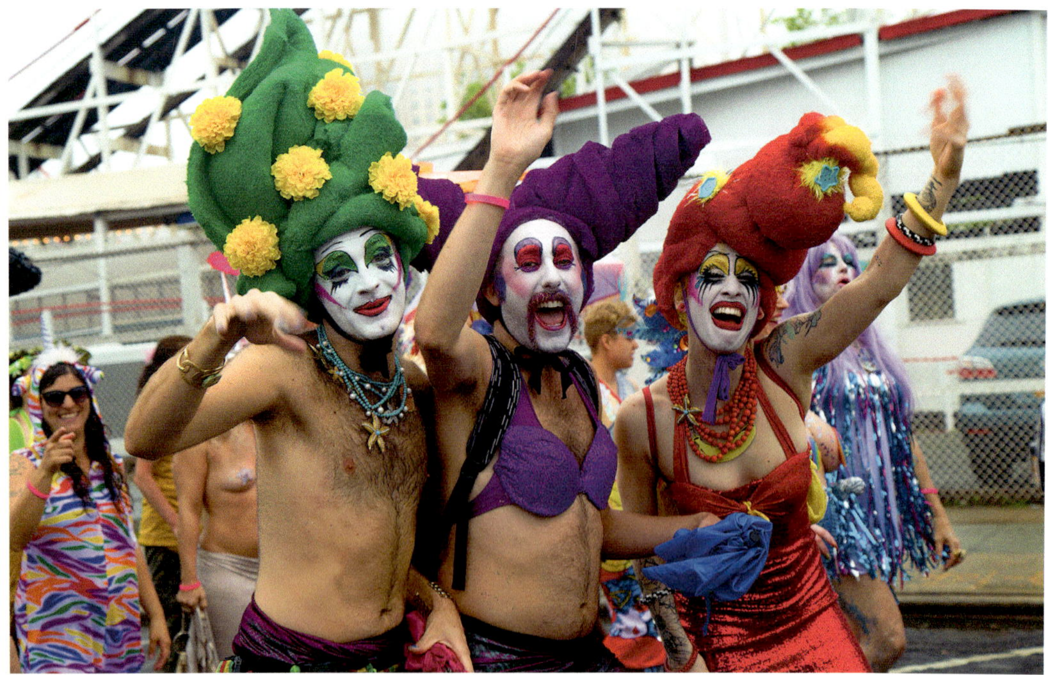

Thousands of costumed revelers participate in the annual Mermaid Parade in Coney Island. A highlight of the day is the crowning of the Royal Couple: King Neptune and Queen Mermaid. (*Photo: Andy Milford*)

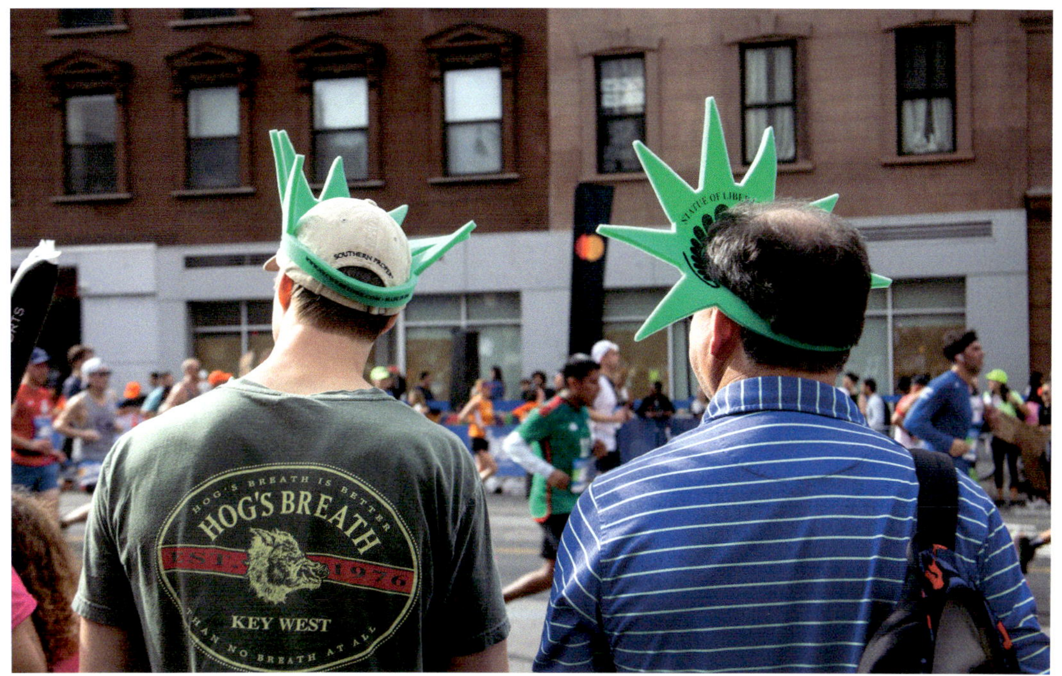

Thousands line the route of the New York City Marathon as it passes through the Brooklyn neighborhoods of Bay Ridge, Sunset Park, Park Slope, and Williamsburg. (*Photo: Andy Milford*)

When it comes to "cultcha," Brooklyn is simply world-class. The Brooklyn Museum, Grand Army Plaza Library, and Brooklyn Academy of Music may be the jewels in the crown of Brooklyn's cultural environment, but for those who prefer a more local experience, Brooklyn serves as a canvas for an incomparable collection of murals, graffiti, and street art. After the middle-of-the-night destruction of 5 Pointz, the legendary "aerosol art space" in Long Island City, some protections have been enforced under VARA (Visual Artists Rights Act of 1990). Legally commissioned works and those considered to have "recognized stature" in the art world may be protected.

The Green-Wood Cemetery in Sunset Park, established in 1838, has hundreds of sculptures, over 7,000 trees, and some 600,000 permanent residents. Green-Wood has long offered a rare opportunity to find peace and solace in the city, and is a favorite destination for birders, photographers and painters. Its landmark gothic entrance gate has been home to a family of colorful monk parakeets for over sixty years.

Completed in 2021, Brooklyn Bridge Park has brought a whole new level of life and energy to Brooklyn's once bustling—and later virtually forgotten—East River waterfront. Here you'll find 1.3 miles of waterfront parkland, a beach, kayaking, sports fields, picnic areas, acres of trails with native plantings, all with stunning views of the lower Manhattan skyline, the Brooklyn Bridge, and the Statue of Liberty.

Set above Brooklyn Bridge Park is a triple-cantilevered engineering marvel deteriorating in plain sight—the Brooklyn Queens Expressway, one of the busiest roadways in the city. Above the busy BQE is the Brooklyn Heights Promenade. In 1941, "master builder" Robert Moses conceived a plan to run the BQE through Brooklyn Heights. Through the efforts of community activists, the Heights was spared and plans were drawn up to build what is now the Promenade. Today, it remains a perfect place to stroll, relax or just enjoy the breathtaking view.

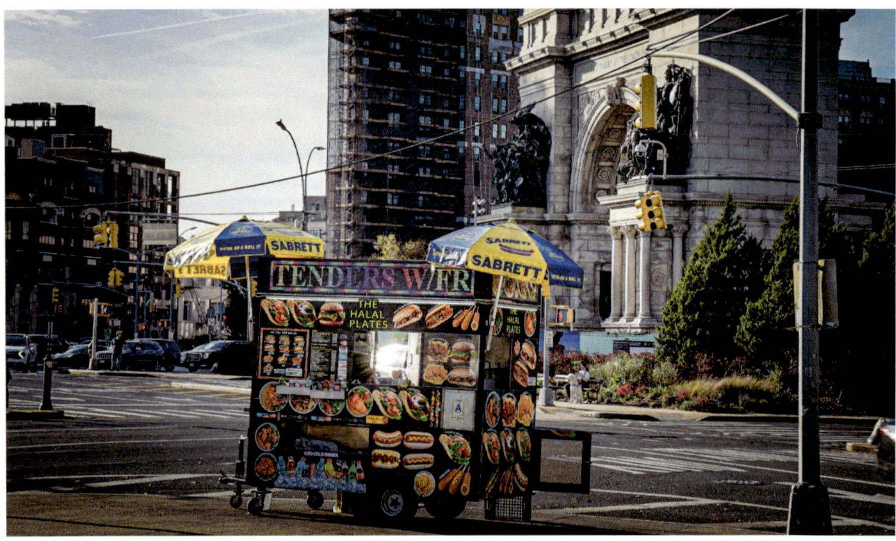

The centerpiece of Grand Army Plaza at the entrance to Prospect Park is the Soldiers' and Sailors' Arch, a Civil War memorial dating from 1892. (*Photo: Liz Cooke*)

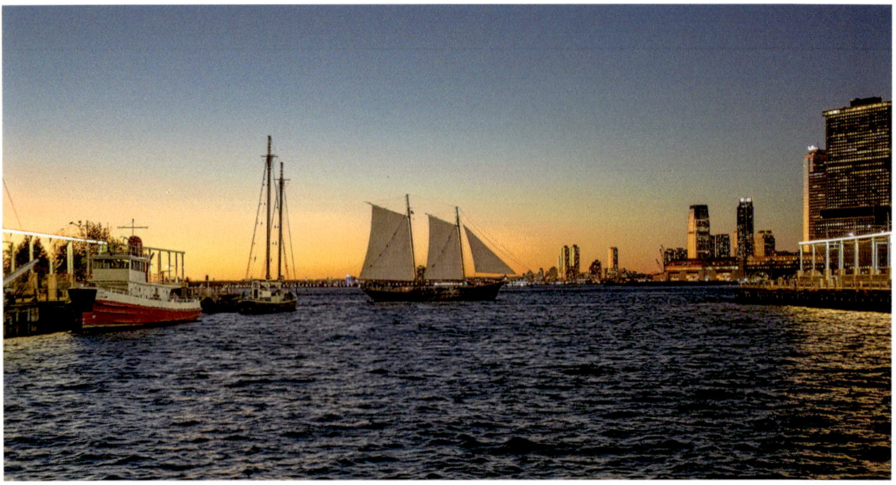

A sunset sail seen from Brooklyn Bridge Park. (*Photo: Andy Milford*)

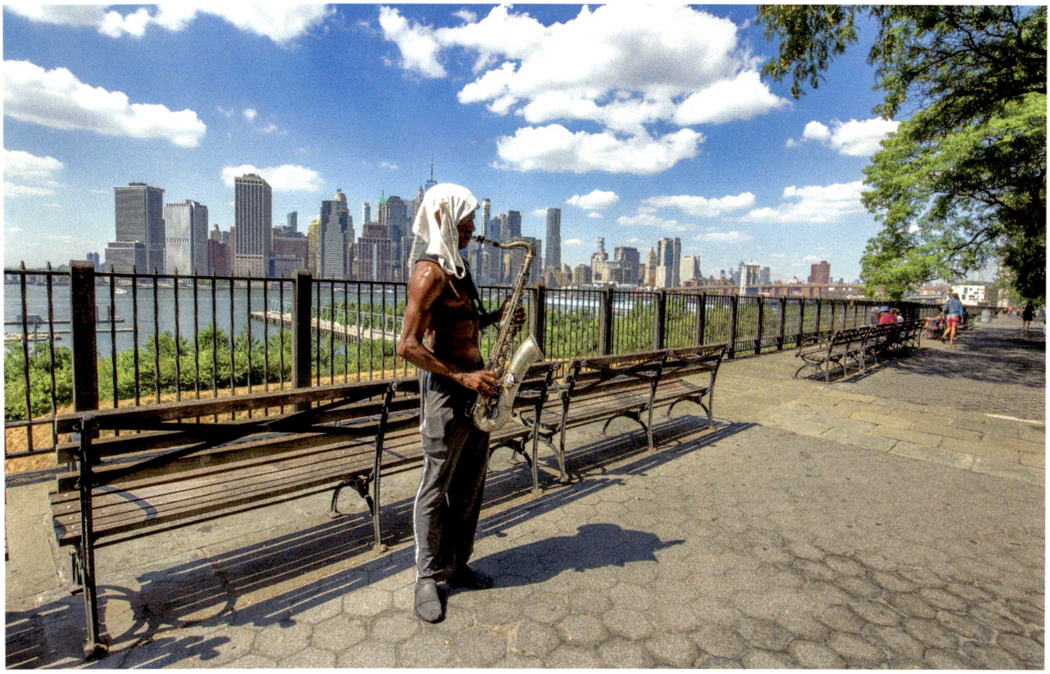

A saxophone player on the Brooklyn Heights Promenade. (*Photo: Andy Milford*)

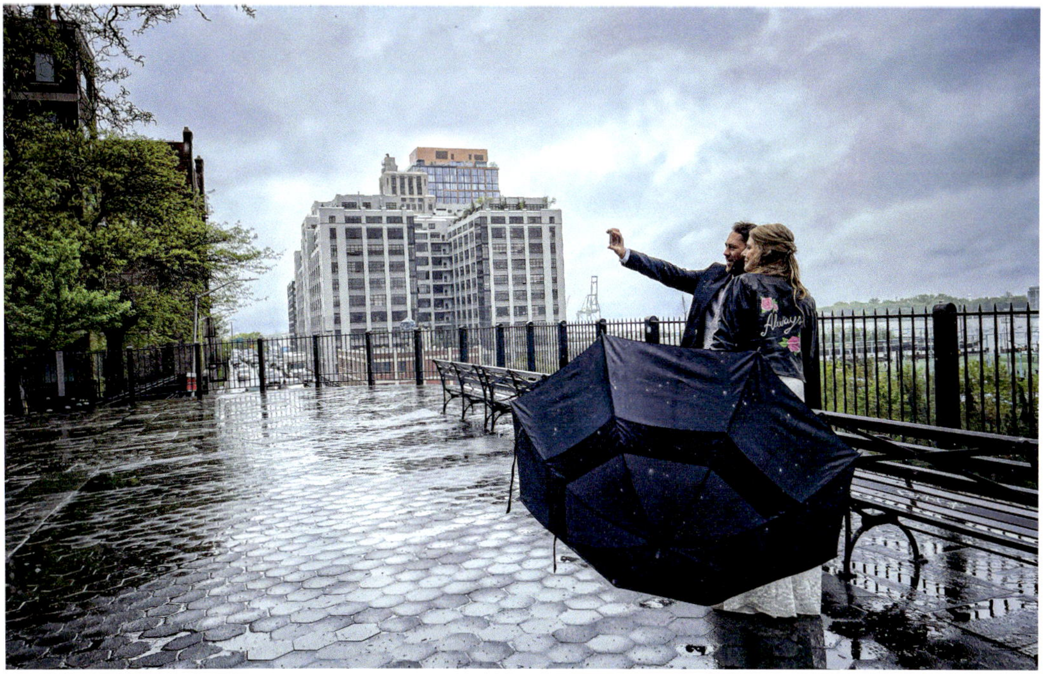

Marriage proposals are frequently seen on the Brooklyn Heights Promenade. This couple celebrates their marriage with a rainy stroll and selfie. (*Photo: Liz Cooke*)

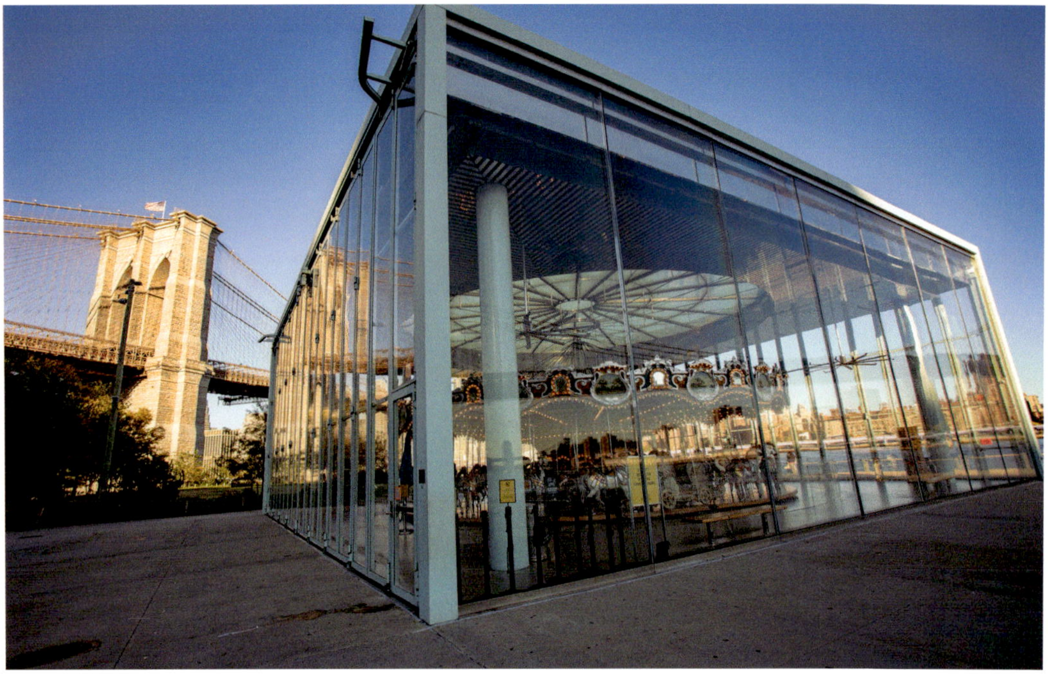

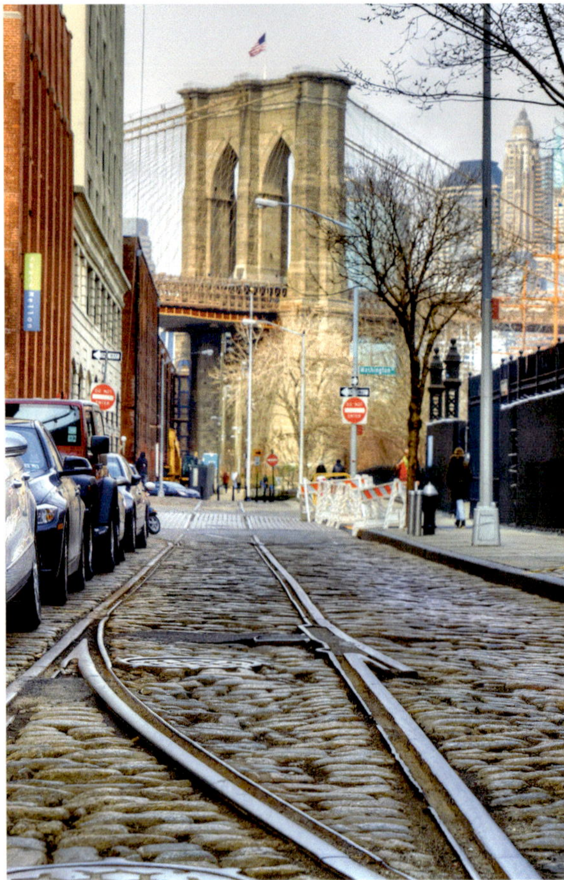

Above: Jane's Carousel is a Dumbo landmark. This fully restored 1922 wooden carousel is housed in a sleek glass pavilion and offers riders stunning views of the Manhattan skyline and Brooklyn Bridge. (*Photo: Andy Milford*)

Left: Trolley tracks and cobblestone streets in Dumbo are a reminder of Brooklyn's industrial past, when horse-drawn carts moved between factories and warehouses. (*Photo: Andy Milford*)

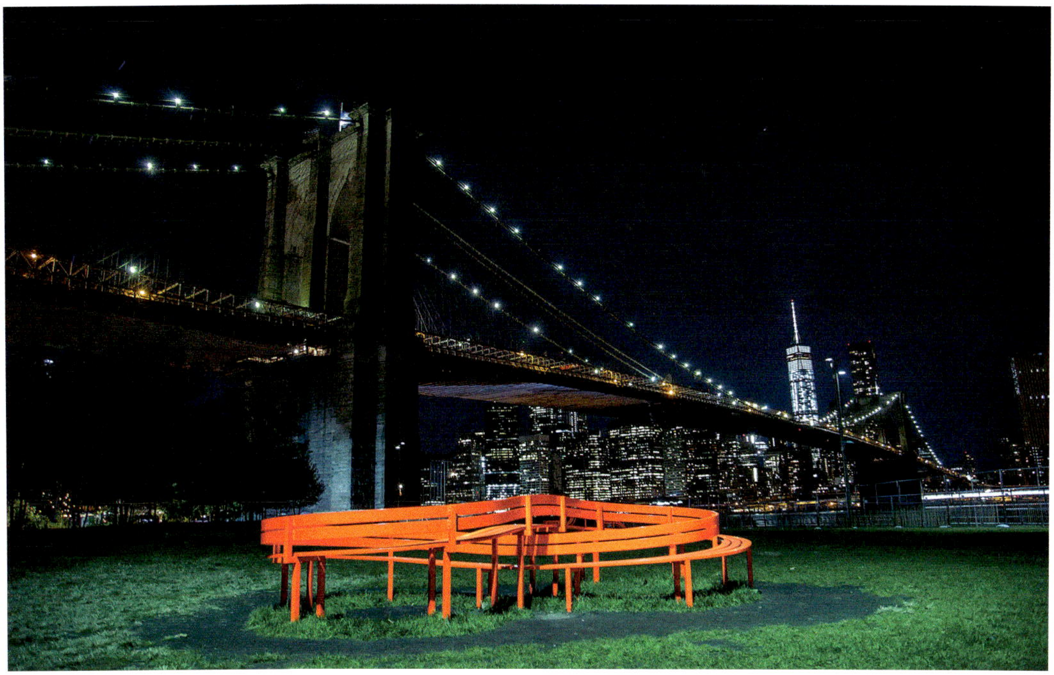

Outdoor art is plentiful in Brooklyn Bridge Park. This work, seen with an illuminated Brooklyn Bridge in the background, is a series of interconnected benches by Danish artist Jeppe Hein. (*Photo: Andy Milford*)

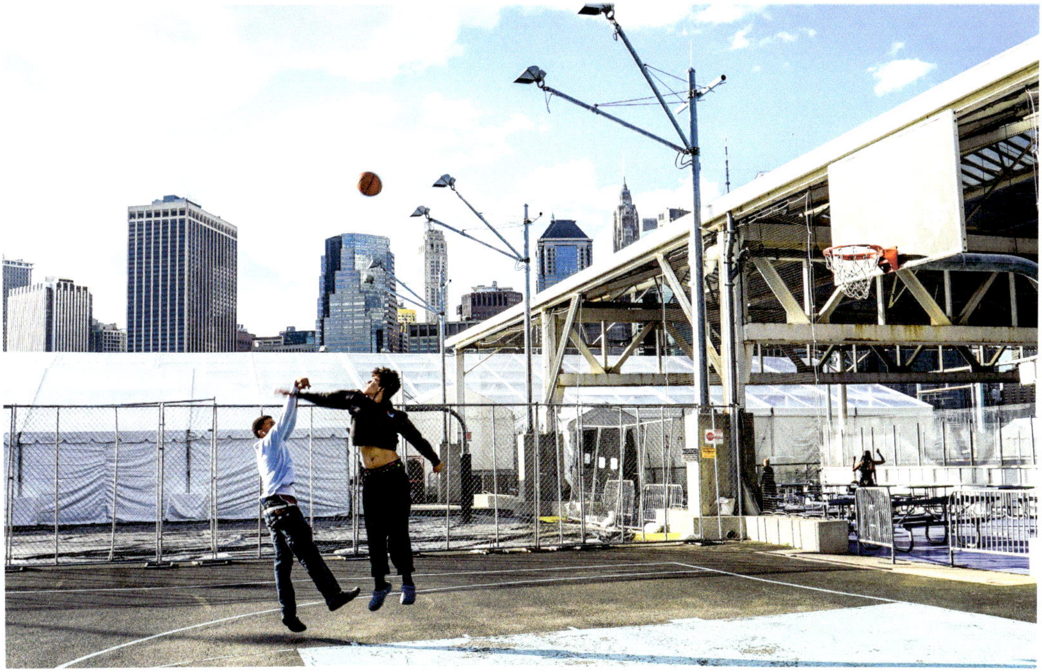

At Brooklyn Bridge Park, players of all ages come to shoot hoops, enjoying everything from casual pick-up games to competitive leagues, all with the Lower Manhattan skyline as a backdrop. (*Photo: Liz Cooke*)

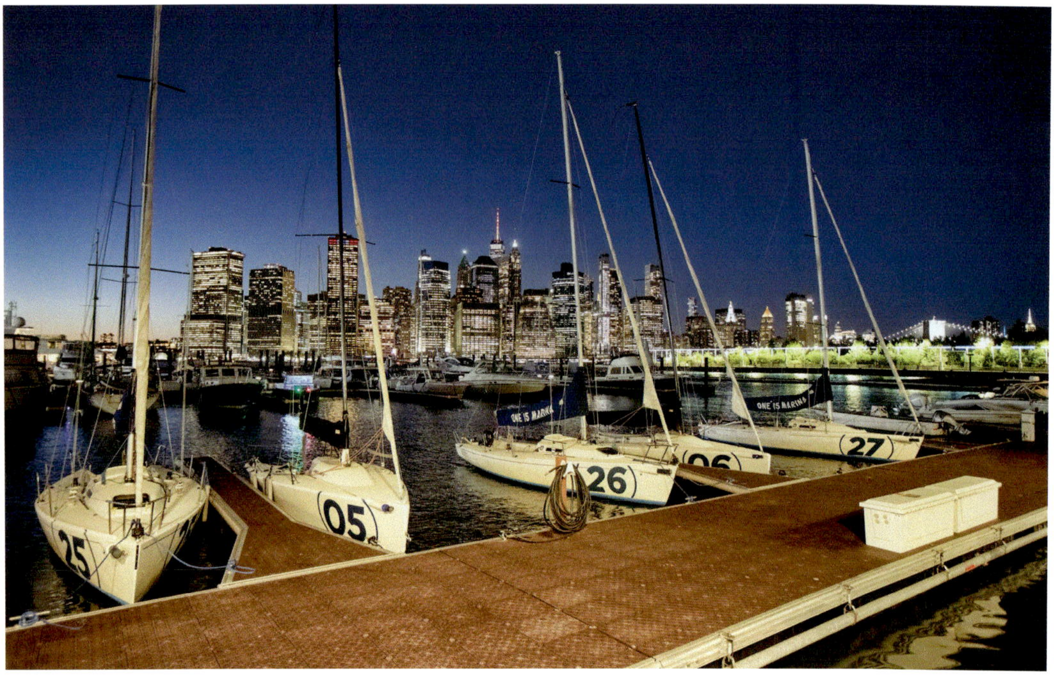

The marina at Brooklyn Bridge Park was developed as part of the park's waterfront revitalization, offering docking space, sailing programs, and access to the water. (*Photo: Andy Milford*)

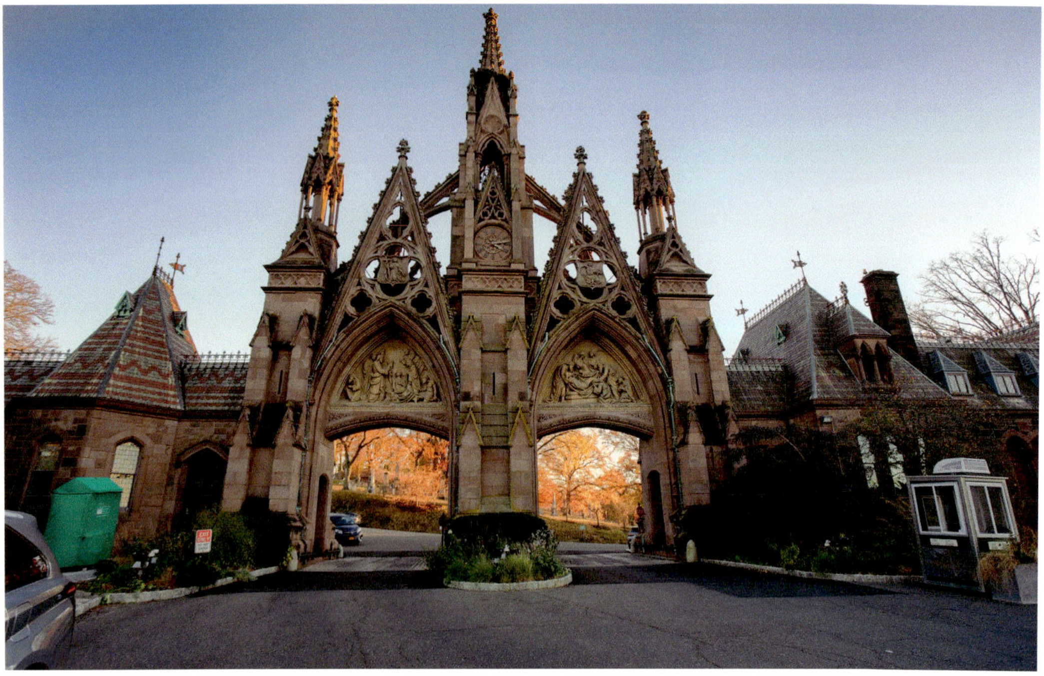

Completed in 1861 and designed by architect Richard Upjohn, the Gothic Revival entrance to Green-Wood Cemetery in Sunset Park is one of its most striking features. (*Photo: Andy Milford*)

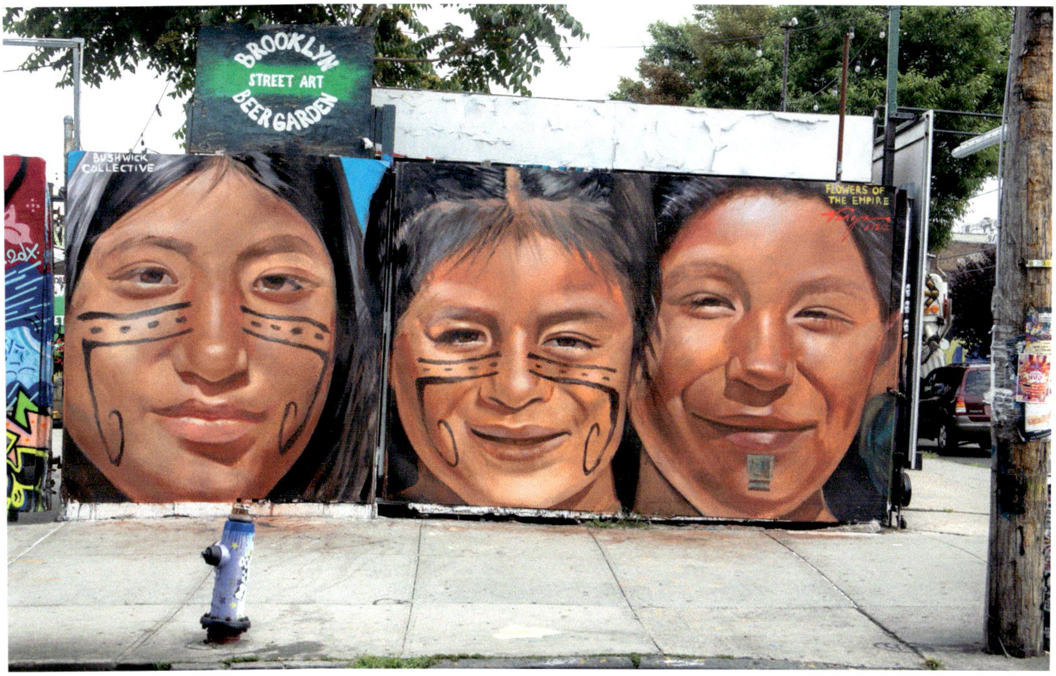

"Flowers of the Empire" by artist Robert Vargas for the Bushwick Collective. (*Photo: Andy Milford*)

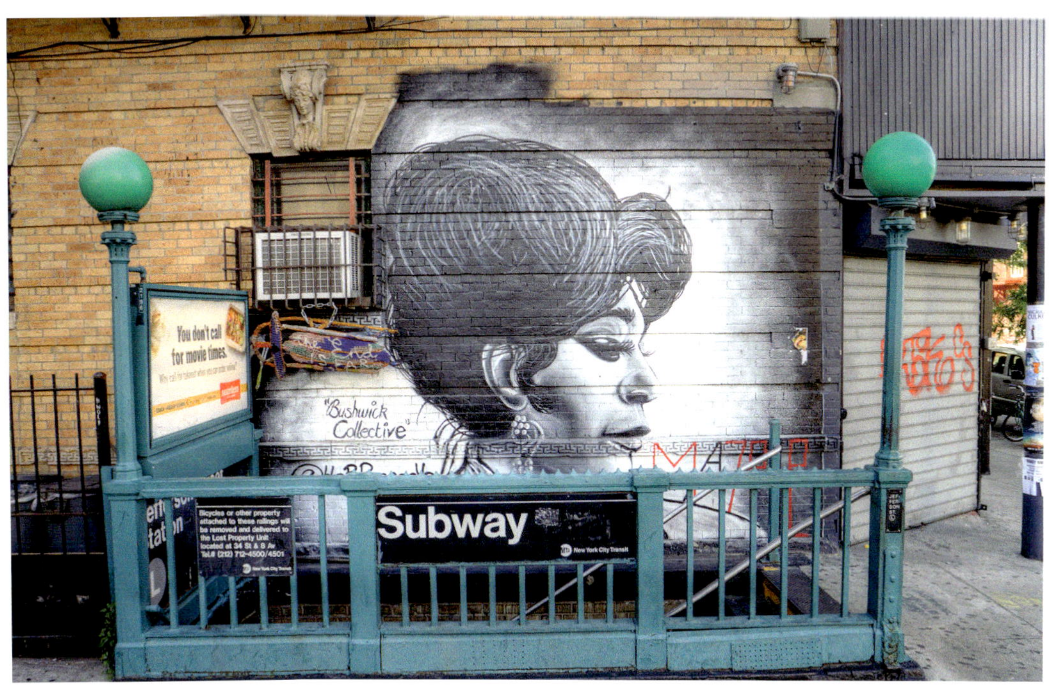

A tribute to the Queen of Soul, Aretha Franklin, at the Franklin Avenue subway station in Bushwick. (*Photo: Andy Milford*)

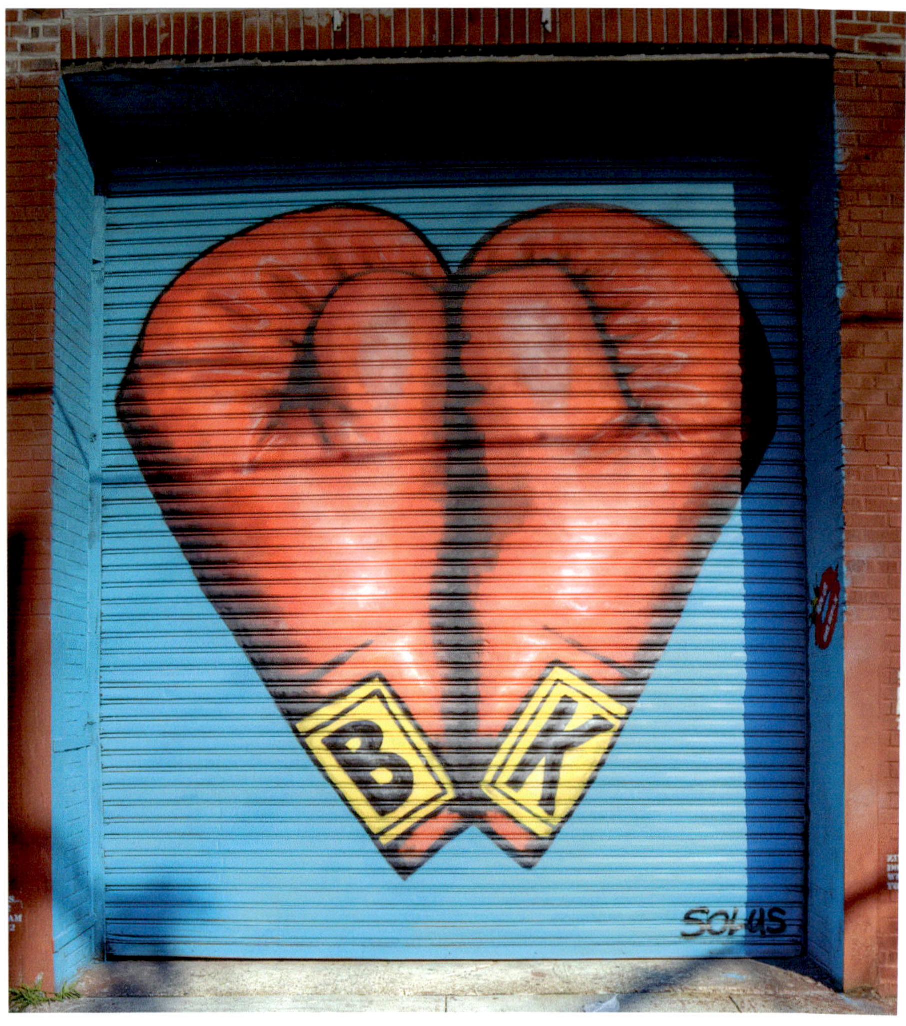

Street art by Solus depicts boxing gloves in the shape of a heart. The initials "BK" could signify Brooklyn or Bushwick. (*Photo: Andy Milford*)

Designed by famed landscape architects Frederick Law Olmsted and Calvert Vaux (the team behind Manhattan's Central Park), Prospect Park's 526 acres sit at Brooklyn's heart and make it one of the most popular green spaces in the city. And in a place as hectic as Brooklyn, an afternoon at the Brooklyn Botanic Garden can be a balm for the soul. Visitors can amble through the Cranford Rose Garden, the stunning plant-filled Steinhardt Conservatory and the tranquil Japanese Hill-and-Pond Garden.

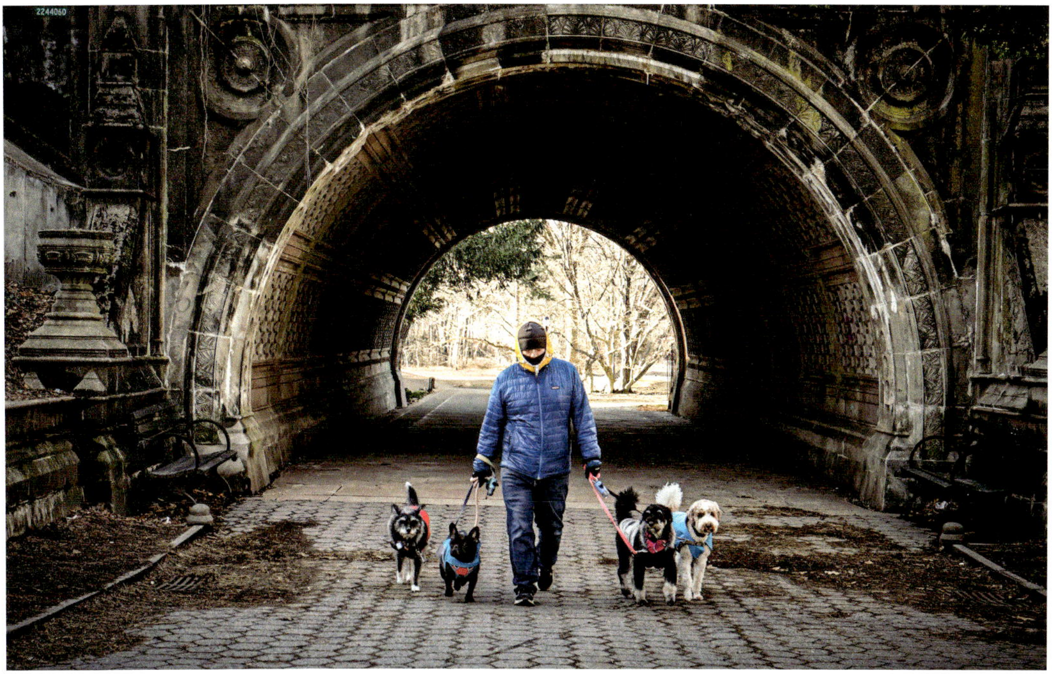

The Cleft Ridge Span Tunnel, built in 1871, is a historic structure in Prospect Park and a lovely place to walk elegantly attired pooches. (*Photo: Liz Cooke*)

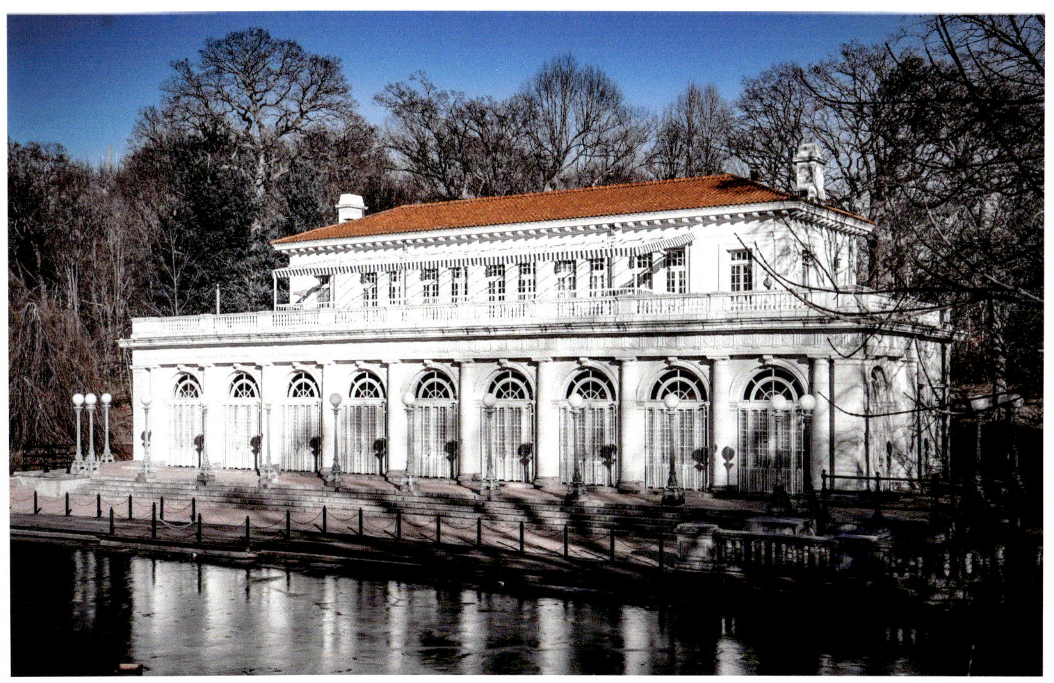

Sitting along the Lullwater, the Prospect Park Boathouse was designed as a resting spot for boaters and park visitors. Over the years, it fell into disrepair but was restored in the 1990s. Today, it serves as a visitor center and event space. (*Photo: Liz Cooke*)

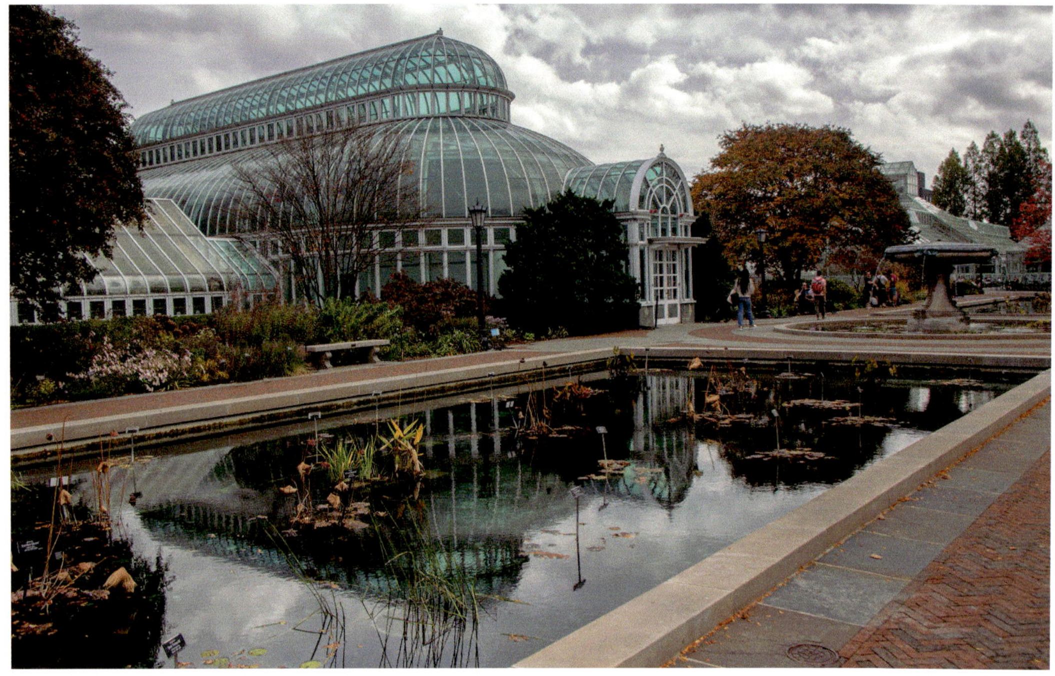

The Steinhardt Conservatory at the Brooklyn Botanic Garden houses a wide variety of tropical and subtropical plants as well as the Bonsai Museum. (*Photo: Andy Milford*)

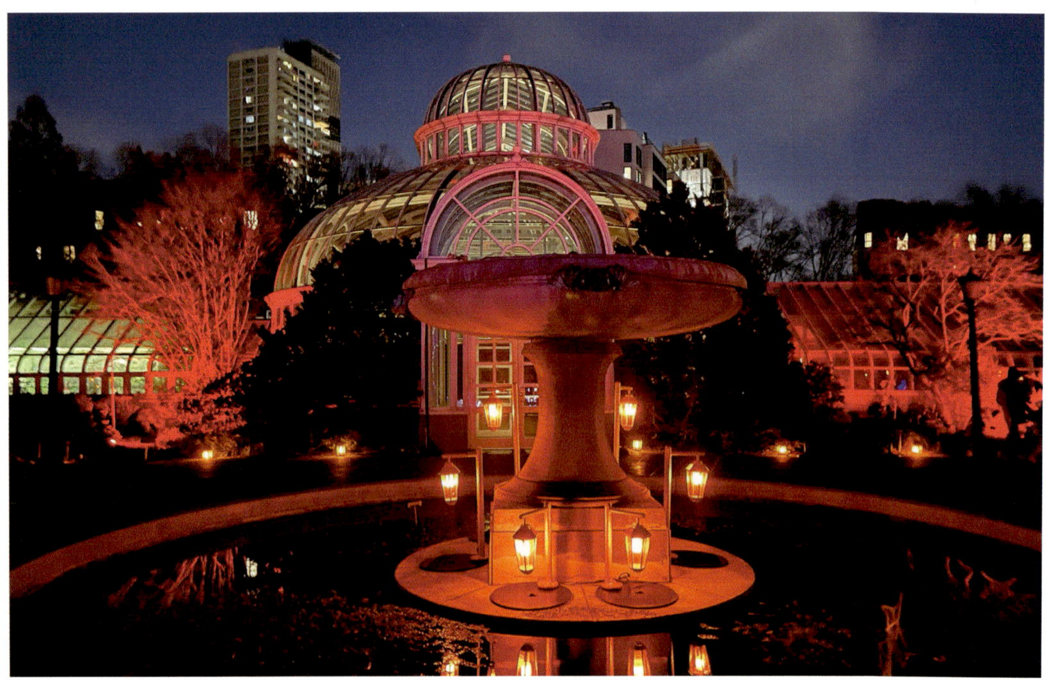

The Brooklyn Botanic Garden comes alive in winter with the holiday light show featuring numerous artist-designed lightworks, illuminating the garden's paths, trees, and sculptures. (*Photo: Liz Cooke*)

With so much to offer—and so many people and interests to serve—it can be hard to fathom the complex task of keeping Brooklyn livable, let alone desirable. Recent years brought huge changes: the construction of Barclays Center at an already chaotic intersection added to the problem of just crossing Flatbush Avenue safely; the development of an entirely new skyline in Downtown Brooklyn begs the question of how to provide essential services like police, schools, and hospitals to so many new residents. Growth is great, until it isn't, and it's hard to know when too much is too much.

So, what does the future hold for Brooklyn? Predicting life in the borough ten or twenty years from now is tricky, but one thing is certain: Brooklyn will continue to evolve, just as it always has. The borough is likely to become even more diverse, with new waves of immigrants bringing fresh perspectives and traditions. Climate resilience will be at the forefront, as waterfront neighborhoods like Sea Gate, Red Hook, and Canarsie adapt to rising sea levels. Gentrification will continue its march across the borough, raising questions about affordability and accessibility.

But some things will remain timeless. The pulse of Brooklyn's street life will continue to thrive. And Brooklynites, whether new arrivals or lifelong residents, will keep finding ways to make the borough their own.

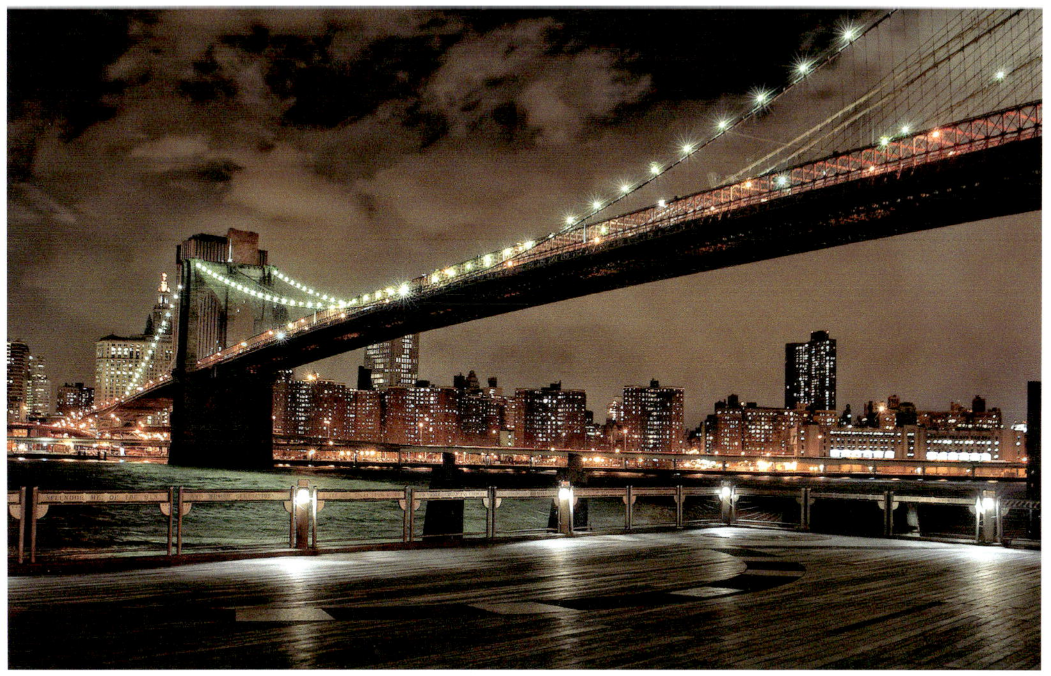

Forever beautiful. The Brooklyn Bridge at night. (*Photo: Richard B. Cooke*)

Epilogue

When Andy and I were first approached about putting together a photography book about Brooklyn, we thought "this won't be hard." We both take a lot of pictures and have huge files to go through. Surely, we will have enough images to do Brooklyn justice. Even if we don't have everything, we love getting together and shooting so what we don't have we can easily get. How naive we were!

It didn't take long before we realized something we should have known all along: Brooklyn is big! And every neighborhood deserves its own book. Because I'm from Brooklyn, I have a lot of loyalty to my fellow Brooklynites and I worried about leaving anyone out. How could I write about Brighton Beach (my childhood neighborhood) without also writing about Bath Beach, or Canarsie, or East New York, or any of a dozen neighborhoods we simply could not get to?

The challenge wasn't just scale; it was also deciding what story to tell. Brooklyn is many things at once—an old city and a modern city, a place of longstanding traditions and constant reinvention, a place of community cohesion and deep social divisions. At one point, Andy and I realized the story we wanted to tell would inevitably be incomplete. Which is why if we have one request it's this: please come see this place for yourself. Take pictures. Start conversations. Smile at strangers. Eat strange food. And enjoy every minute of your time in this exciting, ever-changing place.